"James Barker is one of the most creative a. ..gaging scholars working in Gospels research today. This book combines his pedagogical sensitivities with an encyclopedic knowledge of ancient Christian texts and compositional practices. The end result is a potentially field-altering study that argues for a 'snowballing trajectory' for our canonical gospels and ably demonstrates the Fourth Gospel's awareness of and dependence upon the Synoptics. This book is a game-changer!"

—**Christopher W. Skinner**
Loyola University Chicago

"Utilizing analogies from Pinocchio to Pier Paolo Pasolini, Barker's book seeks to draw attention to where scholars complicate what may have been relatively simple and simplify what may have been extremely complicated in the production of Gospels. A thought-provoking read for anyone interested in the interrelationship of Gospels and how they came to be written. Barker's close attention to detail highlights things that are easy to miss even if you've studied these texts for decades."

—**James F. McGrath**
Butler University

"This entertaining book will shape Gospel scholarship for decades. Barker documents a snowballing trajectory of influence from Mark through Matthew, then Luke, and finally John, each building upon the others. His work on the mechanics of ancient writing will enrich every reader. Although this book is deeply learned, sparkling writing and creative pop culture references make it a joy to read."

—**Greg Carey**
Lancaster Theological Seminary

"*Writing and Rewriting the Gospels* isn't so much a study as a revelation—a convincing glimpse into the hidden processes behind the creation of Matthew, Mark, Luke, and John. Examining a wide range of ancient evidence and drawing on his firsthand experience preparing waxed tablets and papyrus rolls, Barker demolishes many common assumptions about how the gospels were composed. Read it and see the gospel authors come to life."

—**Hugo Méndez**
University of North Carolina at Chapel Hill

WRITING AND REWRITING THE GOSPELS

John and the Synoptics

James W. Barker

WILLIAM B. EERDMANS PUBLISHING COMPANY
GRAND RAPIDS, MICHIGAN

Wm. B. Eerdmans Publishing Co.
2006 44th Street SE, Grand Rapids, MI 49508
www.eerdmans.com

Published 2025

Book design by Lydia Hall

Printed in the United States of America

31 30 29 28 27 26 25   1 2 3 4 5 6 7

ISBN 978-0-8028-7452-8

Library of Congress Cataloging-in-Publication Data

A catalog record for this book is available from the Library of Congress.

To Katy, Jacob, Hannah, and Pumpkin

CONTENTS

Figures

FOREWORD

"TRAJECTORIES" USED TO BE ALL THE RAGE. Books on the development of early Christianity were devoted to the idea that there were multiple divergent "trajectories" that espoused different views of Jesus, his life, his sayings, his death, and the movements that he spawned. Integral to the model was the notion that many of the Christian works that have survived, as well as many of those that have not (like "Q" or the "Signs Gospel"), were independent of one another, and that the overlaps between them are explicable by appealing to a vast ocean of "oral tradition."

The model was a useful one. It taught students and reminded scholars that Christianity did not evolve on an inevitable, proto-orthodox timeline, in which everyone believed pretty much the same thing from the beginning, and those who disagreed were "heretics." The model made sure that we had the appropriate skepticism toward those in power who constructed the idea that "the church" had always believed the same thing from the beginning, and it helped us to think seriously about diversity in Christian origins.

But the model had a fatal flaw. In order to demonstrate that there were multiple, independent works plowing their own furrows from the beginning, the Gospel of Thomas needed to be early and independent, Luke needed to be independent of Matthew, and John needed to be independent of the Synoptics. And that was just for starters. If Luke was independent of Matthew, their common, non-Markan material could be attributed to an unattested early sayings source, "Q." And if Thomas was independent of the Synoptics, it could be an early gospel that, like "Q," witnessed to an early Passion-free Christianity that contrasted radically with the cross-centered theology of the apostle Paul. And then there was John, and if John was independent of the Synoptics, he too had a unique, independent take on the Jesus tradition.

The model of multiple, independent early Christian works, all plowing their own furrows, turns out not to be sustainable, at least if James Barker is right. Barker argues, in my view persuasively, that there was actually a kind of snowballing trajectory, whereby the first gospel, Mark, is used by Matthew and Luke. They rewrite, rework, and reimagine their source. But Luke also knows Matthew's revision of Mark, and he, in turn, copies, corrects, and changes his second source. This does not stop with Luke. The Fourth Gospel, so long thought to have been an independent work of theological but troubling genius, based on the same pool of oral traditions as the Synoptics, actually turns out to have read, reimagined, and rewritten the Synoptics.

In this book, Barker argues compellingly for what is effectively a new paradigm in gospel interrelations, even if it has its precedents. Austin Farrer already argued in 1955 for a model like this, which proceeds from Mark, to Matthew, to Luke, to John. But Barker's book is different, and as someone who is admittedly sympathetic to his approach, I found a great deal to enjoy and appreciate, and, most importantly, to learn from. I am honored to have a chance to endorse *Writing and Rewriting the Gospels* and to write this foreword.

One of the many virtues of this book is that it combines a seriousness of purpose with a lightness of touch. In spite of the sometimes complex subject matter, the book is eminently readable, and its style is lively and compelling. Barker is not afraid to reach for analogies old and new, so that as well as Vergil, Homer, Origen and Augustine, Quintilian, Josephus, and Anselm of Canterbury, we hear about Pinocchio, The Beatles, Peter Jackson, Seinfeld, *Mad Men*, and Monty Python.

Barker has a visual imagination, and I found myself looking at the evangelists, and the books they were writing, in ways that I have not seen before. This is in part because Barker does not stop at describing phenomena. He actually attempts to re-create them. He tells us about how he made his own ancient writing materials so that he—and the readers of this book—can get a sense of what it meant physically to write a gospel. When I was in graduate school, the humanities students used to joke about doing anything "practical" because it was seen as so far from the kind of cerebral work we were doing, but by engaging seriously with ancient writing practices, Barker embraces "the material turn" to shed new light on gospel composition.

A lot of this book is about source-criticism, the question of gospel relationships and the sources used by the evangelists, but while many scholars have been content to focus on the "that" of this question—"that" Matthew and Luke used Mark, "that" John knew the Synoptics, and so on—Barker goes further and answers the key question about "how" one writer used another's work. This involves the kind of contextualizing and historical imagination that bring this book to life, but it also becomes an argument for the particular solution that Barker is advocating, Matthew's use of Mark, Luke's use of Mark and Matthew, and John's use of all three.

The best academic books work whether they are read at the desk or in the armchair. They tell a compelling story that makes sense when it is read in sequence, but they reward excerpting individual elements. This book will work for those professors assigning particular chapters for their different classes, but it will also work for those who want to read the whole thing, on the beach, on the plane, or in the armchair at home. *Writing and Rewriting the Gospels* will cause us to rethink the subject matter of its subtitle, *John and the Synoptics*, and to write and rewrite our own perspectives on these fascinating works.

Mark Goodacre

Abbreviations

1 Apol.	Justin Martyr, *First Apology*
A(Y)B	Anchor (Yale) Bible
ABRL	Anchor Bible Reference Library
Aen.	Vergil, *Aeneid*
AIL	Ancient Israel and Its Literature
AJA	*American Journal of Archaeology*
Ant.	Josephus, *Jewish Antiquities*
Apocr.	Macarius Magnes, *Apocriticus*
APSP	*American Philosophical Society Proceedings*
Argon.	Apollonius of Rhodes, *Argonautica*
ASP	American Studies in Papyrology
ATANT	Abhandlungen zur Theologie des Alten und Neuen Testaments
BDAG	Danker, Frederick W., Walter Bauer, William F. Arndt, and F. Wilbur Gingrich. *Greek-English Lexicon of the New Testament and Other Early Christian Literature.* 3rd ed. Chicago: University of Chicago Press, 2000
BETL	Bibliotheca Ephemeridum Theologicarum Lovaniensium
BibInt	*Biblical Interpretation*
BibInt	Biblical Interpretation Series
BMSEC	Baylor–Mohr Siebeck Studies in Early Christianity
BNTC	Black's New Testament Commentaries
BPC	Biblical Performance Criticism
BR	*Biblical Research*
BTB	*Biblical Theology Bulletin*
BTS	Biblical Tools and Studies
BZNW	Beihefte zur Zeitschrift für die neutestamentliche Wissenschaft
Cat. Min.	Plutarch, *Cato the Younger*
CBQ	*Catholic Biblical Quarterly*
CCS	Classical Culture and Study

CCSA	Corpus Christianorum Series Apocryphorum
CCTC	Cambridge Classical Texts and Commentaries
ClQ	*Classical Quarterly*
Comm. Jo.	Origen, *Commentary on the Gospel of John*
Comm. Matt.	Origen, *Commentary on the Gospel of Matthew*
Cons.	Augustine, *Harmony of the Gospels*
Cont	*Continuum*
CSEL	Corpus Scriptorum Ecclesiasticorum Latinorum
CSML	Cambridge Studies in Medieval Literature
CUASEC	Catholic University of America Studies in Early Christianity
Decr.	Athanasius, *Defense of the Nicene Definition*
Dial.	Justin Martyr, *Dialogue with Trypho*
DJD	Discoveries in the Judean Desert
EC	*Early Christianity*
ECC	Eerdmans Critical Commentary
ECL	Early Christianity and Its Literature
ESV	English Standard Version
ETL	*Ephemerides Theologicae Lovanienses*
GCS	Die griechischen christlichen Schriftsteller der ersten [drei] Jahrhunderte
Gen. Rab.	Genesis Rabbah
Geogr.	Strabo, *Geography*
GRM	Graeco-Roman Memoirs
GTA	Göttinger theologischer Arbeiten
Haer.	Irenaeus, *Against Heresies*
Her.	Philo, *Who Is the Heir?*
Herm. Vis.	Shepherd of Hermas, Visions
Hist. eccl.	Eusebius, *Ecclesiastical History*
Hom. Jo.	John Chrysostom, *Homilies on John*
Hom. Luc.	Origen, *Homilies on Luke*
HThKNT	Herders Theologischer Kommentar zum Neuen Testament
ICC	International Critical Commentary
ICS	*Illinois Classical Studies*
Ign. *Eph.*	Ignatius, *To the Ephesians*
Ign. *Magn.*	Ignatius, *To the Magnesians*
Ign. *Smyrn.*	Ignatius, *To the Smyrnaeans*
Ign. *Trall.*	Ignatius, *To the Trallians*
IJL	Interpreting Johannine Literature
Il.	Homer, *Iliad*

Inst.	Quintilian, *The Orator's Education*
J.W.	Josephus, *Jewish War*
JBL	*Journal of Biblical Literature*
JS	Johannine Studies
JSHJ	*Journal for the Study of the Historical Jesus*
JSJSup	Supplements to the Journal for the Study of Judaism
JSNT	*Journal for the Study of the New Testament*
JSNTSup	Journal for the Study of the New Testament Supplement Series
JSRC	Jerusalem Studies in Religion and Culture
JTS	*Journal of Theological Studies*
LC	*Language and Communication*
LCL	Loeb Classical Library
Leg.	Philo, *Allegorical Interpretation*
Lives	Diogenes Laertius, *Lives of Eminent Philosophers*
LNTS	The Library of New Testament Studies
LSJ	Liddell, Henry George, Robert Scott, and Henry Stuart Jones. *A Greek-English Lexicon*, 9th ed. with revised supplement. Oxford: Clarendon, 1996
LSTS	The Library of Second Temple Studies
LXX	Septuagint
m. Ber.	Mishnah Berakot
Mem.	Xenophon, *Memorabilia*
MTSR	*Method and Theory in the Study of Religion*
Nat.	Pliny the Elder, *Natural History*
Nat. orig.	Augustine, *The Nature and Origin of the Soul*
NHMS	Nag Hammadi and Manichaean Studies
NIV	New International Version
NovT	*Novum Testamentum*
NovTSup	Supplements to Novum Testamentum
NRSV	New Revised Standard Version
NTD	Das Neue Testament Deutsch
NTGF	The New Testament in the Greek Fathers
NTL	New Testament Library
NTMon	New Testament Monographs
NTS	*New Testament Studies*
NTTh	New Testament Theology
NTTS	New Testament Tools and Studies
NTTSD	New Testament Tools, Studies, and Documents

OCD	*Oxford Classical Dictionary*. Edited by Simon Hornblower and Antony Spawforth. 4th ed. Oxford: Oxford University Press, 2012
Od.	Homer, *Odyssey*
OECGT	Oxford Early Christian Gospel Texts
OECS	Oxford Early Christian Studies
OOT	Hugo Grotius, *Opera Omnia Theologica*
Or.	Origen, *Prayer*
P.Oxy.	*The Oxyrhynchus Papyri*. Edited by Bernard P. Grenfell et al. London: Egypt Exploration Fund, 1898–
Pan.	Epiphanius, *Panarion*
PG	Patrologia Graeca. Edited by J.-P. Migne. 162 vols. Paris, 1857–1886
PL	Patrologia Latina. Edited by J.-P. Migne. 217 vols. Paris, 1844–1864
PNTC	Pillar New Testament Commentary
Prax.	Tertullian, *Against Praxeas*
Princ.	Origen, *First Principles*
Ps.-Clem. Hom.	Pseudo-Clementine, *Homilies*
RB	*Revue biblique*
RBL	*Review of Biblical Literature*
[Rhet.]	Dionysius of Halicarnassus, [*Art of Rhetoric*]
RJT	Reception of Jesus in the First Three Centuries
RSECW	Routledge Studies in the Early Christian World
SBLDS	Society of Biblical Literature Dissertation Series
SC	Sources chrétiennes
SHGR	Studies in the History of Greece and Rome
SJT	*Scottish Journal of Theology*
SMART	*Studies in Medieval and Renaissance Teaching*
SNTSMS	Society for New Testament Studies Monograph Series
SNTW	Studies of the New Testament and Its World
SP	Sacra Pagina
Spir.	Basil of Caesarea, *On the Holy Spirit*
StBibLit	Studies in Biblical Literature
StPatrSup	Studia Patristica Supplements
Symp.	Xenophon, *Symposium*
TAPA	*Transactions for the American Philological Association*
TBC	Torch Bible Commentaries
TENTS	Texts and Editions for New Testament Studies
TLG	Thesaurus Linguae Graecae
TT	Textes et traditions

UNT	Untersuchungen zum Neuen Testament
VGPV	Veröffentlichungen der Gesellschaft Pro Vindonissa
Vir. ill.	Jerome, *On Illustrious Men*
VL	Vetus Latina [Old Latin]
VTSup	Supplements to Vetus Testamentum
WGRW	Writings from the Greco-Roman World
WUNT	Wissenschaftliche Untersuchungen zum Neuen Testament
ZAW	*Zeitschrift für die alttestamentliche Wissenschaft*

INTRODUCTION

ONCE UPON A TIME, THERE WAS A living wooden puppet who was helped by a talking cricket and a fairy. The puppet's nose grew longer when he lied, and for a while he became a donkey. But he turned back into a living puppet and eventually transformed into a real boy living with the man who crafted him. Those are elements from the story of Pinocchio, originally written in Italian by Carlo Collodi in the late nineteenth century.[1]

There are many other facets of Collodi's story, which has been retold many times. Three of many film adaptations are the 1940 Disney animated version, the 2022 Disney blend of live-action and computer-generated imagery, and Guillermo del Toro's 2022 stop-motion version.[2] Unlike the book, those films align with one another by giving the cricket a name, making him the narrator, and enhancing his role throughout the story. Also, those films employ the fairy to enliven the puppet initially, whereas in the book, Pinocchio was always a living puppet that had been cut from a magical block of wood. Moreover, the extent and duration of Pinocchio's donkey metamorphosis is either attenuated or excised from the films.[3] The two 2022 films even incorporate a backstory, whereby Pinocchio was carved by Geppetto as he grieved the death of his son. I will not spoil any endings, but Pinocchio's ultimate transformation isn't always the same in the films.

Mine is a book about the Gospels, and I am not trying to label them as fairy tales. I've introduced the Pinocchio story as analogous to the Gospels with re-

1. Carlo Collodi, *Le avventure di Pinocchio: Storia di un burattino* (Florence: Paggi, 1883); Carlo Collodi, *Pinocchio*, trans. Mary Alice Murray, Wordsworth Children's Classics (Ware: Wordsworth, 1995).

2. Ben Sharpsteen and Hamilton Luske, *Pinocchio* (Walt Disney, 1940); Robert Zemeckis, *Pinocchio* (Walt Disney, 2022); Guillermo del Toro, *Pinocchio* (Netflix, 2022).

3. Even in Matteo Garrone's live-action, Italian film *Pinocchio* (Archimede with Rai Cinema and Le Pacte, 2019), which remains remarkably faithful to the book, there are abbreviations; for example, Pinocchio appears before the ape judge but does not go to prison, whereas in the book, Pinocchio serves a four-month sentence.

spect to proliferation and adaptation. A narrative can capture readers' attention and leave them wanting more. So subsequent stories can use the same characters and follow the same narrative arc. Yet some episodes can be omitted or altered, new characters and events can be introduced, and the beginning and ending can be revised and extended. In the case of the Gospels, once Mark established a market for Jesus narratives,[4] Matthew, Luke, and John crowded the market.

To explain the phenomenon of gospel proliferation, I focus on the material production of the Gospels, and I plot simple, snowballing trajectories from Mark to Matthew to Luke to John. I argue that each subsequent evangelist used every preceding gospel. I am willing to risk oversimplification, because in my opinion too much biblical scholarship has produced overly complicated theories to explain relatively easy reading and writing practices.

I hope that scholars find my explanations compelling, but I have also tried to write an accessible book that will appeal to students and laypersons as well. I ended up with more footnotes than I wanted, particularly in this chapter, and no doubt I've left out works that deserved engagement. But in the end, I've avoided as much technical jargon as possible, and I've written in the plain style I use when teaching this subject to students and congregants. In this introductory chapter, I briefly summarize the history of research into the production and reception of the Gospels. I then mention a couple of scholarly approaches I've chosen not to follow. Finally, I highlight some newer approaches that I find quite helpful.

A Brief History of Gospel Research

It cannot be known with certainty who wrote the Gospels, regardless of early traditional identifications. Irenaeus of Lyons (ca. 130–ca. 200) defended the apostolic origins of the canonical gospels: the apostle Matthew originally wrote in Hebrew; Mark wrote what he learned as a disciple of the apostle Peter; Luke was an associate of the apostle Paul; and the Fourth Gospel came from John, the beloved disciple (*Haer.* 3.1.1).[5] Irenaeus's overarching point was that

4. Two recent works on Mark's significance as the first gospel are Helen K. Bond, *The First Biography of Jesus: Genre and Meaning in Mark's Gospel* (Grand Rapids: Eerdmans, 2020); Chris Keith, *The Gospel as Manuscript: An Early History of the Jesus Tradition as Material Artifact* (Oxford: Oxford University Press, 2020).

5. Lorne Zelyck ("Irenaeus and the Authorship of the Fourth Gospel," in *The Origins of John's Gospel*, ed. Stanley E. Porter and Hughson T. Ong, JS 2 [Leiden: Brill, 2015], 239–58) convincingly refutes the notion that Irenaeus considered John, "the disciple of the Lord," anyone other than the son of Zebedee.

the church should read his four, preferred gospels—no more, no less, and no substitutions (*Haer.* 3.11.8). Although his claims regarding authorship were long accepted, they simply cannot be proved.

Nor can it be known when and where the Gospels were written. I date each of the canonical gospels between 70 and 110 CE, sometime after the Roman destruction of the Jerusalem temple but sometime before the early bishop Ignatius of Antioch wrote his letters.[6] I consider that forty-year window to be a narrow range, not a broad one. And within that span, there is no way to discern whether the Gospels were written in rapid succession or after long intervals; either possibility is equally likely.[7]

One area of certainty is that the Gospels were not written independently. More than 90 percent of Mark's Gospel reappears in Matthew and Luke. And it's not just that these gospels tell so many of the same stories: these gospels frequently use the exact same words. Since these three can so easily be "seen together," they are called the Synoptics. The Synoptic problem therefore refers to inferences of which gospel came first and which ones used the others as sources. Less than 20 percent of John's Gospel has parallel material found in one or more of the Synoptics. And when John does have synoptic parallels, the wording typically differs. John diverges so much from the Synoptics that it is fair to ask whether the differences are reconcilable. A related question is whether the Fourth Gospel used one or more of the Synoptic Gospels as source texts. I offer my own answers to these questions throughout this book, so for now I briefly describe how these questions have been answered throughout history.[8]

---

6. My former student Nicholas J. McGrory and I made this argument in "When Were the Gospels Written?" (paper presented at the annual meeting of the Midwest Region of the Society of Biblical Literature, Bourbonnais, IL, 7 February 2016). Regarding composition, I think that John (4:21) and the Synoptics (Matt 24:1–2 // Mark 13:1–2 // Luke 21:5–6) presuppose that the temple has been destroyed. Regarding reception, I think that Ignatius knew Matthew, Luke, and John, which entails that Mark had been written. I accept the middle recension of Ignatius's letters as authentic, and I accept the traditional date of Ignatius's martyrdom prior to 110 CE; see J. B. Lightfoot, *The Apostolic Fathers* (London: Macmillan, 1889–1890; repr., Peabody, MA: Hendrickson, 1989), 3:30.

7. I elaborate these points in my essay "Tatian's Diatessaron and the Proliferation of Gospels," in *The Gospel of Tatian: Exploring the Nature and Text of the Diatessaron*, ed. Matthew R. Crawford and Nicholas J. Zola, RJT 3 (London: Bloomsbury T&T Clark, 2019), 127, 139.

8. There are much more detailed histories available. For the Synoptic problem, see David Laird Dungan, *A History of the Synoptic Problem: The Canon, the Text, the Composition, and the Interpretation of the Gospels*, ABRL (New York: Doubleday, 1999); see also John S. Kloppenborg, "The History and Prospects of the Synoptic Problem," in *The Oxford Hand-*

Readers have observed the Gospels' similarities and differences from the very beginning. In the second half of the second century, Tatian the Assyrian made the so-called Diatessaron, which intricately interwove Matthew, Mark, Luke, and John into a single harmonious narrative. Yet by doing so, Tatian effectively produced a fifth gospel of his own.[9] Origen of Alexandria (ca. 185–ca. 254) appears not to have known the Diatessaron, but he collected and carefully compared the Gospels that would become canonical. In his commentary on John, Origen said that someone would become dizzy if they tried to reconcile the Gospels as historically true (*Comm. Jo.* 10.3), and he realized that some readers would disregard the Gospels as unreliable or uninspired based on their conflicting accounts (*Comm. Jo.* 10.3). Origen nonetheless asserted the spiritual truth of the Gospels, even if they differed in a bodily (i.e., literal) sense. Origen went so far as to say the Gospels' spiritual truth was sometimes preserved in a historical lie (*Comm. Jo.* 10.5).

Origen might have drawn the Gospels' spiritual-bodily distinction from his predecessor Clement of Alexandria (ca. 150–ca. 215). Such a statement by Clement is preserved by Eusebius of Caesarea (ca. 260–ca. 340; *Hist. eccl.* 6.14.5–8),[10] who himself reiterated the spiritual-bodily dichotomy. Eusebius added the tradition that John wrote the last of the four canonical gospels in full awareness of the published Synoptics.[11] Despite being a great admirer of Origen, Eusebius tacitly dissented with regard to the Gospels' discord. In the West, Jerome (ca. 345–420) reinforced Eusebius's claim that John read and intention-

---

book of the Synoptic Gospels, ed. Stephen P. Ahearne-Kroll (New York: Oxford University Press, 2023), 3–26. For John and the Synoptics, see D. Moody Smith, *John among the Gospels*, 2nd ed. (Columbia: University of South Carolina Press, 2001); see also Harold Attridge, "John and Mark in the History of Research," in *John's Transformation of Mark*, ed. Eve-Marie Becker, Helen K. Bond, and Catrin H. Williams (London: T&T Clark, 2021), 9–22. The dates for the figures mentioned below come from F. L. Cross and E. A. Livingstone, eds., *The Oxford Dictionary of the Christian Church*, 4th ed. (Oxford: Oxford University Press, 2005).

9. For the importance of reading the Diatessaron as "a gospel in its own right," see Francis Watson, "Towards a Redaction-Critical Reading of the Diatessaron Gospel," *EC* 7 (2016): 100.

10. Eusebius's "highly selective" reading of Clement has rightly been called into question: Clement undeniably used more than our four canonical gospels, yet Eusebius is using Clement to validate the fourfold gospel. See Francis Watson, *Gospel Writing: A Canonical Perspective* (Grand Rapids: Eerdmans, 2013), 437–38.

11. "However, John [was] last, having perceived that the bodily things had been manifested in the Gospels; having been urged by his acquaintances, [John was] divinely borne in spirit to make a spiritual Gospel" (Eusebius, *Hist. eccl.* 6.14.7). John's "acquaintances" (γνώριμος) could also be considered "pupils," as in Rufinus's Latin translation of Eusebius (*discipulus*).

ally supplemented the Synoptics (*Vir. ill.* 9).[12] In the East, John Chrysostom (ca. 347–407) interpreted the Fourth Gospel's concluding acknowledgments of insufficiency—that all the world's books cannot fully contain the story of Jesus (20:30; 21:25)—to mean that John was well aware that neither he nor the synoptists had told the whole story (*Hom. Jo.* 87).[13]

Early orthodox and catholic tradition regarding the harmonious fourfold gospel was gaining momentum. Nevertheless, Origen's reservations were well founded, for the Neoplatonist philosopher Porphyry (ca. 232–ca. 303) concluded that the Gospels' discord (*asymphōnos; Apocr.* 2.12) rendered them unreliable and untrue.[14] Unlike Origen, Porphyry drew no distinction between historical and spiritual truths, so if the Gospels contradicted each other anywhere, then they were unreliable everywhere. For example, during the crucifixion, Jesus cried out that God had forsaken him (Matt 27:46 // Mark 15:34); Jesus commended his spirit to the Father (Luke 23:46); and Jesus said, "It is finished" (John 19:30). According to Porphyry, the Gospels either recorded the deaths of several men, or the separate evangelists inaccurately reported the death of Jesus (*Apocr.* 2.12).

A century after Porphyry had died, his polemic lived on, so Augustine's (354–430) treatise on the *Harmony of the Gospels* attempted to prove that the Gospels didn't really contradict one another. Augustine assumed that John had read all three Synoptics (*Cons.* 1.4/7). According to Augustine, then, Jesus must have disrupted the commerce in the Jerusalem temple two years before he died, as in the Gospel of John (2:13–17), and Jesus must have done the same thing during passion week, as in the Synoptics (*Cons.* 2.67/129).[15] Not even the Synoptics could contradict one another, so different women must have anointed Jesus on different occasions: an early anointing occurred during the Galilean ministry as Luke narrated (7:36–50), and Jesus was anointed again sometime during passion week as the other gospels said (*Cons.* 2.79/154).[16] Yet in the case of less

---

12. Kurt Aland, *Synopsis Quattuor Evangeliorum*, 14th ed. (Stuttgart: Deutsche Bibelgesellschaft, 1985), 546.

13. For a contemporary reclamation of this argument, see Keith, *Gospel as Manuscript*, 135–46.

14. I consider Porphyry the most likely polemicist in Macarius Magnes's *Apocriticus*; for discussion, see Pieter W. van der Horst, "Macarius Magnes and the Unnamed Anti-Christian Polemicist: A Review Article," in *Jews and Christians in Their Graeco-Roman Context: Selected Essays on Early Judaism, Samaritanism, Hellenism, and Christianity*, WUNT 196 (Tübingen: Mohr Siebeck, 2006), 181–89.

15. Matt 21:10–17 // Mark 11:15–17 // Luke 19:45–46.

16. Matt 26:6–13 // Mark 14:3–9 // John 12:1–8.

glaring discrepancies, such as the timing of Jesus's healing of Peter's mother-in-law, Augustine suggested that the evangelists recorded events in the order they remembered them—not necessarily as the events occurred (*Cons.* 2.21/51).

Thanks in large part to Augustine's treatise, the harmony of the Gospels was not seriously questioned in medieval and early modern European Christendom. Peter Comestor (d. 1278) pointed out key differences, particularly between John and the Synoptics. Yet Comestor did so in the gospel history section of his *Historia Scholastica*, which was his own version of a gospel harmony.[17] When writing commentaries on all the books of the Bible, Nicholas of Lyra (1270–1340) noted differences among the Gospels, but he adhered to Jerome's testimony that John had supplemented the Synoptics. Later, the Protestant Reformer John Calvin reaffirmed John Chrysostom's interpretation of John 20:31 as reflecting John's knowledge of the Synoptics.[18] Conversely, Calvin saved time by writing a commentary on his own harmony of the Synoptics so that he didn't have to write separate commentaries on such similar gospels.[19]

The Protestant Reformation produced seismic shifts and unintended consequences. A Reformer like Calvin could simultaneously challenge medieval scholastic theologians while maintaining patristic testimonies regarding the harmony of the Gospels. Other thinkers were less credulous, and Deism and the Enlightenment allowed scholars to reenvision the gospel writers. In 1642, Hugo Grotius said that the evangelists did not need to be inspired, since "they told stories, not prophecies."[20] A century later, Gotthold Ephraim Lessing called the gospel writers "merely human."[21] Peter Annet revived Porphyry's

---

17. PL 198:1537–1644; Comestor's *Historia evangelica* is his revision of the gospel harmony preserved in Codex Fuldensis, the earliest extant witness to a thoroughgoing recension of Tatian's gospel; see James W. Barker, *Tatian's Diatessaron: Composition, Redaction, Recension, and Reception*, OECS (Oxford: Oxford University Press, 2021), 19–20.

18. John Calvin, *Commentary on the Gospel according to St. John*, trans. William Pringle (Edinburgh: Calvin Translation Society, 1847), 2:281. Calvin's commentary appeared in 1553.

19. John Calvin, *Commentary on a Harmony of the Evangelists, Matthew, Mark, and Luke*, 3 vols., trans. William Pringle (Edinburgh: Calvin Translation Society, 1845–1846).

20. Dirk van Miert, *The Emancipation of Biblical Philology in the Dutch Republic, 1590–1670* (Oxford: Oxford University Press, 2018), 153; van Miert quotes Grotius, *Votum pro pace ecclesiastica*, in *OOT* 3:672, which uses Luke as an example of citing eyewitnesses as his authorities rather than direct, divine inspiration.

21. Gotthold Ephraim Lessing, "Neue Hypothese über die Evangelisten als bloß menschliche Geschichtsschreiber betrachtet," written in 1778 and published in *Theologischer Nachlaß* (Berlin: Voß und Sohn, 1784), 45–72.

line of reasoning that the Gospels' discord undermined their claim to truth,[22] and by the early nineteenth century, Carol Bretschneider could deem the Fourth Gospel nonapostolic and fictitious.[23] Such statements were the exception rather than the rule, however, and plenty of scholars continued reading the Gospels as harmonious.

Contemporary gospel source criticism is deeply indebted to early textual criticism. Although the Greek New Testament had remained the norm throughout the Byzantine Empire, the Greek New Testament did not flourish in Europe until the Renaissance and Reformation eras. By the early 1500s, Greek New Testaments could be mass produced via the printing press. More importantly, in 1550 Stephanus published the first edition with a critical apparatus noting variant readings from various manuscripts; for nearly two hundred years thereafter, "scholars ransacked libraries and museums" to find more manuscripts.[24] The more Greek manuscripts one studies, the more textual variants one discovers, and the tendencies of scribes—whether careful or careless— become readily apparent. So when Henry Owen wrote about gospel origins in 1764, he expressly denied that the Gospels were written independently. On the contrary, subsequent evangelists had "transcribed" the earlier gospels.[25]

At that point in the history of biblical scholarship, Owen represents a crucial and forceful statement of literary dependence. It's not just that one evangelist was familiar with what another gospel had said. Instead, like a scribe attempting to make an exact copy of an exemplar, some of the work of the evangelists required visual contact as they directly copied a source text. The degree of difference between textual criticism and source criticism is that new gospels reworked their sources more freely, although in many episodes, the source material was barely changed.

Irenaeus (*Haer.* 3.1.1) had listed the Gospels in what became the standard order: Matthew, Mark, Luke, and John.[26] Origen had claimed this as the order

22. Peter Annet, *The Resurrection of Jesus Considered: In Answer to the Trial of the Witnesses* (London: Annet, 1743).

23. Carolus Theoph. Bretschneider, *Probabilia de evangelii et epistolarum Joannis, apostoli, indole et origine* (Leipzig: Barth, 1820), 64; I owe this reference to Hans Windisch, *Johannes und die Synoptiker: Wollte der vierte Evangelist die älteren Evangelien ergänzen oder ersetzen?*, UNT 12 (Leipzig: Hinrichs, 1926), 12.

24. Bruce Metzger and Bart D. Ehrman, *The Text of the New Testament: Its Transmission, Corruption, and Restoration*, 4th ed. (New York: Oxford University Press, 2005), 153.

25. Henry Owen, *Observations on the Four Gospels: Tending Chiefly to Ascertain the Times of Their Publication and to Illustrate the Form and Manner of Their Composition* (London: Payne, 1764), 82.

26. The alternate Western order of the Gospels (Matthew, John, Luke, and Mark) was

in which the Gospels were written (*Comm. Matt.* 1.1), and Augustine reiterated this tradition (*Cons.* 1.2/3). Moreover, Augustine acknowledged the different sequence of events in the Gospels, but he did not think that any evangelist was unaware of their predecessors' writings (*Cons.* 1.2/4). That assumption became known as the Augustinian hypothesis, and it endured for centuries.

As gospel composition came into sharper focus during the Enlightenment, scholars reexamined Augustine's presuppositions. Owen daringly rearranged the order of the Synoptics: Matthew came first, Luke was second, and Mark was third; yet Owen followed the tradition that John knew and approved of the Synoptics.[27] Owen's reordering of the Synoptics was elaborated by Johann Jakob Griesbach, and the theory became known as the Griesbach hypothesis. Griesbach made a proper gospel synopsis by arranging each gospel's rendition of sayings and stories in parallel columns; except in the passion narrative and resurrection accounts, Griesbach omitted the Fourth Gospel.[28] He also rejected the ancient tradition that attached the Gospel of Mark to the apostle Peter.[29]

The Griesbach hypothesis took root in the Tübingen school, cultivated by Ferdinand Christian Baur. By the early nineteenth century, reexamination of the Synoptic problem was in full force, and John's relation to the Synoptics was becoming strained. Baur claimed that John knew Mark's and Luke's written gospels, but Baur thought that John's Matthean parallels arose via oral tradition.[30] A stronger argument came from a contemporary of Baur's, Friedrich Lücke, who concluded that John read none of the written Synoptics; John instead relied on a common stock of oral tradition.[31] From then on, the

---

also popular and is known from early Greek witnesses such as Papyrus 45 and Codices Bezae and Washingtonianus as well as several Old Latin manuscripts such as Codex Corbiensis secundus (sigla VL 8, *ff²*).

27. Owen, *Observations on the Four Gospels*, 111–12.

28. Johann Jakob Griesbach, *Synopsis evangeliorum Matthaei, Marci et Lucae una cum iis Joannis pericopis quae historiam passionis et resurrectionis Jesu Christi complectuntur*, 2nd ed. (Halle, 1797).

29. Johann Jakob Griesbach, "A Demonstration That Mark Was Written after Matthew and Luke," trans. Bernard Orchard, in *J. J. Griesbach: Synoptic and Text-Critical Studies 1776–1976*, ed. Bernard Orchard and Thomas R. W. Longstaff, SNTSMS 34 (Cambridge: Cambridge University Press, 1978), 114–15.

30. Ferdinand Christian Baur, *Kritische Untersuchungen über die kanonischen Evangelien: Ihr Verhältniß zu einander, ihren Charakter und Ursprung* (Tübingen, 1847), 280.

31. Friedrich Lücke, *Commentar über die Schriften des Evangelisten Johannes*, vol. 1, 3rd ed. (Bonn: Weber, 1833), 154–56 (198–200 in the 1840 edition).

Griesbach hypothesis weakened, while the theory of Johannine independence strengthened.

Regarding the Synoptic problem, Markan priority—the claim that Mark was the first gospel, which Matthew and Luke each used as a source—had already been advanced.[32] And as Romantic notions of oral tradition gained momentum,[33] scholars entertained the notion of a stock of material common to Matthew and Luke. To make a very long story short,[34] Markan priority became the norm, and Q (short for *Quelle*, the German word for "source") was regarded as the second source used by Matthew and Luke. That formulation is called the two-source hypothesis, since Matthew and Luke relied on the two sources of Mark and Q. The key innovation was that Matthew and Luke were now seen as independent gospels; neither knew the work of the other, but each relied on a long-lost, long list of sayings along with a few narratives. Such a solution to the Synoptic problem emerged slowly in the second half of the nineteenth century, particularly in Germany. Early in the twentieth century, B. H. Streeter synthesized the two-source hypothesis in England and North America.[35] At the turn of the twenty-first century, scholars had painstakingly reconstructed the Q document as it might have existed.[36]

Regarding John and the Synoptics, history repeated itself. Streeter (like Baur a century before) concluded that John used Mark and Luke but not Matthew. Percival Gardner-Smith (like Lücke a century before) argued that all of John's synoptic material arose via oral tradition rather than literary dependence.[37]

32. Gottlob Christian Storr, *Über den Zweck der evangelischen Geschichte und der Briefe Johannis* (Tübingen: Heerbrandt, 1786), 278, 289.

33. For a reasonable and sharp critique of Romanticism's legacy in biblical studies, see Robyn Faith Walsh, *The Origins of Early Christian Literature: Contextualizing the New Testament within Greco-Roman Literary Culture* (Cambridge: Cambridge University Press, 2021), 50–104.

34. To fill in the gaps of nineteenth-century scholarship, see the concise account by Kloppenborg, "History and Prospects," 5–13.

35. B. H. Streeter, *The Four Gospels: A Study of Origins* (London: Macmillan, 1924). Streeter hardly worked in a vacuum. As Dungan (*History of the Synoptic Problem*, 332) points out, Streeter benefited immensely from the works of F. Crawford Burkitt (*The Gospel History and Its Transmission* [Edinburgh: T&T Clark, 1906]) and John C. Hawkins (*Horae Synopticae: Contributions to the Study of the Synoptic Problem* [Oxford: Clarendon, 1898]) among others.

36. James M. Robinson, Paul Hoffmann, and John S. Kloppenborg, eds., *The Critical Edition of Q*, Hermeneia (Minneapolis: Fortress, 2000). John S. Kloppenborg (*The Formation of Q: Trajectories in Ancient Wisdom Collections* [Philadelphia: Fortress, 1987]) has even posited three hypothetical, compositional stages for the hypothetical Q source.

37. Percival Gardner-Smith, *Saint John and the Synoptic Gospels* (Cambridge: Cambridge University Press, 1938).

Even if Gardner-Smith's contribution was largely symbolic,[38] the book marked "the turn of the tide" for C. H. Dodd.[39] Dodd's monograph, soon joined by the landmark commentaries of Rudolf Bultmann and Raymond Brown,[40] formed a strong contingent favoring Johannine independence. Conversely, it is difficult to speak of a twentieth-century consensus, since arguments for John's literary dependence on the Synoptics never evaporated. C. K. Barrett's commentary maintained John's use of Mark.[41] Also, in numerous essays, Frans Neirynck—head of the Leuven school—maintained John's use of all three Synoptics.[42] Currently there is broad support for John's use of Mark.[43] Moreover, Steven Hunt and Wendy North have separately demonstrated John's use of all three Synoptics.[44]

The two-source hypothesis may still be the consensus for solving the Synoptic problem, but there is increasing dissent on several fronts.[45] In the second half of the twentieth century, the Griesbach hypothesis made a revival,[46] but very few scholars have given up Markan priority—a triumph of nineteenth-

38. See Joseph Verheyden, "P. Gardner-Smith and 'the Turn of the Tide,'" in *John and the Synoptics*, ed. Adelbert Denaux, BETL 101 (Leuven: Leuven University Press, 1992), 452.

39. C. H. Dodd, *Historical Tradition in the Fourth Gospel* (Cambridge: Cambridge University Press, 1963), 8 n. 2.

40. Rudolf Bultmann, *The Gospel of John: A Commentary*, trans. G. R. Beasley-Murray, R. W. N. Hoare, and J. K. Riches (Philadelphia: Westminster, 1971); Raymond E. Brown, *The Gospel according to John*, AB 29–29A (Garden City, NY: Doubleday, 1966–1970), 1:xliv–xlvii.

41. C. K. Barrett, *The Gospel according to St. John: An Introduction with Commentary and Notes on the Greek Text*, 2nd ed. (Philadelphia: Westminster, 1978).

42. See, e.g., Frans Neirynck, *Evangelica: Gospel Studies*, ed. Frans Van Segbroeck, BETL 60 (Leuven: Leuven University Press, 1982), 181–488.

43. Eve-Marie Becker, Helen K. Bond, and Catrin H. Williams, eds., *John's Transformation of Mark* (London: T&T Clark, 2021).

44. Steven A. Hunt, *Rewriting the Feeding of the Five Thousand: John 6.1–15 as a Test Case for Johannine Dependence on the Synoptic Gospels*, StBibLit 125 (New York: Lang, 2011); Wendy E. S. North, *What John Knew and What John Wrote: A Study in John and the Synoptics*, IJL (Lanham, MD: Lexington Books/Fortress Academic, 2020).

45. The three-source hypothesis is like the two-source hypothesis, except that Luke also used Matthew; a more complicated version, according to which Q also influenced Mark, is the Q+/Papias hypothesis of Dennis R. MacDonald, *Two Shipwrecked Gospels: The Logoi of Jesus and Papias's Exposition of Logia about the Lord*, ECL 8 (Atlanta: Society of Biblical Literature, 2012).

46. E.g., William R. Farmer, *The Synoptic Problem: A Critical Analysis* (New York: Macmillan, 1964); Allan J. McNicol, ed., with David L. Dungan and David B. Peabody, *Beyond the Q Impasse: Luke's Use of Matthew* (Valley Forge, PA: Trinity International, 1996); David B. Peabody, ed., with Lamar Cope and Allan J. McNicol, *One Gospel from Two: Mark's Use of Matthew and Luke* (Harrisburg, PA: Trinity International, 2002).

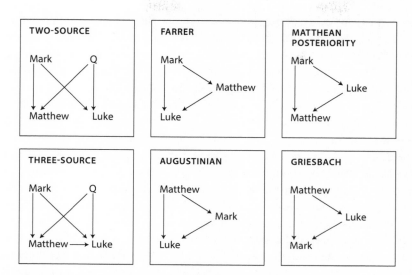

Figure 1.1. Synoptic problem hypotheses

century research. A stronger rival comes from the Farrer hypothesis: Mark wrote first; Matthew used Mark; and Luke used Matthew and Mark. The name comes from Austin Farrer, who outlined the theory in 1955;[47] Michael Goulder, Mark Goodacre, and others have bolstered the theory,[48] which I also defend in this book. As an alternative to the Farrer hypothesis, some scholars propose Matthean posteriority: Mark wrote first; Luke used Mark; and Matthew used both Mark and Luke.[49] Figure 1.1 diagrams the main solutions—past and

47. A. M. Farrer, "On Dispensing with Q," in *Studies in the Gospels: Essays in Memory of R. H. Lightfoot*, ed. D. E. Nineham (Oxford: Blackwell, 1955), 55–88.

48. Michael D. Goulder, *Luke: A New Paradigm*, 2 vols., JSNTSup 20 (Sheffield: JSOT Press, 1989); Mark Goodacre, *The Case against Q: Studies in Markan Priority and the Synoptic Problem* (Harrisburg, PA: Trinity International, 2002); John C. Poirier and Jeffrey Petersen, eds., *Marcan Priority without Q: Explorations in the Farrer Hypothesis*, LNTS 455 (London: Bloomsbury T&T Clark, 2015).

49. Ronald V. Huggins, "Matthean Posteriority: A Preliminary Proposal," *NovT* 34 (1992): 1–22; Robert K. MacEwen, *Matthean Posteriority: An Exploration of Matthew's Use of Mark and Luke as a Solution to the Synoptic Problem*, LNTS 501 (London: Bloomsbury T&T Clark, 2015); Alan Garrow, "Streeter's 'Other' Synoptic Solution: The Matthew Conflator Hypothesis," *NTS* 62 (2016): 398–417; Chakrita M. Saulina, "Competitive Traditions: Luke's and Matthew's (Con)Textualizations of the Beelzebul Controversy," in *The Synoptic Problem 2022: Proceedings of the Loyola University Conference*, ed. Olegs Andrejevs et al., BTS 44 (Leuven: Peeters, 2023), 233–75.

present—to the Synoptic problem; the direction of the arrows indicates which earlier gospel exerted influence. In other words, an arrow extending from one gospel means that it served as a source for whichever subsequent gospel.

Most two-source dissenters hold in common Q skepticism. Q is a hypothetical text, and since Matthew and Luke do not agree word for word when they supposedly used Q, then it might be simpler to ask whether Matthew used Luke or vice versa. Goodacre said it best: "There is surely nothing to lose, except perhaps a document that no one has ever found."[50] Also, Joseph Weaks offers MarQ as an ingenious critique of Q.[51] If one is convinced that Matthew and Luke used Mark, then what happens if one uses the same principles for reconstructing Q to reconstruct Mark out of Matthew and Luke? Such a reconstruction is what Weaks calls MarQ, which ends up being approximately half as long as the actual Gospel of Mark; also, many of Mark's most distinctive attributes disappear in the process of reconstruction. The point is that a hypothetical source text will unavoidably be conformed to the wording of the texts that absorbed it. So if the actual source text were ever discovered, it would most likely differ substantially from any reconstruction made in its absence.[52]

Paths Avoided

There are two main paths I have chosen not to take in this book. One is the study of the historical Jesus. I am certain that the historical Jesus existed, but I am uncertain about how precisely anyone could reconstruct words and sayings of Jesus and the chronology of his ministry. Also, source criticism of the Fourth Gospel has traditionally differed from source criticism as applied to the Synoptic problem. Instead, I study John's relation to the Synoptics much in the same way I study the interrelations of the Synoptics.

The Historical Jesus and the Legend of John Henry

When I describe how subsequent evangelists rewrote earlier gospel stories, I make no attempt to discern what actually happened. Thus I am uninterested in the quest for the historical Jesus. To be sure, scholars have long developed

---

50. Goodacre, *Case against Q*, 18.

51. Joseph Weaks, "Limited Efficacy in Reconstructing the Gospel Sources for Matthew and Luke," in *Empirical Models Challenging Biblical Criticism*, ed. Raymond F. Person Jr. and Robert Rezetko, AIL 25 (Atlanta: SBL Press, 2016), 331–54.

52. Weaks, "Limited Efficacy," 350.

and deployed criteria to ascertain what Jesus really said and did.[53] One criterion was multiple, independent attestation, the notion that Jesus was more likely to have said something if the saying circulated widely and was recorded in independent texts such as Mark's Gospel and Q or the Gospels and Paul's letters.[54] But if there was no Q document, then it cannot count as a multiple source; nonetheless, some scholars maintain that Paul independently recorded some historical information about Jesus.[55] I will argue even more strongly that none of our sources are independent: I do not believe in Q; I will show that John knew all three Synoptics; and I have become convinced that all four evangelists knew at least some of Paul's letters.

To be clear, I am entirely unsympathetic to so-called mythicist claims that Jesus of Nazareth was not a historical person.[56] There was a historical Jesus, but my book makes no attempt to recover his words and deeds. I am more interested in the literary activity of subsequent gospel writers, who could "correct"—that is, rewrite—a predecessor's account even if they had no direct knowledge of actual events.

As a modern analogy, the American folk hero John Henry could hammer steel drills faster than the newly invented, steam-powered rock drill for the construction of railroad tracks—although he tragically died in the process. Scott Reynolds Nelson has identified the historical John Henry as an African American in the Virginia Penitentiary, whose convicts worked alongside steam drills in 1868 on the Chesapeake and Ohio (C&O) Railroad at the Lewis Tunnel in Virginia, near the West Virginia border. The legendary competition between John Henry and the steam drill is often placed at the Big Bend Tunnel in West Virginia. Yet Nelson has explained this discrepancy by identifying Cal Evans as a cook, who relocated from Lewis to Big Bend in 1875. Evans was already telling stories of John Henry, and his stories soon became a ballad.

53. E.g., John P. Meier, "Criteria: How Do We Decide What Comes from Jesus?," in *A Marginal Jew*, vol. 1, *The Roots of the Problem and the Person*, ABRL (New York: Doubleday, 1991), 167–95.

54. Meier, *Marginal Jew*, 1:174.

55. E.g., Mark Goodacre, "Criticizing the Criterion of Multiple Attestation: The Historical Jesus and the Question of Sources," in *Jesus, Criteria, and the Demise of Authenticity*, ed. Chris Keith and Anthony Le Donne (London: T&T Clark, 2012), 168–69.

56. For thoroughgoing refutations of mythicism, see Bart D. Ehrman, *Did Jesus Exist? The Historical Argument for Jesus of Nazareth* (New York: HarperOne, 2013); see also Maurice Casey, *Jesus: Evidence and Argument or Mythicist Myths?* (London: Bloomsbury Academic, 2014).

The first recorded John Henry song dates to 1924, but at least thirty versions were known by 1933.[57]

I deeply admire Nelson's recovery of the historical John Henry, but I am more interested in the ways songwriters reinterpreted the story with no historical knowledge. For example, in most of the traditional renditions, as a baby John Henry could hold a hammer and a piece of steel. It was known even then that he would someday die from hammering steel, a premonition typically revealed as John Henry sat on one of his parent's knees; sometimes it was his mother's,[58] but other times it was his father's.[59] The parentage question opened space for artistic license. Johnny Cash wrote that John Henry was one of twelve children, and Cash implies that each child was conceived whenever their father got out of jail.[60] Jason Isbell wrote instead that John Henry was an illegitimate child.[61] In those two songs, none of John Henry's family history demands historical accuracy. Instead, subsequent songwriters creatively rewrote and reinterpreted earlier recordings. I would not press the analogy to Jesus too far, although I have heard one claim of John Henry's resurrection![62] My point is simply that literary dependence and creative rewriting can be fruitfully explored without regard for historicity.

Source Criticism, but Which Sources and at How Many Stages?

For the Synoptic Gospels, I explain how Matthew used Mark and how Luke used both Mark and Matthew. I pay very little attention to Q as a hypothetical source used independently by Matthew and Luke, because I do not believe that Q existed. Much like my disregard for historical Jesus questions, I do not speculate about how and where any of the synoptic material came from. Matthew contains much more material than does Mark, and Luke adds even more stories and sayings. Yet I do not appeal respectively to M and L sources

57. Scott Reynolds Nelson, *Steel Drivin' Man: John Henry, the Untold Story of an American Legend* (Oxford: Oxford University Press, 2006), 38–40, 89, 104, 122.

58. E.g., Tennessee Ernie Ford, "John Henry," *This Lusty Land!*, Capitol Records, 1957.

59. E.g., Harry Belafonte, "John Henry," *"Mark Twain" and Other Folk Favorites*, RCA Victor, 1954.

60. Johnny Cash, "The Legend of John Henry's Hammer," *Blood, Sweat and Tears*, Columbia Records, 1962.

61. Drive-By Truckers, "The Day John Henry Died," *The Dirty South*, New West Records, 2004.

62. Doc Watson, "John Henry," *Doc Watson Sings Songs for Little Pickers*, Sugar Hill Records, 1990.

for Matthew's and Luke's unique material—an elaboration of the two-source hypothesis known as the four-source hypothesis.[63] The evangelists should be granted sweeping authorial prerogative to omit and rework their sources while inventing or recording unique gospel material. As a general rule, I work with the extant gospels and dispense with hypothetical sources.

Source criticism for the Gospel of John has typically appealed to hypothetical sources and multiple compositional stages.[64] For example, John allegedly used a signs source, which has been reconstructed;[65] maybe there was a pre-Johannine passion narrative;[66] and some scholars have explained how the final form of the gospel developed through various stages.[67] When I talk about source criticism with regard to the Fourth Gospel, I disregard those hypothetical sources and focus instead on John's relation to the Synoptics. Basically I approach John's writing and rewriting as an extension of the Synoptic problem.

I see John as the last of the four canonical gospels, so I do not adhere to Paul Anderson's neologistic, bioptic model of interfluentiality.[68] "Bioptic" replaces "Synoptic," since Anderson argues that Mark and a first edition of John were the earliest gospels. By "interfluential," Anderson means that Markan traditions influenced Johannine traditions, that Johannine traditions influenced Lukan traditions,[69] and that the first written edition of John influenced Matthew's Gospel; but then Matthew's Gospel also influenced the final written

63. For the four-document hypothesis of Mark, Q, M, and L, see Streeter, *Four Gospels*, 223–70.

64. For an overview, see Michael Labahn, "Literary Sources of the Gospel and Letters of John," in *The Oxford Handbook of Johannine Studies*, ed. Judith M. Lieu and Martinus C. de Boer (Oxford: Oxford University Press, 2018), 23–43.

65. E.g., Robert T. Fortna, *The Gospel of Signs: A Reconstruction of the Narrative Source Underlying the Fourth Gospel*, SNTSMS 11 (Cambridge: Cambridge University Press, 1970).

66. E.g., Frank Schleritt, *Der vorjohanneische Passionsbericht: Eine historisch-kritische und theologische Untersuchung zu Joh 2,13–22; 11,47–14,31 und 18,1–20,29*, BZNW 154 (Berlin: de Gruyter, 2007); cf. James W. Barker, review of *Der vorjohanneische Passionsbericht*, by Frank Schleritt, *CBQ* 74 (2012): 397–98.

67. E.g., Bultmann, *Gospel of John*; Urban C. von Wahlde, *The Gospel and Letters of John*, 3 vols., ECC (Grand Rapids: Eerdmans, 2010).

68. Paul N. Anderson, *The Fourth Gospel and the Quest for Jesus: Modern Foundations Reconsidered*, LNTS 321 (London: T&T Clark, 2006).

69. Others have argued for Luke's direct use of John. See, e.g., Barbara Shellard, "The Relationship of Luke and John: A Fresh Look at an Old Problem," *JTS* 46 (1995): 71–98; Mark Matson, *In Dialogue with Another Gospel? The Influence of the Fourth Gospel on the Passion Narrative of the Gospel of Luke*, SBLDS 178 (Atlanta: Society of Biblical Literature, 2001). That is an important perspective to consider, but it's one that I tacitly refute when I point out John's use of Luke.

edition of John.[70] I think there is only one direction of influence running from Matthew to John, and later in this book, I will argue for John's use of Luke rather than the reverse. While Anderson has helpfully highlighted numerous parallels between John and the Synoptics, his overall explanation is highly speculative and needlessly complicated.

PATHS FOLLOWED

If one is to answer chicken-and-egg questions about which gospels influenced the others, then it is fair to ask what the Gospels originally looked like. Ancient manuscripts have noticeable differences, but I do not let those text-critical differences stand in the way of source and redaction criticism—figuring out which gospel came first and then discerning why a later gospel changed the story in large and small ways. Another consideration is what kind of communities were reading and writing the Gospels in the first place. In that regard, I follow the recent approach of looking at the evangelists as ancient writers without making assumptions about churches the authors may or may not have been writing from or for. In line with yet another crucial intervention in current biblical scholarship, I study the proliferation of gospels in terms of rewriting, a standard feature of Second Temple Jewish and Greco-Roman literature.

Finalizing the Gospels

To a very large extent, I am satisfied with ongoing attempts to reconstruct the earliest recoverable form of the Gospels. To be sure, there are thousands of minor variations among manuscripts, but as Michael Holmes puts it, "microlevel fluidity" does not undermine their "macrolevel stability."[71] In this book, then, I predominantly translate from the twenty-eighth edition of the Nestle-Aland

---

70. The only place where Anderson (*Fourth Gospel*, 121–25) sees back-and-forth between Matthew and John is that the binding and loosing saying in Matt 16:19 propelled the similar saying in John 20:23, which boomeranged back to the second binding and loosing saying in Matt 18:18. Elsewhere I have argued that John 20:23 is already responding to Matt 18:18 (James W. Barker, *John's Use of Matthew*, Emerging Scholars [Minneapolis: Fortress, 2015; repr., Eugene, OR: Wipf & Stock, 2021], 37–61).

71. Michael W. Holmes, "From 'Original Text' to 'Initial Text': The Traditional Goal of New Testament Textual Criticism in Contemporary Discussion," in *The Text of the New Testament in Contemporary Research: Essays on the Status Quaestionis*, ed. Bart D. Ehrman and Michael W. Holmes, 2nd ed., NTTSD 42 (Leiden: Brill, 2013), 674.

Greek New Testament published by the German Bible Society.[72] When needed, I cite important variants found in early manuscripts. Some passages are more difficult to reconstruct than others. For example, if one consults just three ancient manuscripts of Matthew's parable of the two sons (21:28–31), one finds three different versions of the parable.[73] If ever there were a case of multiple originals, Matthew's parable could be one, but I would still consider such a scenario highly exceptional. That is, authors likely produced multiple drafts, so an initial text could differ from a final, published form of the same text, and it is conceivable that both versions circulated from the get-go. Even if that were the case, the Gospels' macrostability remains intact.

Early copyists also altered the text by harmonization. That is, scribes found a parallel passage with slightly different wording in another gospel, and then the scribes reworded one version so that both gospels agreed verbatim. The Gospel of Matthew tended to influence the texts of Mark and Luke, but there are plenty of examples where any of the Synoptics could influence any other.[74] Even John's Gospel could influence the Synoptics; the quintessential case is when the piercing of Jesus's side in John 19:34 was inserted into very early and significant manuscripts of Matthew (27:49).[75] The overall point here is that some text-critical variants complicate source-critical questions: if scholars can't know with certainty what the original text of each gospel said, then there will be confusion in some places about which evangelist more likely influenced another.

---

72. I cite a few word choices of contemporary English versions later in this book, but otherwise all the translations of ancient texts are my own. I err on the side of being overly literal; as just one example, I translate Ιακωβ as Jacob, despite the long-standing English rendering of James.

73. See Codices Sinaiticus, Vaticanus, and Bezae: James W. Barker, "Teaching the Bible as a SuperNatural Book: Textual Criticism of Matthew's Parable of the Two Sons," *SMART* 25 (2018): 113–21.

74. On this phenomenon, see Cambry G. Pardee, *Scribal Harmonization in the Synoptic Gospels*, NTTSD 60 (Boston: Brill, 2019); see also James W. Barker, review of *Scribal Harmonization in the Synoptic Gospels*, by Cambry G. Pardee, *JTS* 72 (2021): 392–94.

75. E.g., Codices Sinaiticus and Vaticanus. Matthew R. Crawford ("Severus of Antioch on Gospel Reading with the Eusebian Canon Tables," in *Gospel Reading and Reception in Early Christianity*, ed. Madison N. Pierce, Andrew J. Byers, and Simon Gathercole [Cambridge: Cambridge University Press, 2022], 215–33) conclusively reclaims Severus's argument from late antiquity that the Johannine side-piercing is a later interpolation into Matthew; if it had originally stood in Matthew, then it would have been included in Eusebius's canon 7, the Matthew-John parallels.

In the end, though, the problem of textual variants and their bearing on source criticism has long been recognized.[76] I pay close attention to manuscript evidence at times, and my source-critical conclusions rest on larger-scale compositional and redactional tendencies. I do not think the work of textual criticism will ever achieve complete certainty. Nevertheless, I do think that scholars can study the interrelations of the Gospels with the working assumption that the texts of the Gospels as published and circulated in the late first and early second centuries did not radically differ from the texts we can reconstruct in the twenty-first century.[77]

Redescribing Gospel Communities

A long-lasting side effect of redaction criticism was the endeavor to recreate communities from whom and for whom particular gospels were written.[78] Eventually, an alternative viewpoint held that the Gospels were intentionally written for universal circulation,[79] and a mediating position hypothesized that the Gospels were written within specific communities but with the expectation of an expanding audience.[80] A stronger argument would deem the Johannine

76. E.g., Gordon D. Fee, "Modern Text Criticism and the Synoptic Problem," in *J. J. Griesbach: Synoptic and Text-Critical Studies 1776-1976*, ed. Bernard Orchard and Thomas R. W. Longstaff, SNTSMS 34 (Cambridge: Cambridge University Press, 1978), 154-69; Peter M. Head, "Textual Criticism and the Synoptic Problem," in *New Studies in the Synoptic Problem: Oxford Conference, April 2008; Essays in Honour of Christopher M. Tuckett*, ed. Paul Foster et al., BETL 239 (Leuven: Peeters, 2011), 115-56; Brent Nongbri, "Manuscripts: The Problem with the Synoptic Problem," in *The Oxford Handbook of the Synoptic Gospels*, ed. Stephen P. Ahearne-Kroll (New York: Oxford University Press, 2023), 152-74.

77. The most obvious later interpolations are, of course, the longer ending of Mark (16:9-20) and the adulteress pericope in John (7:53-8:11).

78. E.g., the Matthean, Markan, Lukan, and Johannine communities, respectively, are firm fixtures in the following works: Ulrich Luz, *Matthew*, trans. James E. Crouch, 3 vols., Hermeneia (Minneapolis: Fortress, 2001-2007); Joel Marcus, *Mark*, 2 vols., A(Y)B 27-27A (New York: Doubleday, 2000-2009); Philip Francis Esler, *Community and Gospel in Luke-Acts: The Social and Political Motivations of Lucan Theology*, SNTSMS 57 (Cambridge: Cambridge University Press, 1987); Raymond E. Brown, *The Community of the Beloved Disciple: The Life, Loves, and Hates of an Individual Church in New Testament Times* (New York: Paulist, 1979).

79. Richard Bauckham, ed., *The Gospels for All Christians: Rethinking the Gospel Audiences* (Grand Rapids: Eerdmans, 1998).

80. E.g., David C. Sim, "The Gospels for All Christians? A Response to Richard Bauckham," *JSNT* 84 (2001): 3-27; Margaret M. Mitchell, "Patristic Counter-evidence to the Claim That 'the Gospels Were Written for All Christians,'" *NTS* 51 (2005): 36-79.

community a mere fabrication;[81] a more subtle version of John's environment suggests that, while "a community of sorts may have formed around the book itself, there is no evidence for its existence prior to the Gospel."[82]

Stanley Stowers most forcefully shook the foundations of gospel communities: "The way the concept of 'communities' and 'community' is deployed in scholarship hinders historical work on early Christianity, especially if early Christianity is to be treated as a normal human social phenomenon studied in the non-sectarian university."[83] Stowers has shifted the paradigm by redescribing the evangelists' social formation within networks of literate readers and writers—even ones who didn't personally know each other.[84]

What Stowers argued in nuce Robyn Walsh has brought to fruition. Walsh's *The Origins of Early Christian Literature* brilliantly contextualizes and demystifies the Gospels. Walsh describes the evangelists as "elite cultural producers," but she qualifies that "elite" is a relative term. Simply by virtue of being written, the Gospels come from literate persons, and the overwhelming majority of inhabitants in the Roman Empire were illiterate. Mark, for example, "is not Vergil," and yet "he has enough skill, means, and training to try his hand at a creative piece of writing."[85] I wholeheartedly endorse Walsh's description of the evangelists as well as her doubts that oral tradition is recoverable; I also concur that the proper way to envision gospel communities is as writers writing mainly to impress other writers, not as spokespersons for primitive churches.[86] Anyone who is interested in my book would do well to read Walsh's if they haven't already done so. I hope that my descriptions of material production in chapter 2 are complementary to Walsh's incisive descriptions of the broader social and cultural production of the Gospels.

Redaction criticism was traditionally preoccupied with "the distinctive theological and pastoral concerns of individual editors within their communities."[87] But if the evangelists' writing communities are redescribed along the lines of Stowers and Walsh, then the evangelists' theological motivations

---

81. Hugo Méndez, "Did the Johannine Community Exist?," *JSNT* 42 (2020): 350–74.

82. Adele Reinhartz, *Cast Out of the Covenant: Jews and Anti-Judaism in the Gospel of John* (Lanham, MD: Lexington Books/Fortress Academic, 2018), xiv.

83. Stanley Stowers, "The Concept of Community and the History of Early Christianity," *MTSR* 23 (2011): 238.

84. Stowers, "Concept of Community," 247–50.

85. Walsh, *Origins of Early Christian Literature*, 131.

86. Walsh, *Origins of Early Christian Literature*, 95, 99, 102, 156.

87. E. P. Sanders and Margaret Davies, *Studying the Synoptic Gospels* (London: SCM, 1989), 202–3.

need to be downplayed. I do not deny that gospel writers sometimes revised a source text to make theological points. I simply think that previous scholarship has overemphasized the evangelists' theological agendas. A more basic set of questions comes from ancient rhetoric,[88] particularly how narratives are constructed and comprehended. Oftentimes there are simple and sufficient rhetorical reasons why someone would rewrite their source material. I try to answer those questions about who, what, when, where, and why before I consider that a simple alteration somehow reveals a subsequent evangelist's deep theological convictions.

Rediscovering Rewriting

The proliferation of gospels fits within the broader scribal practices of imitation and rewriting,[89] which were ubiquitous in Jewish and Greco-Roman literature. Molly Zahn defines rewriting as "the deliberate, formally unmarked reproduction and modification of existing texts."[90] I think of the gospels' proliferation as Zahn's term "reuse"; each subsequent gospel became a "new work," even though it was derived from existing sources and remained recognizably connected to them.[91]

Rewriting was a fixture within biblical literature. The book of Deuteronomy, as its Greek name indicates, is literally the second (*deuteros*) version of torah (*nomos*). It repeats dozens of commandments from the earlier law books, most notably the Ten Commandments,[92] even as Deuteronomy revises some laws and adds others. The scribal practice of rewriting torah did not end with Deuteronomy. The book of Jubilees extensively combined, abbreviated, and reinterpreted Genesis and Exodus.[93] Compared with the canonical Torah, Jubilees is—as Eva Mroczek describes—"neither subservient nor hostile"; that is, "proliferation was a value" as new works "took their place alongside

---

88. E.g., Alex Damm, *Ancient Rhetoric and the Synoptic Problem: Clarifying Markan Priority*, BETL 252 (Leuven: Peeters, 2013).

89. For the concept of rewriting (*relecture* in French) applied to the Gospel of John, see, e.g., Jean Zumstein, *Kreative Erinnerung: Relecture und Auslegung im Johannesevangelium*, 2nd ed., ATANT 84 (Zurich: Theologischer Verlag Zurich, 2004); Hunt, *Rewriting*.

90. Molly M. Zahn, *Genres of Rewriting in Second Temple Judaism: Scribal Composition and Transmission* (Cambridge: Cambridge University Press, 2020), 3.

91. Zahn, *Genres of Rewriting*, 38; Zahn adds that rewriting was "a widespread, even ubiquitous scribal technique in early Judaism" (4).

92. Deut 5:6–21 // Exod 20:1–17.

93. Jubilees makes occasional references to Leviticus and Numbers as well.

other scriptures."[94] Besides Torah, the monarchies of Israel and Judah were recounted in the books of Samuel and Kings. Those books were condensed and rewritten in the books of Chronicles, which were later canonized alongside their source texts. Yet the process continued centuries later when Josephus rewrote all the historical books of the Old Testament in his *Antiquities of the Jews*.[95]

Among Greco-Roman literature, Homer was imitated more than anyone. The Gospels themselves may be indebted to Homer,[96] but centuries earlier a series of imitative works became known as the Epic Cycle.[97] The complete cycle comprised prequels, interquels, and a sequel to Homer's epics. The extant fragments also show significant overlap with the *Iliad* and *Odyssey*, including redundancies and incongruities. For example, the *Cypria* described the Trojan war before the *Iliad* commences, but the *Cypria* reinterpreted and even contradicted Homer at times.[98] As it pertains to gospel writing, the point is that subsequent authors could be deeply indebted to a source text while creatively rewriting it.

The Synoptic Gospels are closely intertwined with one another, whereas the Gospel of John diverges more sharply. Nevertheless, I am convinced that John remains deeply indebted to all three Synoptics—even in some instances that are not readily apparent. Here I have in mind the phenomenon of *oppositio in imitando*, a modern term to describe an ancient technique of imitating a classic story while turning elements inside out;[99] I promise that *oppositio in imitando* will be the only pretentious foreign phrase I use in this book.

A prime example comes from Vergil's *Aeneid*. On the whole, Vergil rewrote Homer's *Iliad* and *Odyssey* as a Roman epic so that the descendants of the Trojan losers would eventually conquer the entire Mediterranean world. In Homer's tale, the Greek hero Odysseus sailed to Hades and encountered his

94. Eva Mroczek, *The Literary Imagination in Jewish Antiquity* (Oxford: Oxford University Press, 2016), 142.

95. See especially Louis H. Feldman, *Studies in Josephus' Rewritten Bible*, JSJSup 58 (Leiden: Brill, 1998).

96. E.g., Dennis R. MacDonald, *The Homeric Epics and the Gospel of Mark* (New Haven: Yale University Press, 2000).

97. On the Epic Cycle, see Malcolm Davies, *The Greek Epic Cycle*, 2nd ed. (London: Bristol Classical, 2001); M. L. West, *Greek Epic Fragments from the Seventh to the Fifth Centuries BC*, LCL 497 (Cambridge: Harvard University Press, 2003); West, *The Epic Cycle: A Commentary on the Lost Troy Epics* (Oxford: Oxford University Press, 2013).

98. Davies, *Greek Epic Cycle*, 7, 40, 47.

99. G. Giangrande, "'Arte Allusiva' and Alexandrian Epic Poetry," *ClQ* 17 (1967): 85–97; Stephen M. Wheeler, "Ovid's Use of Lucretius in Metamorphoses 1.67–8," *ClQ* 45 (1995): 200–203.

mother. He didn't even know that she had died, since he had spent so many years away from home. Three times Odysseus tried to hug his mother, but she was a ghost, so he couldn't physically touch her (*Od.* 11.204–209). Vergil rewrote this account in the scene where Aeneas escaped Troy. He left behind his father and wife (*Aen.* 2.861–870), and he soon called out for her (*Aen.* 2.906–908). Come to find out, she had just died, and her ghost appeared before him (*Aen.* 2.911–913). Three times he tried to hug her but could not (*Aen.* 2.936–939). Much later, when Aeneas visited the underworld, he found his father. There, too, he tried three times to hug the ghost but was unable to (*Aen.* 6.828–831).

Vergil undeniably imitated Homer in those scenes, although Vergil rewrote many details and recast the characters. In the underworld, Aeneas meets his father instead of his mother, but it wouldn't make sense for his mother to be there, since she was the goddess Venus. Vergil also doubles the thrice-failed ghost-hugging motif and places one scene much earlier in the story. Aeneas met the ghost of his wife just moments after her death, not years later. Also, the ghost of Aeneas's wife was still in Troy, not yet in the underworld. The differences outnumber the similarities, and yet the similarities outweigh the differences. Vergil could write these scenes only by closely studying Homer, so Vergil was literarily dependent even though he exercised artistic license and literary creativity.

Oppositio in imitando also occurs in biblical texts. Jacob Wright has written extensively about the relationship between King David and Caleb, a hero from the book of Joshua.[100] According to the Bible's chronology, Caleb would have preceded David by a couple of centuries. However, according to Wright's meticulous analysis, the Bible's description of Caleb must have been written after the narratives regarding King David. Caleb is intended to be David's antitype, for the warrior Caleb was retrojected as David's superior, even though David later became king of the very territory Caleb had conquered. The sharpest difference pertains to their vigor: David died at the age of seventy, and he had stopped fighting years earlier; Caleb lived past the age of eighty, and even then he had not stopped fighting. The differences are so striking that they must be intentional.

My favorite example of *oppositio in imitando* in early Christian literature comes from the apocryphal Acts of Thomas, which radically rewrites Luke's story of the rich man and Lazarus (16:19–31). In the Gospel of Luke, a well-dressed rich man feasted daily while poor Lazarus just wanted the crumbs

---

100. Jacob L. Wright, *David, King of Israel, and Caleb in Biblical Memory* (New York: Cambridge University Press, 2014).

(vv. 19–21). In a simple reversal of fortune, both men died, the rich man suffered the flame of Hades, while father Abraham comforted Lazarus (vv. 22–25). The rich man wanted Lazarus to bring him a cool drop of water, but Abraham said it was impossible (vv. 24–26). The rich man then asked Abraham to send Lazarus back to earth to warn the man's five brothers, lest they suffer the same torment (vv. 27–28). Abraham again denied the rich man's request, saying that the brothers should just listen to Moses and the prophets (v. 29). The man insisted that his brothers would repent if they saw someone come back from the dead (v. 30), "but Abraham said to him, 'If they do not obey Moses and the prophets, nor will they be persuaded if someone rises from the dead'" (v. 31).

A very different story appears in the Acts of Thomas (chs. 17–26).[101] The book begins after Jesus's resurrection, and the remaining disciples cast lots to see who would go where to evangelize the world. The lot for India fell to Thomas, and the risen Jesus sold Thomas as a slave to a merchant who had been sent by the king of India to buy a craftsperson (chs. 1–2). Thomas arrived in India, and King Gundaphorus asked him to build a palace (ch. 17). Thomas sketched the design, and the king left money (ch. 18). The king regularly sent money, but instead of building a palace there, Thomas gave the money to the poor (ch. 19). Later the king sent an ambassador to ask what work was left, and Thomas replied that the palace lacked a roof, so the king sent more gold. Now up to this point, Thomas appears to have run quite a ruse. When I first read this story, I was expecting Thomas to take the last sum of money and hastily build the entire palace at a discount. But no, Thomas gave every last penny to the orphaned, widowed, and those who were suffering (ch. 19).

When the king finally came to see his palace, he realized that the apostle had given away the money, preached a new god, and performed healings and exorcisms; Thomas was thus a suspected sorcerer (μάγος; ch. 20). Gundaphorus asked Thomas whether he built a palace (ch. 21). Surprisingly Thomas answered yes, so the king asked to see it. Thomas answered, "Now you are not able to see it, but you will see it when you shall depart from this life" (ch. 21). The angry king imprisoned Thomas and decided to skin him alive and burn him to death (ch. 21).

The king had a brother named Gad, who fell ill and—with his dying words—begged the king to kill the sorcerer; otherwise, "my soul will not rest in Hades" (ch. 21). So Gad died, the king mourned, and he ordered a royal

---

101. My translations and chapter numbers are based on the Greek text via the TLG database: Maximilien Bonnet, *Acta apostolorum apocrypha*, vol. 2 (Leipzig: Mendelssohn, 1903).

burial (ch. 22). Meanwhile, angels led Gad into heaven, showed him houses, and asked him which one he wanted to inhabit. Gad begged for one in particular, but the angels refused, because that house turned out to be the one Thomas had built for Gundaphorus. So Gad asked permission to go back and buy the palace from his brother (ch. 22).

The angels let go of Gad's soul, which reentered his body as it was being prepared for burial (ch. 23). Gad called for his brother and said, "Sell me that palace, which you have in the heavens" (ch. 23), the one built by the imprisoned Christian (ch. 23). At that point, Gundaphorus understood the significance of "forthcoming eternal goods" (ch. 24).[102] The king said, "That palace I cannot sell you, but I pray to enter into it and live and be worthy of its inhabitants. But if you truly want to purchase such a palace, look the person shall live and build you [one] better than that" (ch. 24). The king brought in the apostle Thomas, and Gundaphorus begged forgiveness (ch. 24). The king's brother likewise fell before Thomas and begged to become worthy of Christian ministry (ch. 24). Thomas then praised God for revealing the truth to Gundaphorus and Gad (ch. 25). In the following days, Thomas baptized, anointed, and gave the Eucharist to the king and his brother, but not before they themselves were "assisting the needy, giving to everyone, and relieving everyone" (ch. 26).

As I see it, this scene in the Acts of Thomas could not have been composed independently of Luke's parable of the rich man and Lazarus. For most of the Thomasine version, it is implied that the rich king did not care for his poor subjects, since the apostle did so himself with the king's money. In the end, though, Gundaphorus and Gad clearly understand that repentance entails providing for the material needs of those in poverty. These are characteristically Lukan themes, as is the continuity in Luke-Acts between Moses and the prophets, on the one hand, and repentance and forgiveness through the Lord Jesus Christ, on the other. Yet the setting of India in the Acts of Thomas means that the king and his brother would not be expected to know the law and prophets, so that element has been removed. Perhaps counterintuitively, the strongest link between these episodes is their sharpest difference: as a plot twist, the Acts of Thomas allows the brother to come back to life, and

102. Harold Attridge ("Intertextuality in the *Acts of Thomas*," *Semeia* 80 [1997]: 120) rightly observes that the scene in Acts of Thomas (chs. 17–29) "dramatizes the injunction in the Sermon on the Mount to seek treasures in heaven (Matt 6:19–20)." Attridge isolated clear echoes and allusions of Matthew; I compliment and complement Attridge by suggesting a more subtle and extensive rewriting of Luke's parable.

the brothers repent as an alternate ending. The Acts of Thomas imitates the Lukan parable by substituting characters and by reversing the outcome of the story, a quintessential example of *oppositio in imitando*. I find the same literary technique at play as John rewrote the Synoptics.

WHERE TO GO FROM HERE

Here in chapter 1, I have introduced the interrelations of the Gospels and explained how my work fits into this perennial line of inquiry. Chapter 2 delves deeper into the reading and writing practices of the Greco-Roman

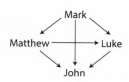

Figure 1.2. John and the Synoptics

world, since that's the Gospels' literary environment. Chapter 3 takes up the Synoptic problem and offers my defense of the Farrer hypothesis. Chapter 4 argues that the Gospel of John used all three Synoptics as source texts. Figure 1.2 diagrams my simple, snowballing solution to the production of the canonical gospels. I did not initially intend to write about the Gospels' claims regarding Jesus's divinity, but I did find places where the evangelists' theological propositions intertwined with source-critical problems. So chapter 5 looks at the Christology of the Gospel of John as it compares with the Synoptic Gospels, Paul's letters, and other pieces of early Christian literature. Chapter 6 concludes the book by tying together strands from each of the earlier chapters and by pointing in other directions for future research.

Chapter 1

How to Write a Gospel

SET IN THE SPRING OF 1960, the series premiere of *Mad Men* featured Peggy Olson (Elisabeth Moss) on her first day in "the steno pool" at the Sterling Cooper advertising agency.[1] As a period piece debuting in 2007, it's funny when Joan Harris (Christina Hendricks) warns Peggy not to be overwhelmed by the technology on her desk: a rotary telephone, an intercom, and a typewriter.[2] Using such antiquated devices may be difficult for some readers to imagine, but my family still had a rotary telephone and a typewriter in our home in 1990. That's when I was a freshman in high school, and I took a yearlong typing course. Our classroom had more than fifty electric typewriters pounding simultaneously at eight in the morning. I would not learn how to use a word processor on a personal computer until 1994, when I was a freshman in college.

Given my firsthand experience of such a radical transition in typing technology, I can at least imagine myself writing this book on a typewriter, but I would prefer not to. "I would prefer not to" was the refrain of Herman Melville's 1853 title character Bartleby,[3] who copied legal documents by hand more than a decade before the typewriter was invented. I definitely prefer not to imagine myself writing this book longhand, but in my lifetime, Umberto Eco expected his students to finish a handwritten draft of a thesis before having it typewritten.[4] Even in the early twenty-first century, former US president Bill

1. Alan Taylor, dir., *Mad Men*, season 1, episode 1, "Smoke Gets in Your Eyes," aired July 19, 2007, on AMC.
2. The typewriter unveiled at the episode's nine-minute mark is an IBM Selectric, which was not released until 1961.
3. Herman Melville, *Bartleby, the Scrivener: A Story of Wall Street*, in *The Texts of Melville's Short Novels*, ed. Dan McCall, Norton Critical Editions (New York: Norton, 2002), 3–34, originally published in *Putnam's Monthly Magazine*, November-December 1853 (p. 3, n. 1).
4. Umberto Eco, *How to Write a Thesis*, trans. Caterina Mongiat Farina and Geoff Farina, foreword by Francesco Erspamer (Cambridge: MIT Press, 2015), 185; the Italian edition was first published in 1977.

Clinton drafted his autobiography longhand, filling "twenty-two big, thick notebooks";[5] the published version was nearly a thousand typeset pages.[6]

Suffice it to say, the process of writing books has rapidly evolved in recent decades—so much so that modern scholars often mischaracterize handwritten book production, which was the norm for millennia. This chapter explains how books were written and studied in the Greco-Roman world. Compared to the present, I emphasize how different it was to use the writing materials of their day. At the same time, I insist that the processes of writing, revising, and rewriting really haven't changed all that much in two thousand years, so analogies to modern media can surprisingly illustrate ancient practices.

In this chapter, I explain briefly why I don't think the Gospels should be considered oral compositions, a model that no longer seems applicable in the first century CE. I then discuss the mental processes and material production of books in the first century. Writers obviously needed to know how to write, and they did so by repetitive reading and by imitating exemplary works. First-century authors predominantly used waxed tablets and bookrolls for drafts, and bookrolls were the medium for publication as well. Codices emerged by the late first century, but scholars should be wary of assuming that gospels were circulating so early in such a new format. Finally, I show several examples of authors who simultaneously used multiple source texts. The rest of the book's snowballing model of gospel proliferation depends on authors being able to manage more than one source at a time, but previous scholarship has misrepresented such a procedure as unfeasible. Authors managed to juggle multiple sources before, during, and after the writing of the Gospels.

ORALITY, AURALITY, AND LITERACY

A typical estimate of early Christian literacy is no more than 10 percent.[7] The Gospels' textualization required literacy on the part of writers and readers, but a much wider audience could listen to the Gospels being read aloud.[8] Orality has to do with speaking, aurality has to do with hearing, and literacy has to do with reading and writing. Some degree of orality could have influenced the Jesus

5. Bill Clinton, interview on *Late Show with David Letterman*, dir. Jerry Foley, CBS, 3 August 2004.

6. Bill Clinton, *My Life* (New York: Knopf, 2004).

7. Harry Y. Gamble, *Books and Readers in the Early Church: A History of Early Christian Texts* (New Haven: Yale University Press, 1995), 5.

8. For the processes of textualization, see Chris Keith, *The Gospel as Manuscript: An Early History of the Jesus Tradition as Material Artifact* (Oxford: Oxford University Press, 2020).

tradition before the Gospels were written. Oral traditions could even circulate thereafter, since Jesus quotes are occasionally found outside of any canonical or extracanonical gospel; for example, Jesus reportedly told his disciples to "become expert bankers."[9] I do not deny the existence of oral tradition, but I think it is utterly unrecoverable,[10] so I am primarily concerned with literacy.

My ensuing portrait of authors drafting, revising, and publishing gospels is therefore incompatible with oral composition.[11] The oral composition model goes back to the work of Milman Parry, a classicist who wanted to know how the Homeric epics were composed. Parry conducted fieldwork in former Yugoslavia in the early 1930s,[12] and he observed at least twenty South Slavic bards. He concluded that the Homeric epics were not only composed orally but also recited orally. Albert Lord accompanied Parry when they met Avdo Međedović, their "Yugoslav Homer," whose recitations could exceed fifteen thousand lines.[13]

Some biblical scholars have applied the oral composition model to the Gospels.[14] One version envisions the Gospel of Mark as a "composition in performance, but with a reed and ink as mouth."[15] A slightly different version suggests that the Gospels were "written 'transcriptions' of oral narratives that had

---

9. E.g., Ps.-Clem. *Hom.* 3.50.2; Origen, *Comm. Jo.* 19.7.2.

10. I am closely allied with Robyn Faith Walsh's (*The Origins of Early Christian Literature: Contextualizing the New Testament within Greco-Roman Literary Culture* [Cambridge: Cambridge University Press, 2021], 156) position that any elements of oral tradition known to the gospel writers "are irretrievable to us, if they existed at all."

11. I differentiate "oral composition" from "oral performance"; for the latter, Whitney Shiner's *Proclaiming the Gospel: First Century Performance of Mark* (Harrisburg, PA: Trinity International, 2003) helpfully contextualizes public readings of the written gospel.

12. "Milman Parry Collection of Oral Literature," Harvard Library, https://curiosity.lib. harvard.edu/milman-parry-collection-of-oral-literature.

13. Stephen Mitchell and Gregory Nagy, "Introduction to the Second Edition," in Albert B. Lord, *The Singer of Tales*, ed. Stephen Mitchell and Gregory Nagy, 2nd ed. (Cambridge: Harvard University Press, 2000), 14.

14. E.g., Joanna Dewey, "The Survival of Mark's Gospel: A Good Story?," *JBL* 123 (2004): 495–507; David Rhoads, "Performance Criticism: An Emerging Methodology in Second Testament Studies—Part I," *BTB* 36 (2006): 118–33; Antoinette Clark Wire, *The Case for Mark Composed in Performance*, BPC 3 (Eugene, OR: Cascade, 2011); Pieter J. J. Botha, *Orality and Literacy in Early Christianity*, BPC 5 (Eugene, OR: Cascade, 2012), 188. Nicholas A. Elder (*The Media Matrix of Early Jewish and Christian Narrative*, LNTS 612 [London: T&T Clark, 2019], 3) attempts a nuanced characterization of Mark's Gospel as "an oral tradition that was committed to the written medium via dictation," but he allows for "multiple rounds of revision" to the written product (32), which no longer sounds to me like oral composition.

15. Wire, *Case for Mark*, 58.

been composed in performance," although the performers neither read nor memorized scripts; in that case, surviving transcripts came from listeners remembering lengthy performances "with great faithfulness."[16] I am highly skeptical that either version of oral composition explains the Gospels' origins.[17]

For the composition-in-performance model, a contemporary analogy is improvisational comedy, but such performances are very short in duration—not hours long, as a gospel performance would run. By contrast, contemporary, hour-long stand-up comedy routines have been slowly crafted and committed to writing and to memory before a performance—usually with minimal if any notes on hand. Jerry Seinfeld famously retired decades of jokes after performing them one last time.[18] He later documented the arduous process of composing new material.[19] Very early on, Seinfeld lost his train of thought in the middle of a joke, looked through a stack of notes on stage, and asked himself—and his audience—what his point was. After three months, he had a solid twenty minutes of material. A month later, he was up to forty minutes, and after six months, he had reached a full hour. Even then, before a performance, he would read through a list of jokes or themes while reciting shorthand references such as "beauty contest."

Seinfeld's method is in fact attested in the Greco-Roman era. According to the master rhetorician Quintilian (ca. 35–ca. 96 CE), an orator could keep brief annotations in hand for occasional reference during a performance (*Inst.* 10.7.31), and everything could be written out in full if the entire performance needed to be memorized (*Inst.* 10.7.32). It was also possible for an accomplished orator such as Cicero (106–43 BCE) to write out the most important parts of a speech in a notebook and refer to it as needed. But mainly Cicero could rely on his quick thinking and improvisation during the performance. Cicero also had speeches transcribed during the performance via the innovation of shorthand.[20] Granted, Cicero shows that it was possible to compose extemporaneously with relatively little preparation and that speeches could be transcribed in the moment. Yet Cicero was the exception rather than the rule, and Quintilian warned that extemporaneous orations usually ended up looking foolish (*Inst.* 10.7.21).

16. Rhoads, "Performance Criticism," 118, 123, 124.

17. My skepticism was shared by Larry W. Hurtado ("Oral Fixation and New Testament Studies? 'Orality', 'Performance' and Reading Texts in Early Christianity," *NTS* 60 [2014]: 335) and Eric Eve (*Writing the Gospels: Composition and Memory* [London: SPCK, 2016], 67–72).

18. Marty Callner, dir., *Jerry Seinfeld: "I'm Telling You for the Last Time,"* HBO, 1998.

19. Christian Charles, dir., *Jerry Seinfeld: Comedian*, Miramax Films, 2002.

20. Plutarch, *Cat. Min.* 23.3.

When it comes to rhetorical savvy, I would not place any of the evangelists on par with Cicero. Besides very low literacy rates overall, extremely few people could transcribe via shorthand in the first century. It would also be highly extraordinary for someone to write out a gospel by remembering a performance of it. Despite having trained his memory since childhood, Quintilian found it difficult to memorize something by having someone read it to him—even if the work was broken down and read repetitively (*Inst.* 11.2.34). Moreover, prose was more difficult than poetry to memorize (*Inst.* 11.2.39).

To be sure, there were exceptional feats of memorization in antiquity. Augustine's friend Simplicius knew Vergil's *Aeneid* forward and backward.[21] However, such memorization requires a stable, written text that could be read repetitively. Hayden Pelliccia has forcefully pressed this point by scrutinizing performances in the ancient city of Dionysia.[22] Each year, a thousand choristers performed long poetic works verbatim,[23] an impossible feat if the literary work was in flux or if each performance was a bit different from another; both are tenets of the oral composition model.

Another problem for the oral composition model is relying on Parry's work on Homer as the foundation. The *Iliad* and *Odyssey* became relatively fixed in writing by 600 BCE.[24] It is at least conceivable that they emerged via oral composition. The same could be true of the subsequent works known as the Greek Epic Cycle, which were composed by 500 BCE.[25] Yet there was a marked shift in the Hellenistic period that I have not seen accounted for among biblical performance critics.

As Peter Bing has noted, Homer depicts himself as an oral poet appealing directly to the Muses for help in reciting the catalogue of ships and captains embarking for Troy (*Il.* 2.484–492).[26] After the conquest of Alexander the

21. Augustine, *Nat. orig.* 4.7.9; Mary Carruthers, *The Book of Memory: A Study of Memory in Medieval Culture*, 2nd ed., CSML (Cambridge: Cambridge University Press, 2008), 21–22. The *Aeneid*'s Latin word count (ca. sixty-four thousand) is comparable to the fourfold gospel in Greek (ca. sixty-five thousand).

22. Hayden Pelliccia, "Two Points about Rhapsodes," in *Homer, the Bible, and Beyond: Literary and Religious Canons in the Ancient World*, ed. Margalit Finkelberg and Guy G. Strousma, JSRC 2 (Leiden: Brill, 2003), 97–116.

23. Pelliccia, "Two Points," 100.

24. Martin West, "The Homeric Quest Today," *APSP* 155 (2011): 392.

25. Benjamin Sammons, *Device and Composition in the Greek Epic Cycle* (Oxford: Oxford University Press, 2017), 3. For the Epic Cycle's similarity to the Gospels vis-à-vis proliferation, see my essay "Tatian's Diatessaron and the Proliferation of Gospels," in *The Gospel of Tatian: Exploring the Nature and Text of the Diatessaron*, ed. Matthew R. Crawford and Nicholas J. Zola, RJT 3 (London: Bloomsbury T&T Clark, 2019), 114–15.

26. Peter Bing, *The Well-Read Muse: Present and Past in Callimachus and the Hellenistic*

Great, however, poets began taking dictation from the Muses. That is, first the poet had to hear the Muses while writing in solitude, and only later through the written medium could readers indirectly experience their inspiration. An Egyptian poet in the early third century BCE invoked the Muses, but he asked for their song to be written on tablets; another Hellenistic writer similarly invoked the Muses for aid in the first column of a writing tablet. Bing gives many other examples to make the crucial point: "It seems that the Muses have learned to write!"[27]

A final indication of oral composition's obsolescence comes from Greco-Roman Homeric imitations. I will discuss the work of Apollonius of Rhodes in more detail later. For now, I note that Apollonius imitated Homer masterfully, but the imitation was not an oral composition.[28] Similarly, albeit in Latin, Vergil wrote an innovative Homeric imitation, but when later artists envisioned him composing the *Aeneid*, the poet sat in a chair and inscribed a bookroll on his knee while listening to the Muses.[29] The point is that if Hellenistic and Roman imitations of Homeric epics were not being composed orally, then I don't see a strong foundation for applying the oral composition model to the Gospels.

MENTAL PROCESSES AND MATERIAL PRODUCTION

I view the Gospels as compositions that were drafted and extensively revised before publication. Literary production required education, and we know a lot about Greco-Roman pedagogy, because several *Progymnasmata* have survived;[30] these are the preliminary exercises for students transitioning from elementary education to higher rhetorical training. Also, in much more detail than the *Progymnasmata*, Quintilian wrote the *Orator's Education*, a twelve-volume work that is longer than the entire New Testament. The gospel writ-

---

Poets, Hypomnemata 90 (Göttingen: Vandenhoeck & Ruprecht, 1988; repr., Ann Arbor: Michigan Classical, 2008), 11–12.

27. Bing, *Well-Read Muse*, 14, 15, 19; by extension, Stephen King (*On Writing: A Memoir of the Craft* [New York: Scribner, 2000], 144) says that the Muse comes to "your typewriter or computer station."

28. Richard L. Hunter, "Apollonius Rhodius," *OCD* 122.

29. Charles Martindale, ed., *The Cambridge Companion to Virgil* (Cambridge: Cambridge University Press, 1997), 110–11, plate 1a.

30. George A. Kennedy, ed., *Progymnasmata: Greek Textbooks of Prose Composition and Rhetoric*, WGRW 10 (Atlanta: Society of Biblical Literature, 2003); see also Mikeal C. Parsons and Michael Wade Martin, *Ancient Rhetoric and the New Testament: The Influence of Elementary Greek Composition* (Waco, TX: Baylor University Press, 2018).

ers were by no means as accomplished as Quintilian, but he helpfully describes how students learned to write, the materials they used, and the mental processes involved.

Imitation and Recollection

According to Quintilian, the ability to paraphrase, abridge, and embellish Aesop's fables was a prerequisite to a rhetorical education (*Inst.* 1.9.1–3), and students should learn to imitate the best authors (*Inst.* 10.2.1). By reading Torah and the Prophets, the synoptists found ways to imitate Moses and Elijah.[31] For example, Matthew tells of Herod the Great's slaughter of the innocents in response to Jesus's birth (2:13–18), which recalls Pharaoh's infanticide when Moses was born (Exod 2:1–10). Jesus also resuscitates a widow's son (Luke 7:11–16), just as Elijah had done (1 Kgs 17:17–24). Jesus is said to have conversed with Moses and Elijah at the transfiguration,[32] so there is little doubt that the evangelists not only imitated Old Testament characters and episodes but also intended readers to recognize at least some of the parallels. I'll also show throughout the book how gospel writers imitated one another by copying verbatim or rewriting earlier stories and sayings.

It was important for an ancient author to have a good memory, but students were not typically memorizing entire literary works.[33] Instead, students memorized "sayings of brilliant men and selections from the greatest poets" (*Inst.* 1.1.36) as well as "selections from orators and historians" (*Inst.* 2.7.2). Quintilian himself frequently quoted phrases from Vergil's *Eclogues* (e.g., *Inst.* 10.1.12, 56, 92). To memorize a passage, Quintilian said to write it out in full, to break it into manageable portions, and to read the sections aloud repeatedly (*Inst.* 11.2.2, 27, 33).

As the fourfold gospel was becoming canonical, Eusebius of Caesarea (ca. 260–ca. 340 CE) described the upbringing of Origen of Alexandria (ca. 185–ca. 254 CE). Origen learned Scriptures by heart through daily recita-

---

31. See, e.g., Dale C. Allison Jr., *The New Moses: A Matthean Typology* (Minneapolis: Fortress, 1993); Thomas L. Brodie, *The Birthing of the New Testament: The Intertextual Development of the New Testament Writings*, NTMon 1 (Sheffield: Sheffield Phoenix, 2004); in reply to Brodie's thesis, see John S. Kloppenborg and Joseph Verheyden, eds., *The Elijah-Elisha Narrative in the Composition of Luke*, LNTS 493 (London: Bloomsbury, 2014).

32. Matt 17:1–9 // Mark 9:2–10 // Luke 9:28–36.

33. Contra Eve, *Writing the Gospels*, 82–83; and Alan Kirk, *Q in Matthew: Ancient Media, Memory, and Early Scribal Transmission of the Jesus Tradition*, LNTS 564 (London: Bloomsbury T&T Clark, 2016), 96–97.

tion as his father exacted (*Hist. eccl.* 6.2.7–8). Origen's Scripture memorization deserves scrutiny, however. John 12:45 says, "The one who sees me sees the one who sent me," and John 14:9c says, "The one who has seen me has seen the Father." Origen repeatedly writes, "The one who has seen me has seen the Father who sent me,"[34] a conflation arising "almost certainly from memory."[35]

On different occasions, Origen would quote the same verse in slightly different ways. Not only that, but sometimes Origen's quotations also correspond to known textual variants. For example, in Origen's *Commentary on the Gospel of John* (20.41.387), the quotation of John 6:51—where Jesus says, "I am the bread of life"—matches Codex Bezae exactly; yet in Origen's treatise on prayer (*Or.* 27.4), he quotes the same verse with exactly the same alterations found in Codex Koridethi.[36] This is a recurring phenomenon in Origen's writings,[37] and at times he explained to his readers that he had found different readings in different manuscripts of the same biblical text.[38] I suggest, then, that the longer the quotation and the closer the agreement with a known manuscript, the more likely it is that an author or reviser had visual contact with a written source. Origen could have read from manuscripts or quoted from memory while he was dictating to a scribe, and either way, the Scripture references could have been checked and revised prior to publication.

I have jumped ahead in time to Origen, a prolific author with extensive knowledge of Jewish and Christian Scriptures. While the scale of Origen's library and scriptorium was probably far greater than any of the evangelists', I find him a helpful analogy for the production of the Gospels.[39] Some material could have been recalled from memory, but there was plenty of time to go back and make revisions, although some mistakes might have gone uncorrected. For example, Matthew quotes a prophet as saying, "He shall be called a Nazorean" (2:23), but no such Old Testament prophecy exists. Yet when Mark (4:12) alluded to Isaiah 6:9–10, that people would hear a prophet

---

34. Origen, *Cels.* 7.43 [three times]; *Comm. Jo.* 13.25.153; 19.6.35; 32.29.359; *Hom. Luc.* 1.4.

35. Bart D. Ehrman, Gordon D. Fee, and Michael W. Holmes, *The Text of the Fourth Gospel in the Writings of Origen*, NTGF 3 (Atlanta: Scholars Press, 1992), 1:299 n. 1.

36. Ehrman, Fee, and Holmes, *Text of the Fourth Gospel*, 173 n. 3.

37. Gordon D. Fee, "Origen's Text of the New Testament and the Text of Egypt," *NTS* 28 (1982): 348–64.

38. Bruce M. Metzger, *Historical and Literary Studies: Pagan, Jewish, and Christian*, NTTS 8 (Grand Rapids: Eerdmans, 1968), 88–103.

39. According to Eusebius (*Hist. eccl.* 6.23.2), Origen dictated to more than seven shorthand writers taking turns; at least seven others were involved: some wrote out full drafts, and young women finished the works in calligraphy.

but not really understand the message, Matthew (13:14–15) added forty-seven words verbatim from Isaiah; Matthew most likely copied directly from a book of Isaiah at that point.

Given the exceptionally high degree of verbatim agreement among the Synoptic Gospels, scribal copying can also help us envision the emergence of a new gospel. I imagine Matthew first as a scribe making copies of Mark.[40] Perhaps the copyist Matthew altered a word or phrase here and there. But over time, the author Matthew figured out how to rewrite Mark much more extensively. Similarly, I think of Luke as a scribe making copies of Matthew and Mark. But Luke was also a scholar of these texts. By comparing the earlier gospels' similarities and differences, Luke could have decided how to rewrite them both. John shows far less dependence on the Synoptics. But where there is overlap, John reveals that he has carefully studied all his predecessors.

I take for granted that the gospel writers had good recollection of their literary sources and that the evangelists imitated and altered their sources. I have in mind, though, that the authors knew a source text well enough to seek and find parallel passages when needed. It would take exponentially more time to memorize a text by repetitive reading than simply knowing a text well enough to skim it and find a passage to work with. So I reject the assumption that the evangelists "made little or no use of direct eye contact with any of them while composing their own work."[41] Whether drafting or revising, I envision the gospel writers maintaining visual contact with their sources.[42]

Writing on Waxed Tablets

Once they attained enough familiarity with their source materials, authors could begin writing. Quintilian teaches to write slowly and to make frequent revisions (*Inst.* 10.3.5–11). Writers should make further revisions, specifically additions, deletions, and alterations (*Inst.* 10.4.1–2). The first draft should be written on waxed tablets, which can be easily erased, and some boards should leave room for corrections and insertions (*Inst.* 10.3.31–33). Parchment note-

---

40. For building a library by copying manuscripts yourself, see George W. Houston, *Inside Roman Libraries: Book Collections and Their Management in Antiquity*, SHGR (Chapel Hill: University of North Carolina Press, 2014), 13–14.

41. Contra Eve, *Writing the Gospels*, 41; see also 54: "In all probability, most authors worked from memory."

42. In this regard, I agree with R. A. Derrenbacker Jr., "Matthew as Scribal Tradent: An Assessment of Alan Kirk's *Q in Matthew*," *JSHJ* 15 (2017): 221.

books (*membrana*) and reused scrolls could also be used for drafts, but tablets were the most common.

There is ample archaeological evidence of Roman-era waxed tablets.[43] Boards from multiple sites measure around fourteen by twelve centimeters;[44] for comparison, the pages of Loeb Classical Library editions are around sixteen by ten centimeters. A single wooden board was usually between four and six millimeters thick. A student might learn to write the alphabet on a tablet with a single board with just one writing surface, but polyptychs had multiple pages for longer compositions.

The outside-facing boards were solid wood and served as covers. The inner boards had margins, usually between one and two centimeters, which surrounded the writing area. The writing area was recessed about one millimeter into the wood and filled with wax. Diptychs had two covers and two inner pages for writing, but additional inner boards were double sided. So triptychs had four pages, tetraptychs had six pages, and so forth; there are even octoptychs with fourteen pages.

Like codices, tablets were bound inside the long edge. Unlike codices, tablets were typically written horizontally with top and bottom pages rather than *transversa* with left and right pages. A writing area of twelve by ten centimeters could comfortably hold three hundred letters.[45] There is a nice wall painting of an open pentaptych in a house at Herculaneum,[46] a tablet that could fit two thousand letters while leaving blank space for revisions. Triptychs could fit a thousand letters and still leave empty space.[47]

---

43. On the use of waxed tablets in schools, see Raffaella Cribiore, *Writing, Teachers, and Students in Graeco-Roman Egypt*, ASP 36 (Atlanta: Scholars Press, 1996), 65–69.

44. Elizabeth A. Meyer, "Roman Tabulae, Egyptian Christians, and the Adoption of the Codex," *Chiron* 37 (2007): 295–347; Michael Alexander Speidel, *Die römischen Schreibtafeln von Vindonissa: Lateinische Texte des miltärischen Alltags und ihre geschichtliche Bedeutung*, VGPV 12 (Brugg: Gesellschaft Pro Vindonissa, 1996), 24; R. S. O. Tomlin, "'The Girl in Question': A New Text from Roman London," *Brittania* 34 (2003): 41.

45. E.g., Tomlin, "'Girl in Question.'"

46. E. G. Turner, *Greek Manuscripts of the Ancient World* (Princeton: Princeton University Press, 1971), 34, plate 10.

47. I typically use a conservative approximation of two thousand letters per pentaptych, but I note here that boards could be smaller or larger and that tablets could contain fewer or additional boards; the following measurements refer to the board, not the margined writing area: ca. 250 letters fit 11.2 × (4.5) cm (Speidel, *Die römischen Schreibtafeln*, 98); ca. four hundred letters fit 17 × 14 cm (P.Mich. 3.166; Francis W. Kelsey, "A Waxed Tablet of the Year 128 A.D.," *TAPA* 54 [1923]: 187–95); ca. five hundred letters would fit 17.6 × 13.9 cm if the writing area were filled (P.Berol. 14004); and a very large heptatych from Herculaneum

To test the feasibility of working with waxed tablets, I made a triptych. I used six-millimeter-thick walnut and cut three boards measuring fifteen by twelve centimeters. I left two-centimeter margins, so the writing area is approximately eleven and a half by nine centimeters. I used a router to recess the writing boards by one millimeter and filled them with melted beeswax and a dab of coconut oil; I also added some soot from burned papyrus to give the writing surface a charcoal color, which is easier to read. I have always written rather small, and I can easily fill a single writing surface with twelve lines and twenty letters per line. I can fit a few more letters per board if the wax is a bit harder, but the harder the wax, the more difficult it is to erase.

For a stylus, at times I have used an awl to write and a flathead screwdriver to erase. Mostly I just use a bamboo skewer that I have turned into a stylus: the pointy end can be sharpened like a pencil, and I filed and sanded the back end as a flat edge for erasing; the disadvantage of my skewer is that the erasing surface is smaller than would be found on a typical Roman-era stylus. In some archaeological finds, letters were written on waxed tablets, and the writing is preserved despite the wax having evaporated. The reason is that the metal stylus scrawled through the wax and inscribed the wood. That makes sense to me, since boards inevitably require less wax than I anticipate.

My triptych is relatively small, and—compared to my years of education— I still have very little experience using waxed tablets. I can nonetheless write out 175 Greek words (840 letters) with half a board left blank. For comparison, Luke's (5:17–26) story of Jesus's healing a paralyzed man is less than 1,100 letters; Mark's (2:1–12) version is less than 1,000 letters; and Matthew's (9:1–8) is less than 750 letters. Matthew could have easily drafted his scene on a triptych, while Mark and Luke could have used a triptych or tetraptych. Figure 2.1 shows that two boards could fit all of Matthew's version except for the closing sentence about the crowd's reaction to the miracle.

Luke would have needed sixteen pentaptychs to draft the entire gospel in one-third increments, as John Poirier suggested.[48] Or Luke could have

---

measures 29 × 14 cm: Elizabeth A. Meyer, "Writing Paraphernalia, Tablets, and Muses in Campanian Wall Painting," *AJA* 113 (2009): 572.

48. John C. Poirier, "The Roll, the Codex, the Wax Tablet and the Synoptic Problem," *JSNT* 35 (2012): 3–30. In response to Poirier, F. Gerald Downing's ("Waxing Careless: Poirier, Derrenbacker and Downing," *JSNT* 35 [2013]: 391) estimated five hundred letters per board, which would be the uppermost limit (e.g., P.Berol. 14004); however, Downing doesn't seem to know about polyptychs, so he vastly overestimated that 180–200 tablets were necessary for Luke's Gospel or 60–70 for each of Poirier's three suggested divisions; Eve (*Writing the Gospels*, 144) uncritically accepted Downing's estimates. I defended Poirier's position in

used just twelve pentaptychs and transferred their contents whenever he could fill most of a bookroll. The more tablets an author filled initially, the more time it would take later when transferring the draft onto a bookroll. Conversely, an author might lose momentum if they stopped too often to copy the contents of their tablets into a scroll. I estimate that ancient authors would have possessed at least enough waxed tablets to fill a bookroll, something like ten pentaptychs or their equivalents, which could hold twenty thousand letters. That much text would still leave plenty of room for revisions in a typical bookroll.[49]

When it comes to handwriting, biblical scholars have often overlooked just how much time it took to think about what to write and then write it out longhand. Having been spoiled by modern technology, we can make revisions almost instantaneously on computers. If I simply copy a text by typing it on my work processor, I can easily type sixty words per minute, approximately three hundred English letters without spaces. It takes me exactly twice as long to copy the same amount of

```
ANDGETTINGINTOABOATHEY
CROSSEDOVERANDCAMEINTOHIS
OWNCITYANDLOOKTHEYWERE
CARRYINGTOHIMAPARALYZED
PERSONHAVINGBEENPUTONABED
ANDJESUSSEEINGTHEIRFAITHSAID
TOTHEPARALYZEDPERSONHAVE
CONFIDENCECHILDYOURSINSARE
FORGIVENANDLOOKSOMEOFTHE
SCRIBESSAIDTOTHEMSELVESTHIS
PERSONBLASPHEMES
```

```
ANDJESUSSEEINGTHEIRTHOUGHTS
SAIDWHYDOYOUTHINKEVILIN
YOURHEARTSFORWHATISEASIER
TOSAYYOURSINSAREFORGIVEN
ORRISEANDWALKSOTHATYOU
CANKNOWTHATTHESONOFMAN
HASAUTHORITYONTHEEARTHTO
FORGIVESINSTHENHESAYSTO
THEPARALYZEDPERSONGETUP
PICKUPYOURBEDANDDEPARTIN
TOYOURHOUSE
```

Figure 2.1. Modeling Matthew's use of a waxed tablet

"The Use of Sources in Ancient Compositions," in *The Oxford Handbook of the Synoptic Gospels*, ed. Stephen P. Ahearne-Kroll (Oxford: Oxford University Press, 2023), 53. Poirier has now offered his own defense: "Luke and the Wax Tablet Revisited: An Assessment of Supposed Difficulties," in *The Synoptic Problem 2022: Proceedings of the Loyola University Conference*, ed. Olegs Andrejevs et al., BTS 44 (Leuven: Peeters, 2023), 335–55.

49. According to Pliny the Elder (*Nat.* 13.74–82), there were not more than twenty sheets in a papyrus roll, which would measure approximately 340 cm long: T. C. Skeat, "The Length of the Standard Papyrus Roll and the Cost-Advantage of the Codex," repr. in J. K. Elliott, ed., *The Collected Biblical Writings of T. C. Skeat*, NovTSup 113 (Leiden: Brill, 2004), 65–66.

text by hand with a pencil on a legal pad. It takes a bit longer (two and a half minutes) to copy the same amount of text on my waxed tablet. The point is that handwriting causes much more fatigue than typing does.

Anselm of Canterbury provides a concrete example of writing on tablets and bookrolls in the late eleventh century. Anselm drafted the *Proslogion* (more than twenty-three thousand letters) on waxed tablets. Anselm's first draft mysteriously disappeared, but he had more tablets on hand, so he wrote another draft. Unfortunately, the wax from the second draft was chipped to pieces, so Anselm finally wrote the *Proslogion* on a parchment roll.[50] Assuming that Anselm's drafts did not differ much from the published version, his set of tablets could contain nearly half of Luke's Gospel.

Writing the *Proslogion* in ink would have taken a minimum of two full days. This figure comes from the colophon of an early ninth-century manuscript of one of Augustine's works (Munich BSB Clm 14437 f. 109r). Two scribes copied for seven days, and a third scribe corrected the manuscript on the eighth day.[51] Factoring in half a day each for corrections, the scribes averaged between thirteen thousand and fourteen thousand letters per day.[52] These scribes worked during the Carolingian Renaissance, an unprecedented era of literary output. And these professionals wrote at exceedingly high rates, so we should not assume that any of the evangelists could write so fast. Nevertheless, the work of those rapid medieval scribes set absolute minimums for copying each gospel: four days for Mark, five days for John, and seven days each for Matthew and Luke.

Revisions and Publication on Bookrolls

Readers may start at the beginning of a book and read straight through to the end, but I doubt that any author ever wrote a book from start to finish. Although the point has not gone completely unacknowledged,[53] biblical scholars have not emphasized enough that authors from antiquity to the present typically wrote in multiple stages. Quintilian likened writing books to birthing

50. Richard H. Rouse and Mary A. Rouse, "Wax Tablets," *LC* 9 (1989): 179.

51. Michael Gullick, "How Fast Did Scribes Write? Evidence from Romanesque Manuscripts," in *Making the Medieval Book: Techniques of Production*, ed. Linda L. Brownrigg (Los Altos Hills, CA: Anderson-Lovelace, 1995), 46, 49. Gullick gives column counts, but I have calculated the number of letters, since manuscripts' column sizes vary considerably.

52. For comparison, the twelfth-century scribe of BL Royal MS 5 F XII also copied ten thousand letters per day: Gullick, "How Fast Did Scribes Write?," 50.

53. See, e.g., Eve, *Writing the Gospels*, 61, regarding "multi-stage collaborative composition."

livestock: the larger the animal, the longer the gestation period (*Inst.* 10.3.4). He also said to revise while you're initially writing (*Inst.* 10.3.6) but also to make further revisions after having put aside the draft for a while (*Inst.* 10.3.7; 10.4.2).

Modern music production offers a glimpse at writing, revising, and finalizing works. Peter Jackson's *The Beatles: Get Back* documents the band's last performance and final album.[54] Paul McCartney played piano and sang "The Long and Winding Road" while road manager Mal Evans transcribed lyrics and suggested changing one occurrence of "waiting" to "standing" (I, 1:43–1:45), a revision depicted on the typed copy of the song a few days later (II, 0:17). When McCartney first dictated lyrics of "Get Back" to John Lennon, the character Jo Jo had the family name Jackson (I, 2:20), but a few days later the last name turned into a birthplace—first Arizona, then northern Arizona, and finally the city of Tucson, Arizona (II, 0:17–18).

Evans also wrote out lyrics as McCartney sang the first verse and chorus of "Let It Be," originally called "Mother Mary." The band recorded twenty-eight takes of the song, the twenty-seventh of which was the album version (III, 2:17).[55] On the twenty-eighth take,[56] McCartney sings "no sorrow" rather than "an answer" in the last verse and chorus. As tape continued to roll, McCartney, Lennon, George Harrison, and engineer Glyn Johns consider it the best take, although McCartney observes, "I didn't get quite the words I had written here, though" (4:34–4:36).

For the Beatles' album, there were sixty hours of film and 150 hours of audio documenting the writing, revising, and recording processes. For the Gospels, we have no way of knowing how many rounds of revisions there might have been or how long it would have taken the evangelists to think through, draft by hand, revise by hand, and rewrite by hand precisely what they wanted to publish.

By the time the Gospels were written, scrolls had been the norm for a thousand years, so it shouldn't have been difficult for a literate person to use a bookroll. Yet the cumbersomeness of bookrolls has been greatly exaggerated by biblical scholars.[57] I can't help but wonder whether some scholars have

54. Peter Jackson, dir., *The Beatles: Get Back*, Disney+, 2021.

55. The Beatles, *Let It Be*, Apple Records, 1970, track 6; George Harrison appears to have overdubbed different guitar solos later.

56. The Beatles, *Let It Be: Special Edition (Super Deluxe)*, Apple Records, 2021: disc 3, song 12.

57. On this point, I concur with Hurtado, "Oral Fixation," 327–30. Those who overemphasize bookrolls' cumbersomeness include R. A. Derrenbacker Jr., "The 'External and Psychological Conditions under Which the Synoptic Gospels Were Written': Ancient Compositional Practices and the Synoptic Problem," in *New Studies in the Synoptic Problem:*

ever read a printed newspaper: just think of how cumbersome it is to have multiple, multicolumned articles on a single page, and yet to continue reading one article, you often have to skip several pages. Modern readers nevertheless mastered the use of printed newspapers for more than a century.

To see what reading a scroll might have been like, I made one for the Gospel of John using the Greek text of the fourth-century Codex Vaticanus. Although the codex is a different medium, its text is arranged into ninety-six full columns, each with forty-two rows and approximately seven hundred letters total. That would have made a normal-sized prose bookroll in earlier centuries.[58] I printed my scroll on eleven-by-seventeen-inch paper and had to standardize the margins, so my intercolumnar widths are a bit wider than an ancient text would have been. But that just means my bookroll of John is slightly longer than an ancient one actually would have been. When rolled up, my scroll's diameter is six centimeters, and when unrolled, the length is just over ten meters. I usually keep two columns in view when reading, and I can roll from one end to the other in five minutes. As T. C. Skeat concluded by experimenting with wallpaper more than forty years ago, I can confirm that rerolling a scroll is neither irksome nor time-consuming.[59]

A Note about Codices

For contemporary readers who use a tablet for electronic books, swiping a screen from right to left is like scrolling through an ancient text. Yet most readers probably think of a book as having pages bound within outside covers. In ancient terms, that is a codex, which emerged in the first century CE. By 85 CE, Martial (14.184–192) gave the earliest description of parchment codices,[60] but their legal status had been debated a few decades earlier.[61] The earliest material remains of a codex (P.Oxy. 1.30) date near 100 CE.[62]

Oxford Conference, April 2008; Essays in Honour of Christopher M. Tuckett, ed. Paul Foster et al., BETL 239 (Leuven: Peeters, 2011), 437; F. Gerald Downing, "A Paradigm Perplex: Luke, Matthew and Mark," NTS 38 (1992): 21; Kirk, Q in Matthew, 54–58; Rhoads, "Performance Criticism," 123.

58. See William A. Johnson, Bookrolls and Scribes in Oxyrhynchus (Toronto: University of Toronto Press, 2004), 217–30 (table 3.7).

59. T. C. Skeat, "Two Notes on Papyrus," repr. in Elliott, Collected Biblical Writings, 60–64.

60. Mario Citroni, "Martial," OCD 905.

61. Adam Bülow-Jacobsen, "Writing Materials in the Ancient World," in The Oxford Handbook of Papyrology, ed. Roger S. Bagnall (Oxford: Oxford University Press, 2009), 18.

62. Jean Mallon, "Quel est le plus ancien exemple connu d'un manuscrit latin en forme de codex?," Emerita 17 (1949): 7.

It is not impossible that the Gospels were read in codex form in the first century, but that would be exceptionally early. Whenever the Gospels were first made into codices, each gospel would likely have been a single codex. The simplest design is a single-quire codex, where the pages are folded in the center and bound by tacketing. With this design, the first two pages and the last two pages of the text have to be written on the same sheet. The most important element of constructing a single-quire codex is that you have to know exactly where the midpoint of the text is. And the easiest way to find the midpoint was to have a completed draft on a bookroll.

I made my first single-quire codex in the summer of 2015. Since then I have made others, including separate full-scale models of the Gospels of Luke and John. I use single-columned pages, which typically have forty-five rows and approximately 1,250 letters.[63] The Gospel of John codex has twenty-four double-sided pages, as compared with thirty-six double-sided pages for the Gospel of Luke. Since codices have writing on both sides and since the columns are wider, codices are much more portable than bookrolls. Again, though, a gospel had to be drafted on a bookroll before it could be turned into a codex. In the late first century, the safest bet is that the Gospels were published as bookrolls, and scholars should not appeal to codices as though they were easier to manage than bookrolls.[64]

Managing Multiple Sources

The central thesis of my book is that each subsequent gospel writer knew and used every gospel that came before. Even in a single episode, Luke could combine Matthew and Mark, just as John could combine all three Synoptics. Some scholars think that would have been too difficult and that the gospel writers worked as simply as possible by using one source text at a time.[65] I have

63. My pages are approximately the same size as the longer pages in Papyrus 75; for example, f. 46v has forty-five rows and 1,230 letters, although not every page has as many rows. Brent Nongbri (*God's Library: The Archaeology of the Earliest Christian Manuscripts* [New Haven: Yale University Press, 2018]) has also crafted models of early Christian books, particularly later, multiquire codices.

64. Contra R. A. Derrenbacker Jr., *Ancient Compositional Practices and the Synoptic Problem*, BETL 186 (Leuven: Leuven University Press, 2005), 225.

65. See esp. Derrenbacker, *Ancient Compositional Practices*, followed by Eve, *Writing the Gospels*, 55–57. See also F. Gerald Downing, "Compositional Conventions and the Synoptic Problem," *JBL* 107 (1988): 69–85. All three are influenced by Christopher Pelling, *Plutarch and History: Eighteen Studies* (London: Duckworth, 2002). I suspect that Plutarch himself used multiple sources at times. For example, there are nine attested lives of Cato the Younger,

challenged that misperception,[66] but some scholars remain unconvinced.[67] I have attempted to clarify my position,[68] and I extend my analysis here.

Scribes could work alone when they copied texts, as the early Christian visionary Hermas described himself doing (Herm. Vis. 2.4). Reading from one source while writing a new text would thus be unproblematic. There is also abundant evidence of authors—whether Greek or Roman, Jewish or Christian—working with multiple sources while writing their own compositions. Below I give examples from scholars in Oxyrhynchus, Egypt; the Jewish recensionists of the Septuagint; Josephus's use of conflicting Old Testament narratives; and Tatian's monumental harmony of the fourfold gospel.

There are endless possibilities for the ways authors could have worked with their sources. Perhaps a single author worked in solitude. If so, then paperweights could hold four different texts open in a semicircle. That takes up the same amount of space if today someone harmonized the four canonical gospels by laying open four copies of the Greek New Testament, one for each gospel. Alternatively, a group of five people could harmonize the Gospels by assigning each gospel to an individual while the fifth person drafted the harmony. Different authors would have figured out what worked best for themselves, and contemporary scholars shouldn't exaggerate the difficulty of managing multiple sources.

Greco-Roman Scholars of Homer's Epics

In Homer's *Odyssey*, after Odysseus departed Hades, Circe warned him about dangers in the voyage ahead, first the Sirens and then the sea monsters Scylla and Charybdis (*Od.* 12.37–68, 73–126).[69] Circe mentions in passing the ship Argo, which was piloted by Jason with divine assistance from Hera; Jason was the only one ever to have successfully made this passage (*Od.* 12.69–72).

---

but Plutarch's is the only one to survive; Caesar accused Cato of incest, but Plutarch must have juxtaposed another source to insist that Cato honorably cared for his widowed sister (*Cat. Min.* 54).

66. James W. Barker, "Ancient Compositional Practices and the Gospels: A Reassessment," *JBL* 135 (2016): 109–21.

67. E.g., John S. Kloppenborg, "Macro-conflation, Micro-conflation, Harmonization and the Compositional Practices of the Synoptic Writers," *ETL* 95 (2019): 629–43.

68. Barker, "Use of Sources"; the discussion here regarding the Septuagint, Josephus, and Tatian overlaps with some of pp. 46–52 in that essay.

69. I thank William A. Johnson for his generous and helpful feedback on an earlier version of this section.

Centuries after Homer's works first appeared, that brief reference to Jason's Argo provided a golden opportunity to write a prequel. Rudimentary imitation was an important way for students to learn to write, but an accomplished author could also publish a refined imitation. In stunning detail, Apollonius of Rhodes employed Greek hexameter and recounted Jason's legendary retrieval of a golden ram's fleece. Apollonius composed the *Argonautica* in the third century BCE. To do so, Apollonius had memorized the *Iliad* and the *Odyssey* "inside out and back to front."[70]

I am not convinced that the gospel writers worked extensively with Homer's works,[71] and I doubt that subsequent evangelists had memorized the earlier gospels. Nevertheless, the *Argonautica* is a helpful example of readers collecting and studying related literary works. The textual transmission of the *Argonautica* even shows that readers sometimes changed Apollonius's wording to match its Homeric model. The same phenomenon occurs in the composition and transmission of the Gospels.

Oxyrhynchus is a city in Egypt where in the late nineteenth century thousands of papyri were excavated. William Johnson has synthesized evidence of scholars at Oxyrhynchus collecting, collating, and commenting on texts in a particular genre, including epics.[72] Along these lines, papyrus fragments of the *Argonautica* show that readers were annotating their texts by glossing Homeric parallels. For example, Apollonius imitated Homer to describe how a hero killed his foes in rapid succession. *Argonautica* 1.994 begins with the word "bow" (*toxon*), the weapon Homer put in Heracles's hands when fighting monsters, which "one after another he brought to the ground."[73] When the bow (*toxon*) is mentioned in P.Oxy. 4414, the word "all" (*pantas*) is written right above, in between the lines. "All" and "bow" are definitely not synonyms, so in this case an advanced reader has recalled the phrase from Homer's *Iliad*, which Apollonius was imitating: "all, one after another, he brought to the bounteous earth" (*Il.* 12.194; 16.418).[74]

---

70. Michael W. Haslam, "Apollonius Rhodius and the Papyri," *ICS* 3 (1978): 61. On memorization of Homer's works in antiquity, see, e.g., Xenophon, *Symp.* 3.5 (Raffaella Cribiore, *Gymnastics of the Mind: Greek Education in Hellenistic and Roman Egypt* [Princeton: Princeton University Press, 2001], 213); see also Xenophon, *Mem.* 4.2.10 (Pelliccia, "Two Points," 110).

71. Cf. Dennis R. MacDonald, *The Homeric Epics and the Gospel of Mark* (New Haven: Yale University Press, 2000).

72. William A. Johnson, *Readers and Reading Culture in the High Roman Empire: A Study of Elite Communities*, CCS (Oxford: Oxford University Press, 2010), 179–92.

73. *Argon.* 1.994: ἐπασσυτέρους πέλασε χθονί.

74. *Il.* 12.194; 16.418: πάντας ἐπασσυτέρους πέλασε χθονὶ πολυβοτείρ. See U. Wartenberg,

As another example, to signify mourning, Homer used the phrase "tearing out his hair" on just one occasion (*tillonto te chaitas*; *Od.* 10.567). Also on just one occasion, Homer elsewhere used the phrase "shearing his hair" (*keironto te chaitas*; *Od.* 24.46). Apollonius employed one of these phrases at *Argon.* 1.1057—"shearing" according to medieval manuscripts but "tearing" in P.Oxy. 2696. Regardless of which came first, the alteration came from someone who recognized the Homeric doublet.[75]

The same phenomenon of textual contamination occurs in early manuscripts of the Synoptic Gospels. When Jesus teaches not to be anxious, he says to "look at the birds in the sky" in Matthew 6:26, but in Luke 12:24, Jesus says to "consider the ravens." Codex Bezae gives a harmonistic variant by replacing Luke's "ravens" with Matthew's "birds in the sky." Papyrus 45 presents a harmonizing variant in Luke, which adds Matthew's wording: "consider the birds of the sky and the ravens." These are not careless errors, like when a copyist skipped or doubled a word or a line. Instead, these technical, harmonistic and harmonizing variants arise from readers' study of multiple gospels, and I grant that such short alterations might have been recalled from memory.

Recensions of the Septuagint

Contemporary Bible readers often own more than one Bible, and many readers use more than one translation. The same was true of ancient Bible readers, as is clearly evident in Greek translations of the Hebrew Scriptures. Although the term "Septuagint" originally applied only to the Greek translation of the Torah, Septuagint became a catchall for the Greek Jewish Scriptures. As with any translation, the Septuagint sometimes diverged from its Hebrew sources, so full-scale revisions emerged very early to make the Greek sound more like the Hebrew.[76]

"Apollonius Rhodius, *Argonautica* I (POxy 4413–4422)," in *The Oxyrhynchus Papyri*, ed. E. W. Handley et al., GRM 84 (London: Egypt Exploration Society, 1997), 64:89.

75. Haslam, "Apollonius Rhodius," 59; see also p. 67 for the contamination of the *Argonautica*'s text from the outset of its transmission.

76. In this subsection, I have drawn on "Tatian's Diatessaron and the Proliferation of Gospels"; I have also culled from "The Equivalence of *Kaige* and *Quinta* in the Dodekapropheton," in *Found in Translation: Essays on Jewish Biblical Translation in Honor of Leonard J. Greenspoon*, ed. James W. Barker, Anthony Le Donne, and Joel N. Lohr (West Lafayette, IN: Purdue University Press, 2018), 127–52.

The earliest evidence of a Septuagint recension is the Greek Minor Prophets Scroll from Nahal Hever, which dates just before the turn of the era.[77] The translation is very wooden and was called *kaige* because of its tendency to translate the Hebrew words *ve-gam,* meaning "also," as *kaige* (even).[78] Sometimes *kaige*'s work is hardly detectable—for example, changing just three out of twenty-three words in Hab 2:18. At other times, a verse from *kaige* looks like a completely independent translation, as in Hab 3:14, where the preposition *en* is the only one of fifteen words left unchanged.[79] Most of the translation falls somewhere in the middle, but overall *kaige* successfully realigned the Septuagint toward the Hebrew text. The only way to do so was for the recensionist to maintain constant, close comparison of the Hebrew text and the Septuagint while drafting the full-scale revision.

The Minor Prophets Scroll is part of a much broader *kaige* tradition revising different books at different times, especially Job and Daniel. As part of the *kaige* tradition, Theodotion made a complete recension of the Septuagint around the turn of the era.[80] Aquila likewise revised the Septuagint to align with the Hebrew, and his recension is dated to around 125 CE. Aquila's translation was even more literal than Theodotion's, but yet another recensionist reversed course. Around 200 CE, Symmachus rendered the Greek more idiomatically, although he was clearly indebted to the earlier versions.

My main point here is that the Septuagint recensionists collected and compared the work of their predecessors. Symmachus was the last of the three main Jewish recensionists, and he worked word by word through all of his predecessors. For the biblical book of Joshua, Michaël N. van der Meer has painstakingly isolated Symmachus's decision-making processes.[81] At various

77. Emanuel Tov, with the collaboration of R. A. Kraft and a contribution by P. J. Parsons, *The Greek Minor Prophets Scroll from Nahal Hever (8HevXIIgr),* DJD 8/The Seiyâl Collection 1 (Oxford: Clarendon, 1990), 26.
78. Dominique Barthélemy, "Redécouverte d'un chaînon manquant de l'histoire de la Septante," *RB* 60 (1953): 18–29; Barthélemy, *Les Devanciers d'Aquila: Première publication intégrale du texte des fragments du Dodécaprophéton,* VTSup 10 (Leiden: Brill, 1963).
79. Barker, "Equivalence of *Kaige* and *Quinta,*" 128–29.
80. Following Peter J. Gentry ("Pre-hexaplaric Translations, Hexapla, Post-hexaplaric Translations," in *Textual History of the Bible,* vol. 1A, ed. Armin Lange [Leiden: Brill, 2016], 211–34), the traditional dating of Theodotion ca. 180 CE is inaccurate. For an overview of the Greek Jewish Scriptures, see Emanuel Tov, "Septuagint," in Lange, *Textual History of the Bible,* vol. 1A, 191–210.
81. Michaël N. van der Meer, "Symmachus's Version of Joshua," in Barker, Donne, and Lohr, *Found in Translation,* 53–93.

points, he preserved readings from the Septuagint, from Aquila, and from Theodotion. Yet Symmachus also used the Hebrew text to make numerous additional corrections to each of the earlier Greek versions.

Ancient readers similarly collected and compared multiple versions. In the mid-second century, Justin Martyr read both *kaige* and the Septuagint. When the two differed, Justin sometimes conflated them to preserve alternate readings—for example, the quotation of Zech 9:9 in *Dialogue with Trypho* (53.3).[82] On a much grander scale, Origen's Hexapla (ca. 250 CE) worked through the entire Old Testament. "Hexapla" refers to the six main columns, which were the Hebrew text, Origen's Greek transliteration, and the Septuagint alongside the recensions of Aquila, Symmachus, and Theodotion.

The Hexapla was an extraordinarily long set of books, and the work was lost by the early medieval period. Yet we do have the Syro-Hexapla,[83] a Syriac translation of the Septuagint as revised by Origen. This Syriac text includes important marginal annotations of alternate wording from the recensions. For example, the Hebrew text of Zechariah 12:10 says that Jerusalem will mourn when they look at the one they "pierced" (*daqar*). The Septuagint referred to "dancing triumphantly" (*katorcheomai*) over someone, not "piercing" him. The Hebrew word for "dance" (*raqad*) is so graphically similar that it could easily be confused with "pierce."[84] The Syro-Hexapla's glosses reveal that Theodotion and Aquila changed the Septuagint's "dance" to "pierce" (*d-q-r*), which must have matched their Hebrew text.

For my purposes, the Syro-Hexapla's glosses provide a working analogy for how a subsequent gospel writer could combine source materials. For example, Luke could have used Matthew and Mark when narrating Jesus's healing of a paralyzed man. Luke could have worked in stages, beginning with a collation of Matthew and Mark. Luke decided mainly to follow Mark while incorporating a few elements from Matthew, so those Matthean details could have been glossed directly onto the manuscript of Mark. To indicate a deletion, it was common to put dots beneath the letters of a word, and alternate words could be written interlinear. Figure 2.2 illustrates how Luke might have glossed Mark's text. That way, Luke could look at one sheet of one gospel, but Luke's story would still have been simultaneously combining two gospels.

82. James W. Barker, "The Reconstruction of *Kaige/Quinta* Zechariah 9,9," *ZAW* 126 (2014): 584–88.

83. Antonio Maria Ceriani, *Codex Syro-Hexaplaris Ambrosianus* (London: Williams & Norgate, 1874).

84. In Hebrew, the letters *d* (ד) and *r* (ר) look very much alike.

Figure 2.2. Modeling collation, annotation, and composition

Mark 2:1–12 with *alterations* and <u>deletions</u> from Matt 9:1–8	**Luke 5:17–26**
And entering again into Capernaum days later, it was heard that he is in a house. And many gathered so as to have no more room, not even toward the door, and he was speaking to them the word.	And it happened on one of the days he also was teaching, and there were sitting Pharisees and torah-teachers who had come from every village of Galilee and Judea and Jerusalem. And the power of the Lord was unto him to heal.

look *on a bed* And they came carrying toward him a paralyzed person, being picked up by four people. And not being able to carry toward him because of the crowd, they unroofed the roof where he was, and having dug out, they let down the pallet where the paralyzed person was lying.	And look, men carrying on a bed a person who was paralyzed, and they were seeking to bring him in and put him before him. And not finding how they could bring in because of the crowd, climbing up on the house, they let him down through the tiles with the stretcher into the middle in front of Jesus.

said And <u>Jesus</u>, seeing their faith, says <u>to the paralyzed person</u>, "Child, your sins are forgiven."	And seeing their faith, he said, "Person, your sins have been forgiven you."
Some of the scribes were there sitting and debating in their hearts, "Why is this one talking like this? He blasphemes! Who is able to forgive sins except one, God?"	And the scribes and the Pharisees started to debate, saying, "Who is this who talks blasphemy? Who is able to forgive sins except God alone?"
And immediately Jesus, knowing in his sprit that they are debating in themselves like this, says to them, "Why are you debating these things in your hearts? What is easier to say to a paralyzed person: 'your sins are forgiven' or to say 'Get up, pick up your pallet, and walk?'	Jesus, recognizing their debatings, answering, said toward them, "Why are you debating in your hearts? What is easier to say: 'Your sins have been forgiven you' or to say 'Get up and walk around'?
So that you can know that the Son of Man has authority to forgive sins on the earth," he says to the paralyzed person, "I say to you: Get up, pick up your pallet, and go away into your house."	So that you can know that the Son of Man has authority on the earth to forgive sins," he said to the one who has been paralyzed, "I say to you, 'Get up, pick up your little bed, proceed into your house.'"
And he got up and immediately picking up the pallet, *away into his house* he went out in front of everyone so as to amaze everyone *fear* and to glorify God saying, "We never saw something like this!"	And suddenly standing up in front of them, having picked up what he was lying on, he went away into his house glorifying God. And everybody took stunned and glorified God and were full of fear saying, "we saw paradoxes today."

Josephus's Use of 2 Samuel and 1 Chronicles

Josephus published the *Antiquities of the Jews* in the last decade of the first century CE, around the same time the Gospels were written. The first half of the *Antiquities* follows the chronology of the Old Testament, and Josephus paraphrased, condensed, expanded, and reinterpreted his sources. Josephus lacks the extended verbatim agreements that are so common among the Synoptic Gospels. Yet Josephus remains a helpful comparison for gospel writing, because he had to decide what to do when two books told the same story in different ways. Already in the Bible, 1–2 Chronicles had rewritten 1–2 Samuel and 1–2 Kings. Josephus wrote his own version that combined parallel accounts.

A classic example of Josephus's modus operandi is the interweaving of 2 Samuel and 1 Chronicles when King David rose to power (*Ant.* 7.46–64).[85] Most significantly, Josephus identified and incorporated details unique to one of his sources. As in 2 Samuel, Josephus recounted the assassination of Ishbaal, the son who had succeeded Saul as king after his death;[86] the Chronicler had omitted Ishbaal entirely. Josephus proceeds to the city of Hebron, where David was anointed king according to both 2 Samuel and 1 Chronicles.[87] There Josephus repeated the Chronicler's reference to the prophet Samuel (1 Chr 11:3); Samuel had anointed David as king long before (1 Sam 16:13), but later the prophet died (1 Sam 25:1), and he wasn't mentioned at all in 2 Samuel.

Early in 2 Samuel (3:20) there is a passing reference to a feast at Hebron, when Abner and twenty men defected from Saul's dynasty to join David in the civil war. The Chronicler embellished this story so that David held a three-day feast at Hebron with an army of more than three hundred thousand troops (1 Chr 12:23–40). Josephus used the Chronicler's version of the feast at Hebron (*Ant.* 7.53–60).

After reigning in Hebron for seven and a half years, David's army captured Jerusalem.[88] In the biblical accounts, the Chronicler omitted a line from 2 Samuel (5:6), where David was taunted as though hypothetically disabled people could defeat him in battle (2 Sam 5:6). Josephus not only included the episode from 2 Samuel but also rewrote it so that literally disabled people were

85. Christopher Begg, *Flavius Josephus: Translation and Commentary*, vol. 4, *Judean Antiquities Books 5–7* (Leiden: Brill, 2005), 218–23.

86. *Ant.* 7.46–52 // 2 Sam 4:1–12.

87. *Ant.* 7.53 // 2 Sam 5:1–5 // 1 Chr 11:1–3.

88. 2 Sam 5:6–10 // 1 Chr 11:4–9.

the ones mocking David (*Ant.* 7.61). When rewriting 2 Samuel, the Chronicler added a detail about Joab becoming commander of the army, since he was the first one to attack Jerusalem (1 Chr 11:6); Josephus incorporated that tidbit (*Ant.* 7.63–64). These examples suffice to show that Josephus could not have composed this section of his history without scrupulously and continuously comparing both of his biblical source texts.

New Testament scholars have studied this section of Josephus's work, but they have reached the wrong conclusions. Robert Derrenbacker is correct that 2 Samuel provides the frame for Josephus's sequence, but Derrenbacker wrongly claimed that Josephus did not use the Chronicler's wording.[89] Also, Derrenbacker stressed that Josephus does not move "back and forth between sources *within* episodes,"[90] but that is precisely what happened in several instances.

Gerald Downing has also looked at this passage, but he mischaracterized Josephus as giving up and writing "a completely fresh account of his own."[91] Josephus did write a new account, but there was nothing to give up: Josephus straightforwardly combined elements from both sources. For the use of both biblical sources, Downing granted, "Just occasionally [Josephus] seems to glance across at Chronicles, to check a list of names."[92] Downing has in mind several lists of David's descendants,[93] and Josephus included David's daughter Tamar, who was named only in 1 Chronicles 3:9. The problem with saying Josephus "glanced" at Tamar is that he had advanced at least as far as 1 Chronicles 11. To get back to 1 Chronicles 3, Josephus had to cover more than thirty thousand Greek letters, which would have filled a minimum of fifteen very wide columns in an ancient scroll—more than one-third of the width of a scroll of 1 Chronicles.

It has been claimed that ancient writers worked "as simply as possible," particularly with "little or no scrolling to and fro."[94] Josephus definitely could have worked more simply, but he chose not to. Besides scrolling forward and backward within one source, he managed to work with multiple sources simultaneously. And it's not just that Josephus was using 2 Samuel and 1 Chronicles:

89. Derrenbacker, *Ancient Compositional Practices*, 102–3.

90. Derrenbacker, "External and Psychological Conditions," 441.

91. F. Gerald Downing, "Redaction Criticism: Josephus' *Antiquities* and the Synoptic Gospels (I)," *JSNT* 8 (1980): 62.

92. Downing, "Redaction Criticism," 61.

93. *Ant.* 7.70; cf. 2 Sam 5:13–16 // 1 Chr 3:5–9 // 1 Chr 14:3–7; see Begg, *Flavius Josephus*, 4:223.

94. F. Gerald Downing, "Actuality versus Abstraction: The Synoptic Gospel Model," *Cont* 1 (1991): 111.

occasionally he tips his hand to show that he was comparing the Hebrew and the Greek versions of the same text.[95] Josephus may not have worked as simply as possible, but I do think that he worked simply: as I see it, collation, conflation, harmonization, and scrolling to and fro with multiple scrolls would have been relatively simple processes for a competent first-century author.

Tatian's Diatessaron

In the late second century, Tatian the Assyrian composed a famous gospel harmony.[96] It was later called the "Diatessaron," meaning "out of the four,"[97] to signify that Tatian meticulously harmonized the Gospels of Matthew, Mark, Luke, and John. Tatian did not add any unique stories of his own. Nor did he significantly alter the wording of whichever source he was using at the time. So in those regards, Tatian is less of an author compared to the earlier evangelists. However, Tatian's accomplishment should by no means be devalued, and Francis Watson rightly points out that the Diatessaron's combination of sources "is on a continuum with Luke's or Matthew's."[98]

With the exception of Luke's prologue and perhaps Jesus's genealogies, Tatian's gospel did not leave out a single episode from the fourfold gospel. Yet by carefully interweaving all their overlapping materials, the Diatessaron ended up approximately 25 percent shorter than the four canonical gospels combined. Tatian managed to work simultaneously with more sources than any of the canonical evangelists did. It is highly inaccurate to describe "the major part

---

95. For example, Josephus combines "ransoming" [= Hebrew] Jonathan with "praying for" [= Greek] him (1 Sam 14:45 // *Ant.* 6.128); see Michael Avioz, *Josephus' Interpretation of the Books of Samuel*, LSTS 86 (London: Bloomsbury T&T Clark, 2015), 199–200; see also Begg, *Flavius Josephus*, 4:25–26. Moreover, the ghost of Samuel tells Saul that his children will "fall" [= Greek] in battle and "be with me" [= Hebrew] (1 Sam 28:19 // *Ant.* 6.336); see Avioz, *Josephus' Interpretation*, 200. Derrenbacker (*Ancient Compositional Practices*, 115) undervalued Josephus's text-critical conflations.

96. The Diatessaron did not survive in Tatian's original form, but much of it can be reconstructed. For Tatian's narrative sequence, see my book *Tatian's Diatessaron: Composition, Redaction, Recension, and Reception*, OECS (Oxford: Oxford University Press, 2021); chapter 2 (pp. 29–43) goes into much more detail regarding "Tatian's Compositional Practices."

97. Eusebius of Caesarea uses the name Diatessaron (τὸ διὰ τεσσάρων) in *Hist. eccl.* 4.29.6, but I agree with Matthew R. Crawford ("Diatessaron, a Misnomer? The Evidence from Ephrem's Commentary," *EC* 4 [2013]: 365) that Tatian probably just called his work "the gospel."

98. Francis Watson, "Towards a Redaction-Critical Reading of the Diatessaron Gospel," *EC* 7 (2016): 96.

of the Diatessaron" as block by block,[99] because—by my calculations—approximately 75 percent of the Diatessaron required Tatian's simultaneous use of three or four gospels.

The following block quotation shows how the feeding of the five thousand was combined in Codex Fuldensis, a sixth-century Latin witness to the Diatessaron.

> When it became evening, the Twelve approaching said to (Jesus), "Send the crowd away, so that going out into the surrounding villages and lands, they can lodge and find provision, because here we are in a deserted place." He said to them, "They have no need to go away; you give them [something] to eat." Philip answered him, "Loaves of two hundred denarii are not enough for them that each can take a bite." He says to them, "How many loves do you have? One of his disciples says to him, Andrew the brother of Simon Peter, "There is a little boy here who has five barley loaves and two little fish, but what are these unto so many unless going out we buy this food for all the people?" He said, "Give them here to me." And he commanded them all to lie down, a symposium—a symposium on green grass. And they fell back, group [to] group, by a hundred and by fifty. Taking the five loaves and the two fish, looking up into the sky, he blessed and broke them and was giving to the disciples to serve the crowd. He gave to the disciples, and the disciples to the crowds. And everyone ate and was filled, and they took up the leftovers of morsels filling twelve baskets. And there were about five thousand men eating apart from women and children.

That is a fine encapsulation of the feeding miracle. And even without consulting a synopsis, some readers may recognize certain details, such as Philip's and Andrew's individual speaking parts from the Gospel of John (6:7–9). To get an idea of just how intricately Tatian moved across the fourfold gospel, the underlined portions of figure 2.3 show which gospel Tatian used at any given time, and the arrows indicate each time he switched between gospels. The story begins and ends with Matthew's wording, but the text switches sources ten times within one short scene.

Before Tatian could harmonize parallel stories, he first had to locate them. Numerous episodes had to be relocated simply because the canonical gospels did not always put the same story in the same place. And Tatian sometimes

---

99. Contra Sharon Lea Mattila, "A Question Too Often Neglected," *NTS* 41 (1995): 205.

created new narrative sequences that did not match any of his sources.[100] At one point in Luke, a random woman from a crowd raises her voice to tell Jesus, "Blessed is the womb that bore you and the breasts that you nursed at" (11:27–28); earlier his mother and brothers had come to see him but could not get to him because of the crowd (8:19). Tatian cleverly juxtaposed those events so that Mary was present in the crowd when the woman blessed Jesus's mother.[101] That is just one example of a technique Tatian employed throughout the Diatessaron.[102] Tatian also moved back and forth within each gospel, and at various points he covered more than 20 percent (twenty thousand Greek letters) of each gospel. Some modern scholars exaggerate such dexterity as "mind-boggling" and "extreme,"[103] or perhaps an ancient authors' scrolling was "absurdly furious."[104] Obviously it wasn't too hard for Tatian, and his endeavor was far more complicated than any of the canonical evangelists. We shouldn't think of such relocations as too difficult for any of the earlier gospel writers.

CONCLUSION

I titled this chapter "How to Write a Gospel," but I've written an awful lot about reading. That's because not all readers are writers, but all writers are readers. As gospels proliferated, subsequent evangelists studied the works of their predecessors. The main questions are how authors wrote and how they used their source materials. For these questions, there is plenty of evidence from antiquity, and I have adduced modern media analogies. In the end, it's not difficult to reconstruct the gospel writers' methods, and those methods wouldn't have been difficult.

I do not think that the Gospels are oral compositions or transcriptions of oral performances. Such Homeric models appear to have died out by the Hellenistic era, so scholars should no longer apply them to the Roman era. Instead of inspiring rhapsodes, the Muses dictated to authors writing on waxed tablets. That was the medium for authors to draft literary works for centuries, including the era in which the Gospels were written. Waxed tablets could be easily erased and reused, so they were highly practical. Anyone who

100. Contra Downing, "Paradigm Perplex," 36.

101. Arabic harmony 16.11–18.

102. See my *Tatian's Diatessaron*, 44–58 (ch. 3).

103. Andrew Gregory, ed., *The Gospel according to the Hebrews and the Gospel of the Ebionites*, OECGT (Oxford: Oxford University Press, 2017), 187.

104. Alan Kirk, "The Synoptic Problem, Ancient Media, and the Historical Jesus: A Response," *JSHJ* 15 (2017): 250; see also scrolling "furiously" in Kirk, *Q in Matthew*, 218.

Luke 9:12-17

The day came down. Approaching, the Twelve said to (Jesus), "Send the crowd away, so that going out into the surrounding villages and lands, they can lodge and find provision, because here we are in a deserted place." He said to them, "You give them to eat." They said, "We have no more than five loaves and two fish, unless going out we buy this food for all the people."

For there were about five thousand men. He said to his disciples, "Have them lie down, groups up to fifty." And they did this and had everyone lie down. Taking the five loaves and the two fish, looking up into the sky, he blessed and broke them and was giving to the disciples to serve the crowd. And they all ate and were filled, and their leftovers were taken up—twelve baskets of morsels.

Matt 14:15-21

When it became evening, the disciples came to him saying, "The place is a desert, and the hour has already passed; send away the crowds so that going away into the villages they can buy themselves food."

He said to them, "They have no need to go away; you give them [something] to eat." They say to him, "We have nothing here except five loaves and two fish."

He said, "Give them here to me." And ordering the crowds to lie down on the grass, taking the five loaves and the two fish, looking up into the sky, he said a blessing; and breaking the loaves, he gave to the disciples, and the disciples to the crowds. And everyone ate and was filled, and they took up the leftovers of morsels filling twelve baskets. And there were about five thousand men eating apart from women and children.

Mark 6:35-44

And more hours already having passed, his disciples said coming to him, "The place is a desert, and already an hour more; send them away so that going away into the surrounding fields and villages they can buy themselves something to eat." Answering he said to them, "You give them [something] to eat." And they say to him, "Going away, should we buy loaves for two hundred denarii and give them to eat?" He says to them, "How many loaves do you have? Go see." And finding out, they say, "Five, also two fish."

And he commanded them all to lie down, a symposium—a symposium on green grass. And they fell back, group [to] group, by a hundred and by fifty. And taking the five loaves and the two fish, looking up into the sky, he said a blessing and broke apart the loaves and gave to the disciples so that they could provide them; and he divided the two fish to everyone. And everyone ate and was filled. And the ones eating were five thousand men.

John 6:5-13

So Jesus, lifting up (his) eyes and seeing that a large crowd comes to him, says to Philip, "Where can we buy loaves so that these can eat?" This he said testing him, for he knew what he was about to do. Philip answered him, "Loaves of two hundred denarii are not enough for them that each can take a bite."

One of his disciples says to him, Andrew the brother of Simon Peter, "There is a little boy here who has five barley loaves and two little fish, but what are these unto so many?" Jesus said, "Make the people fall back." There was a lot of grass in the place. So the men fell back, the number about five thousand. So Jesus took the loaves and, giving thanks, distributed to the ones lying back, and likewise of the fish as much as they wanted. As they were filled up, he says to his disciples, "Gather together the leftover fragments so that nothing is lost." So they gathered together and filled twelve baskets of fragments from the five barley loaves that remained among the ones who had eaten.

Figure 2.3. Feeding the Five Thousand according to Codex Fuldensis

claims that they had "limited capacity" likely has little hands-on experience making or using waxed tablets.[105]

Scholars frequently appeal to ancient writers' memory skills, and memorization was an essential part of ancient education. However, students did not typically memorize entire literary works verbatim. A word or short phrase here and there could easily be recalled from memory, such as replacing or combining Luke's ravens (12:24) with Matthew's birds of the sky (6:26). But the longer the passage and the higher degree of verbatim agreement, the more likely a subsequent author was reading directly from a source.

To whatever extent an author used tablets for writing a draft, at some point there had to be a full draft on a bookroll. There is no way to know how many rounds of revisions the Gospels went through, but any publication was expected to have been thoroughly edited by expanding portions that needed further explanation, cutting superfluous material, and rewording anything that needed clarification. When the Gospels were composed, codices were just beginning to emerge, so the most probable scenario is that the Gospels were first published as scrolls. And whenever a single-quire gospel codex was first made, a scroll was prerequisite for the bookmaker to find the midpoint of the gospel and calculate the number of sheets needed for the codex. Given how long bookrolls had been the primary medium for literary works, ancient writers knew how to handle them. My own experimentation has shown them to be easily manageable, so uninformed claims about unwieldy scrolls should be disregarded.

Authors could work alone or in group settings. In either case, writers could also manage multiple source texts simultaneously. In particular, recensions of the Septuagint, Josephus's *Antiquities*, and Tatian's Diatessaron could not have been composed without consistent, close reference to two, three, or four biblical source texts. It was not difficult for a reader to reposition within a scroll, and scrolling time is negligible compared to the time it takes to copy or to rewrite source material. For example, it takes less than one minute for me to reposition ten columns in a bookroll, but it takes me more than fifteen minutes to copy a single column using a stylus on a waxed tablet or using quill and ink on papyrus or parchment. Josephus managed Old Testament texts in this way around the same time the Gospels were being written. And Tatian constantly

---

105. Kirk (*Q in Matthew*, 49) references Baldric of Bourgueil, who wrote a poem about his octoptych (Vatican MS Reg. lat. 1351 ff. 24v–25v), which by my count was large enough to fit 3,785 letters; that was rather large, but Kirk seems to think it quite limited.

traversed each of the four canonical gospels to compose the Diatessaron within a century of their publication.

Based on these findings, my standpoint throughout the remainder of this book is that the gospel writers usually maintained visual contact with their source texts and that each subsequent evangelist could easily reposition within every previous gospel.

Chapter 2

SYNOPTIC TRAJECTORIES

IN THE PREVIOUS CHAPTER, I explained how Josephus simultaneously used the Old Testament books of Samuel and Kings along with Chronicles as sources. There is a very broad consensus that Samuel and Kings came first and that Chronicles represents a later rewriting; there is no doubt that Josephus wrote much later and used all the earlier texts. By contrast, we have no absolute dates for the composition of the Gospels, and the lines of influence and dependence among the Synoptics have proven much more difficult to disentangle.

The Synoptic problem is the study of why Matthew, Mark, and Luke are so similar and yet so different. Others have written histories of the Synoptic problem,[1] and there are excellent guides for studying the issue.[2] My introductory chapter diagrammed the main solutions, and my purpose in this chapter is to defend the Farrer hypothesis. The theory is named for Austin Farrer, who published an essay in 1955 affirming that Mark was the first gospel while dispensing with the hypothetical document Q; as opposed to the view that Matthew and Luke independently used a long-lost sayings source, Luke simply used Matthew's Gospel.[3] Michael Goulder bolstered the Farrer hypothesis in his commentary on Luke.[4] Mark Goodacre took up the torch and has solidified

---

1. E.g., David Laird Dungan, *A History of the Synoptic Problem: The Canon, the Text, the Composition, and the Interpretation of the Gospels*, ABRL (New York: Doubleday, 1999); see also John S. Kloppenborg, "The History and Prospects of the Synoptic Problem," in *The Oxford Handbook of the Synoptic Gospels*, ed. Stephen P. Ahearne-Kroll (New York: Oxford University Press, 2023), 3–26.

2. E. P. Sanders and Margaret Davies, *Studying the Synoptic Gospels* (London: SCM, 1989); Mark Goodacre, *The Synoptic Problem: A Way through the Maze* (London: T&T Clark, 2001).

3. A. M. Farrer, "On Dispensing with Q," in *Studies in the Gospels: Essays in Memory of R. H. Lightfoot*, ed. D. E. Nineham (Oxford: Basil Blackwell, 1955), 55–86.

4. Michael D. Goulder, *Luke: A New Paradigm*, 2 vols., JSNTSup 20 (Sheffield: JSOT Press, 1989).

the Farrer hypothesis as a viable and increasingly attractive alternative to the two-source hypothesis.[5]

The Synoptic problem has been debated for centuries, and by no means can I settle the question in just one chapter. My more modest goal is to highlight examples where I find the Farrer hypothesis most compelling. Surely there are abundant counterexamples and even counterarguments to the case studies I've selected. I try not to ignore rival theories altogether, so at times I explain why the Farrer hypothesis works better than the Augustinian, Griesbach, two-source, or Matthean posteriority hypotheses. For the most part, though, I am content to plot progressions from Mark to Matthew and then to Luke. This sets up a snowballing trajectory that will run into the next chapter, where I argue that John used all three Synoptic Gospels.

In what follows, I begin with a brief discussion of notebooks, specifically the notion that the Gospel of Mark might have been intentionally left unfinished. I then offer a macroview of the Synoptic Gospels, where the explanatory power of the Farrer hypothesis is the strongest. Thereafter I focus extensively on Luke's use of Matthew and Mark. One area is the tricky phenomenon of conflations and doublets. Sometimes two sayings or stories can be combined into one, but at other times a single episode is doubled. No author is entirely predictable, but I find good rhetorical reasons why Luke might create a conflation here or a doublet there, depending on the circumstances.

The so-called minor agreements are another thorny issue.[6] Those are places where Matthew and Luke differ from Mark in the same ways and at the same place—a hard thing to explain if Matthew and Luke were written independently. So I look at Jesus's healing of paralysis, which has a trove of minor agreements. I then turn to Luke's depiction of crowds, for they comprise a large group of devoted disciples as opposed to the fickle mob that eventually forms in Matthew and Mark. Next I isolate a tendency whereby Luke finds something surprising in a source text and carefully eliminates the element of surprise.

---

5. Mark Goodacre, *The Case against Q: Studies in Markan Priority and the Synoptic Problem* (Harrisburg, PA: Trinity International, 2002); see also John C. Poirier and Jeffrey Petersen, eds., *Marcan Priority without Q: Explorations in the Farrer Hypothesis*, LNTS 455 (London: Bloomsbury T&T Clark, 2015).

6. See, e.g., Frans Neirynck, *The Minor Agreements of Matthew and Luke against Mark with a Cumulative List*, BETL 37 (Leuven: Leuven University Press, 1974); Georg Strecker, ed., *Minor Agreements: Symposium Göttingen 1991*, GTA 50 (Göttingen: Vandenhoeck & Ruprecht, 1993); Andreas Ennulat, *Die "Minor Agreements" Untersuchungen zu einer offenen Frage des synoptischen Problems*, WUNT 2/62 (Tübingen: Mohr Siebeck, 1994).

I end with the parousia or second coming of Jesus—the end that never seems to come according to the Gospel of Luke.

A NOTE ABOUT NOTEBOOKS

Recent scholarship has described Mark, the earliest gospel,[7] as *apomnēmoneumata* or *hypomnēmata*,[8] each of which can mean "memoranda." Both Greek words are in the domain of *mnēma*, which—like the word "mnemonics"—refers to memory. As *apomnēmoneumata* or *hypomnēmata*, Mark would have been written as something memorable, but the recent idea is that Mark's text was more like a set of rough notes rather than a proper narrative.[9] Along these lines, Lucian's second-century *How to Write History* (48) used the singular *hypomnēma* in the sense of "draft," since it would still lack order (*taxis*) and beauty (*kallos*).[10] Similarly, Galen lectured to friends or students who might make notes (*hypomnēmata*), but sometimes a transcription of the lecture was published without Galen's authorization.[11] In the early church, Clement of Alexandria reportedly thought of the Gospel of Mark as a written record of the apostle Peter's spoken teaching—a "memoir via writing."[12] Since Mark was called *hypomnēmata*, the gospel can be read "as unfinished notes."[13]

First and foremost, I commend scholars for contextualizing gospel writing within Greco-Roman categories and conventions. I certainly do not deny that *hypomnēmata* and *apomnēmoneumata* can refer to notebooks or that Mark

---

7. For Markan priority, see, e.g., Goodacre, *Case against Q*, 19–45. See also the selection of classic arguments for "the case for the priority of Mark" in Arthur J. Bellinzoni Jr., ed., *The Two-Source Hypothesis: A Critical Appraisal* (Macon, GA: Mercer University Press, 1985), 23–93. I also endorse the approach taken in Alex Damm's *Ancient Rhetoric and the Synoptic Problem: Clarifying Markan Priority*, BETL 252 (Leuven: Peeters, 2013). Markus Vinzent (*Marcion and the Dating of the Synoptic Gospels*, StPatrSup 2 [Leuven: Peeters, 2014]) has argued that the gospel used by the arch-heretic Marcion in the second century was actually the first gospel written; I find Vinzent's theory wholly unconvincing, as does Clare K. Rothschild, whose review relegates Vinzent's monograph to "a nonscientific genre such as historical fiction, philosophical speculation, or personal reflection" (*RBL*, 15 March 2016).

8. Nicholas A. Elder (*The Media Matrix of Early Jewish and Christian Narrative*, LNTS 612 [London: T&T Clark, 2019], 43) correctly uses both terms synonymously.

9. Matthew D. C. Larsen, *Gospels before the Book* (New York: Oxford University Press, 2018), 86.

10. Larsen, *Gospels before the Book*, 12; Elder, *Media Matrix*, 43 n. 142

11. Galen, *On My Own Books (De libris propriis)* 11, 14–15; Elder, *Media Matrix*, 45.

12. διὰ γραφῆς ὑπόμνημα (Eusebius, *Hist. eccl.* 2.15.1); Elder, *Media Matrix*, 48.

13. Larsen, *Gospels before the Book*, 122.

can be read in this way. Nevertheless, I offer two words of caution against reifying Mark's Gospel as an unfinished text.

One has to do with the terminology itself, since there were finished, published, and cited ancient books that went by the title *hypomnēmata* and *apomnēmoneumata*. Xenophon wrote his five-volume *Memorabilia* about Socrates in the fourth century BCE,[14] and the book was cited for centuries as *apomnēmoneumata*.[15] Around the turn of the era, Strabo referred readers to his "sixth book of *Historical Memoirs*."[16] The *Memoirs* did not lack order, since Strabo called his *Geography* a composition (*syntaxis*) of the "same kind" (*homoeidēs*) as the *Memoirs,* and both works were intended for an elite audience (*Geogr.* 1.1.23). A century or so later, Plutarch explicitly cited Strabo's *Historical Memoirs* when writing the life of the Roman general Lucullus (28.8). Therefore, even if Mark's Gospel was called *apomnēmoneumata* or *hypomnēmata,* those names do not entail that the work was rough and unfinished or that the gospel was an oral transcription.

A related point of caution has to do with aesthetic judgments regarding the unfinished nature of Mark. Mark certainly appears less complete when compared to Matthew and Luke. Looking at the ending, Mark has a young man in sparkly clothes tell some women that Jesus has risen from the dead and that he will appear to the disciple in Galilee; the women are supposed to convey the message, but they don't—the end (Mark 16:1–8).[17] Matthew (ch. 28) rewrote the story so that the young man was explicitly called an angel, the women did as commanded, and the risen Jesus physically encountered the women and remaining disciples. Luke (ch. 24) likewise has women tell the disciples that Jesus was resurrected, and Jesus encountered them in the flesh. Once we can compare all three Synoptics, Mark undoubtedly appears less complete.

Conversely, when Mark was first written, an early collection of Paul's letters was likely the only available literature about Jesus. Paul repeatedly claims that Je-

---

14. For comparison, Xenophon's *Memorabilia* is nearly thirty-six thousand words, approximately the length of two gospels combined.

15. In the first century BCE, see Dionysius of Halicarnassus, [*Rhet.*] 9.11.51; in the third century CE, see Diogenes Laertius, *Lives* 2.6.

16. ἐν τῇ ἕκτῃ τῶν Ἱστορικῶν Ὑπομνημάτων βίβλωι (Strabo, *Geogr.* 11.9.3). For all that can be known about this lost work, see Delfino Amgaglio, *Gli historikà hypomnemata di Strabone: Introduzione, traduzione italiana e commento dei frammenti,* Memorie 39, fasc. 5 [pp. 377–425] (Milan: Instituto Lombardo di scienze e lettere, 1990).

17. On reading Mark 16:1–8 as "suspended" rather than "incomplete," see Michal Beth Dinkler, "Narrative Design in the Synoptics," in Ahearne-Kroll, *Oxford Handbook of the Synoptic Gospels,* 142–48.

sus was raised from the dead, but there is no narration of an empty tomb. The most Paul says about the resurrection is that Jesus arose, appeared to Peter (aka Cephas) and the Twelve, and to many others, including Paul himself (1 Cor 15:4–8). That discourse on resurrection also draws a strong distinction between a physical body and a spiritual body (v. 44). Hypothetically, then, Jesus's physical body could still be rotting in a tomb, even as his imperishable spiritual body was visiting Peter, Paul, and Mary. Mark at least tells us that Jesus's physical body was resurrected and remained no longer in the tomb. Relative to Paul's letters, Mark's Gospel is more complete when it comes to Jesus's resurrection. Relative to Mark, though, Matthew and Luke are more complete, since the risen Jesus appears in the flesh.

Subsequent evangelists routinely added clarification and entire stories to supplement the work of their predecessors. Nevertheless, Mark's Gospel could stand on its own as a finished text. Moreover, no matter how closely the Synoptics resemble one another, readers clearly discerned them as different books.[18] Once again, the first-century reader Josephus undeniably differentiated the highly similar works of 2 Samuel and 1 Chronicles, and it's worth noting here that the Chronicler added to the beginning and ending of Samuel and Kings.[19] Similarly, Matthew and Luke added material to the beginning, middle, and end of Mark. But that doesn't render Mark an unfinished work, since that gospel is itself a narrative with a beginning, middle, and end of its own.

An Overview of the Farrer Hypothesis

Beginning at the beginning, Mark presents John the Baptizer and Jesus with practically no introduction. To be sure, Mark's opening sentences espouse belief in Jesus as the Messiah (1:1), and readers soon learn that he comes from Nazareth (1:9). Later Jesus's mother and brothers appear (3:31), and later still we learn their names, that Jesus had sisters as well, and that he worked as a carpenter (6:3). Those snippets comprise Jesus's entire backstory according to Mark, and the text gives no way to discern how old Jesus is.

Matthew begins with a genealogy from Abraham to Jesus, and the nativity story is told from Joseph's perspective. By itself, the nativity marks a significant

18. Contra Larsen, *Gospels before the Book*, 106, where he thinks it "highly unlikely" that readers of Matthew and Mark "would have thought of these manuscripts as two different books."

19. Larsen (*Gospels before the Book*, 182 n. 7) draws an analogy, according to which Matthew is like a version of Mark, similar to the Greek expansion of the Hebrew book of Esther. A much closer analogy for the proliferation of highly similar and yet clearly distinguishable biblical literature is Matthew : Mark :: Chronicles : Samuel and Kings.

supplementation of Mark's Gospel. Matthew not only tells that Jesus was born prior to the death of Herod the Great but also that Jesus died during the governorship of Pontius Pilate. Accordingly, ancient and modern historians can deduce that Jesus probably did not reach the age of forty, although Matthew nowhere says so explicitly.

Luke's Gospel opens with additional supplementation. Compared to Mark, the genealogy and a nativity story show that Luke has added the same kind of material as Matthew did—albeit with noticeable differences. For the Christmas story, Luke complements Matthew by presenting Mary's perspective. There is also a nativity story for John the Baptist, who turns out to be a relative of Jesus. Luke's genealogy appears in a different place and is notoriously different from Matthew's, but Luke most distinctively expands the lineage from Adam to Abraham. Moreover, Luke states explicitly that Jesus was around thirty years old when he began his ministry (3:23), and Luke presents one episode to fill in the gap between Jesus's birth and the beginning of his ministry, namely, the twelve-year-old Jesus's trip to the Jerusalem temple for Passover (2:41–52).

Bracketing the question of historicity entirely, subsequent evangelists added stories to fill in gaps in the life of Jesus, thereby incrementally increasing the amount of biographical details about Jesus and John the Baptist. Such a tendency in the canonical gospels continues in the extracanonical Infancy Gospels of Jacob (aka James) and Thomas, which respectively added much more detail to the characters of Mary and Joseph as well as the birth and childhood of Jesus.[20]

In the middle of the Synoptic Gospels, there is a similar expansive tendency, particularly relating to Jesus's teaching and his apostles' work. Matthew's Sermon on the Mount and Luke's Sermon on the Plain are significant teaching blocks. As Mark Goodacre has elucidated, there are plenty of redaction- and narrative-critical reasons why Luke would have abbreviated, altered, and redistributed various pieces of Matthew's sermon.[21] Such revisions hardly amount to "unscrambling the egg with a vengeance!"[22] And Luke's general reordering of double tradition does not make him a "crank."[23]

I find the Farrer hypothesis most plausible for these sermons. After Mark's one-sentence report of the temptation (1:13), Jesus calls the first four disciples

---

20. On this topic, see esp. Mark Goodacre, "The *Protevangelium* of James and the Creative Rewriting of *Matthew* and *Luke*," in *Connecting Gospels: Beyond the Canonical/Non-canonical Divide*, ed. Francis Watson and Sarah Parkhouse (Oxford: Oxford University Press, 2018), 57–76.

21. Goodacre, *Case against Q*, 81–132 (chs. 4–6).

22. Reginald H. Fuller, *The New Testament in Current Study* (London: SCM, 1963), 87.

23. B. H. Streeter, *The Four Gospels: A Study of Origins* (London: Macmillan, 1924), 183.

(vv. 16–20) and teaches in the Capernaum synagogue (v. 21). Mark adds, "And they were amazed at his teaching, for he was teaching them like someone having authority and not like the scribes" (v. 22). Yet Jesus's only teaching thus far in Mark is his proclamation that "the time has been fulfilled, and the kingdom of God has come near; repent and believe in the gospel" (1:15).

Matthew took advantage of Mark's lack of teaching. So after a detailed temptation story (Matt 4:1–11), Jesus calls the first four disciples (vv. 18–22) and soon gains a reputation as a preacher and healer (vv. 23–25). Although Jesus stayed in Galilee, his fame spread widely: people came from Syria for healing (v. 24), and many crowds from Galilee, the Decapolis, Jerusalem, Judea, and the Transjordan followed him (v. 25). Then Matthew inserts the Sermon on the Mount, at the conclusion of which "the crowds were amazed at his teaching, for he was teaching them like someone having authority and not like their scribes" (Matt 7:28–29). Matthew adds the possessive pronoun "their" and identifies the subject as "the crowds," but otherwise Matthew has copied Mark 1:22 verbatim.

Luke kept Mark's statement about the crowd's amazement in the same place. To set up the Sermon on the Plain, Luke brings forward Jesus's designation of the twelve apostles (6:13–16). All apostles are disciples, but not all disciples are apostles. That is, a larger group of disciples remains in view, and they are joined by a crowd that had come for healing from Judea and Jerusalem as well as the coast of Tyre and Sidon (vv. 17–19). All of these groups are present at Luke's sermon, since Jesus looks at his disciples (v. 20) but does not depart from the crowd.

Given the differences between Matthew and Luke, Saint Augustine harmonized the accounts so Jesus gave two similar sermons in succession, first on the mountain and then down on the plain (*Cons.* 2.19/45). According to the Farrer hypothesis, Luke moved the sermon from a mountain (*horos*, Matt 5:1) to a level place (*topos pedinos*, Luke 6:17); Luke also clarified the audience and abbreviated the content. As a modern-day analogy to Luke's shortening of Matthew's sermon, Goodacre has shown how even Pier Paolo Pasolini's film adaptation *The Gospel according to St. Matthew* cuts more than half of the Sermon on the Mount.[24] And while I've mentioned Luke's tendency to moving things forward, Luke can also save things for later. In this regard, I wholeheartedly endorse Francis Watson's elucidation of how Luke could have used a notebook to preserve teachings that would be placed later in the gospel.[25]

---

24. Goodacre, *Case against Q*, 125, originally published as Mark Goodacre, "The Synoptic Jesus and the Celluloid Christ: Solving the Synoptic Problem through Film," *JSNT* 80 (2000): 36; Pier Paolo Pasolini, dir., *The Gospel according to St. Matthew* (Arco Films, 1964).

25. Francis Watson, *Gospel Writing: A Canonical Perspective* (Grand Rapids: Eerdmans,

I have already mentioned Matthew's and Luke's expansions of the resurrection story. I would add that the last sentence of Matthew's Gospel records Jesus's promise to remain with the disciples "all the days until the culmination of the aeon" (28:20). Such a statement raises questions about Jesus's whereabouts and availability, so Luke added the ascension (24:51) to clarify that, from then on, Jesus would be with the disciples in spirit but not in the flesh.[26] The risen Jesus had indeed appeared in the flesh. Matthew (28:17) says that some of the disciples doubted (*distazō*) when they saw Jesus, so Luke has Jesus not only show them his hands and feet but also eat a piece of fish (24:37–43).[27] Again there is a simple synoptic snowball, where Matthew augmented Mark's account, and Luke augmented Matthew's.

Doublets and Conflations

Text-critical conflations are easily identified, like when Papyrus 45 added Matthew's "birds of the sky" to the "ravens" in Luke 12:24. Source-critical conflations are more difficult to determine. The reason is that every solution to the Synoptic problem must have conflations at one point or another.[28] As E. P. Sanders observed, "The evidence for conflation in each of the Synoptics is more or less even. It thus follows that the Synoptic problem cannot be solved by appeal to conflation."[29]

Doublets are the flip side of conflations. Rather than combining two orig-

---

2013), 170. I would give Luke 16:16–18 as an example where Luke might have simply copied some leftover Matthean sayings and then erased his notebook.

26. I have made this point before in "Tatian's Diatessaron and the Proliferation of Gospels," in *The Gospel of Tatian: Exploring the Nature and Text of the Diatessaron*, ed. Matthew R. Crawford and Nicholas J. Zola, RJT 3 (London: T&T Clark, 2019), 127; however, I failed to notice that Jeffrey Peterson had already done so: "Matthew's Ending and the Genesis of Luke-Acts: The Farrer Hypothesis and the Birth of Christian History," in Poirier and Peterson, *Marcan Priority*, 154–55.

27. Luke 24:40 is missing in a few manuscripts, such as Codex Bezae, but Jesus already told the disciples to see his flesh-and-bone hands and feet in v. 39, which always stands in Luke.

28. For example, according to the Griesbach hypothesis, Mark (10:33) appears to conflate Matthew's (20:18) chief priests and scribes with Luke's (18:32) gentiles. According to the Matthean posteriority hypothesis, Matthew (4:11) appears to conflate Mark's (1:13) ministering angels with Luke's (4:13) statement that the devil left Jesus at the end of the temptation narrative. According to the Augustinian and Farrer hypotheses, Luke (9:11b) appears to conflate Mark's (6:34) teaching with Matthew's (14:14) healing as a setup for the feeding of the five thousand.

29. E. P. Sanders, *Tendencies in the Synoptic Tradition*, SNTSMS 9 (Cambridge: Cambridge University Press, 1969), 271.

inally separate details into one, an author can divide or multiply a single episode into separate events. Each synoptist has doublets: Matthew has the most,
twenty-two according to John Hawkins's classic study *Horae Synopticae*;[30]
Mark has the fewest; and Luke falls in the middle. To further complicate mat-
ters, one evangelist's conflation can be another evangelist's doublet, depending
on one's preferred solution to the Synoptic problem.

Aelius Theon's *Progymnasmata* is likely a first-century example of the
preliminary exercises for rhetorical education. Theon described six elements
of narration: person, action, place, time, manner, and cause; he also listed
clarity, conciseness, and credibility as narrative virtues.[31] Eliminating doublets and creating conflations would be a viable way to achieve conciseness,
but this virtue is inconclusive, since each evangelist must sometimes conflate
and sometimes double. I find the virtue of credibility more promising, particularly when focusing on person, time, and place. If one simply asks who,
what, when, and where, Luke shows some consistency in setting the stage and
casting characters.

Differentiating Allies from Adversaries

In the Gospel of Mark (9:38), the disciples encounter someone who uses the
name of Jesus to cast out demons. The disciples try to stop him, because "he
does not follow with us." But Jesus said not to stop him, because Jesus seems to
think that anyone who does a miracle in his name is doing a good thing (v. 39).
Jesus adds, "For whoever is not against us is for us" (v. 40).

Matthew seems to have a problem with that section of Mark. In the Sermon on the Mount, Jesus says that at final judgment, some people will be
rejected even though they cast out demons in Jesus's name and did miracles
(7:21–23). In other words, Jesus approves of a stranger doing these exact things
in Mark 9:38–39, but Matthew has rewritten the scenario as something Jesus

30. John C. Hawkins, *Horae Synopticae: Contributions to the Study of the Synoptic Problem*, 2nd ed. (Oxford: Clarendon, 1909), 80–107. For example, for the healing of blindness
at Jericho (Matt 20:29–34 // Mark 10:46–52 // Luke 18:35–43), Matthew not only doubles the
character so that there are two blind men, but Matthew doubles the entire narrative, since
Jesus elsewhere heals two blind men (9:27–31). A Markan doublet would be the saying that
whoever wants to be first should be enslaved to everyone (9:35b; 10:43–44). Luke doubles
the saying that "everyone who exalts themselves will be humbled, and the one who humbles
themselves will be exalted" (14:11; 18:14).

31. George A. Kennedy, ed., *Progymnasmata: Greek Textbooks of Prose Composition and
Rhetoric*, WGRW 10 (Atlanta: Society of Biblical Literature, 2003), 28–42, esp. 28–29.

might oppose. Later in the gospel, Matthew says, "The one who is not with me is against me, and the one who does not gather with me scatters" (12:30). Luke uses Mark's and Matthew's material on separate occasions. Mark's outsider exorcist shows up in Luke 9:49–50, and Luke agrees with Mark nearly verbatim. Luke omits the line about miracle workers not speaking ill of Jesus (Mark 9:39), but the point of the brief episode is that "whoever is not against us is for us" (Luke 9:50c).

In all three Synoptics, Jesus is accused of casting out demons by the power of Beelzebul, the "Lord of the Flies" or the ruler of demons; Jesus retorts that a house divided against itself cannot stand, so Satan cannot be divided against himself.[32] Toward the end of the story, Matthew and Luke add the verbatim statement, "Whoever is not with me is against me, and whoever does not gather with me scatters."[33]

The Beelzebul controversy occurs in all the Synoptics, but Matthew and Luke align against Mark for several sentences totaling more than fifty words verbatim.[34] The two-source hypothesis claims that both Mark and Q contained this story and that Matthew and Luke independently combined their separate sources in nearly identical ways. The circularity of the two-source hypothesis is at its highest in these kinds of cases, and the entire category of "Mark-Q overlap" has rightly been criticized,[35] since Q was originally conceived as a way of isolating material that was in Matthew and Luke but not in Mark.

No matter how similar the wording and structure, there is all the difference in the world between "not with me is against me" and "not against me is for me." Matthew uses the former, Mark uses the latter, and Luke clarifies that Jesus made both statements on different occasions. To be sure, conflations tend to cancel each other out, but not all conflations are created equal. The two-source and Matthean posteriority hypotheses do not account for this pair

32. Matt 12:24–26 // Mark 3:22–26 // Luke 11:15–18; Matthew (9:32–34) created a doublet to foreshadow the Beelzebul controversy.

33. ὁ μὴ ὢν μετ' ἐμοῦ κατ' ἐμοῦ ἐστιν, καὶ ὁ μὴ συνάγων μετ' ἐμοῦ σκορπίζει (Matt 12:30 // Luke 11:23).

34. Matt 12:26–30 // Luke 11:18–23.

35. See Goodacre, *Case against Q*, 163–65, where "Mark-Q overlap passages" are renamed "major agreements" (163); see also Mark Goodacre, "Taking Our Leave of Mark-Q Overlaps: Major Agreements and the Farrer Theory," in *Gospel Interpretation and the Q-Hypothesis*, ed. Mogens Müller and Heike Omerzu, LNTS 573 (London: T&T Clark, 2018), 201–22. For a defense of the Farrer hypothesis in this pericope, particularly appealing to orality and memory, see Eric Eve, "The Devil in the Detail: Exorcising Q from the Beelzebul Controversy," in Poirier and Petersen, *Marcan Priority*, 16–43.

of opposite sayings. For the Beelzebul controversy, Luke's use of Matthew and Mark is the likeliest scenario.

Scribes and Pharisees in the Beelzebul Controversy and Sign of Jonah

Another striking aspect of the Beelzebul controversy is that Luke can't seem to decide who started the argument. Mark (3:22) says that scribes from Jerusalem accused Jesus of relying on Beelzebul to cast out demons. Matthew (12:24) has the Pharisees make that accusation. Luke (11:15) generically says that "some of those" claimed that Jesus was colluding with Beelzebul. It would have made perfect sense to conflate Mark's scribes with Matthew's Pharisees, since Luke has Jesus argue against both groups soon thereafter (11:37–54) and again as the setup for the three parables about the lost (15:1–2).

Nevertheless, Luke combines the Beelzebul controversy with the saying about the demand for a sign, which occurs in all three Synoptics. In combining these episodes, Luke had to streamline a potentially convoluted cast of characters. In Mark 8:11, Pharisees tempt Jesus to show them a sign from heaven, but Jesus replies that this generation will not receive a sign (v. 12), and he soon warns his companions about the yeast of the Pharisees and Herod (v. 15). A similar thing occurs twice in Matthew. In Matthew 12:38–42, scribes and Pharisees want to see a sign from Jesus, but he says that the sign of Jonah is the only one that this evil and adulterous generation will see. In Matthew 16:1–4, Pharisees and Sadducees request a sign, and Jesus says that an evil and adulterous generation seeks after a sign, but the sign of Jonah is the only one that will be given; then Jesus warns the disciples about the yeast of Pharisees and Sadducees.

At the beginning of the Beelzebul controversy (Luke 11:15), Luke inserts, "Other tempters were seeking a sign from heaven from him" (v. 16). Luke eventually returns to this point and has Jesus call this generation evil and say that the sign of Jonah is the only one they would receive (v. 29). According to Matthew and Mark, the Pharisees would be the common denominator to ask Jesus for a sign.[36] But when Matthew and Mark are combined, Herod, scribes, and Sadducees are also associated with the question. Matthew's Sadducees (16:1) appear especially out of place, since Mark (12:18) and Luke (20:27) only

---

36. Chakrita M. Saulina finds it "somewhat strange" that Luke would not have named the Pharisees in the Beelzebul controversy. Saulina, "Competitive Traditions: Luke's and Matthew's (Con)Textualizations of the Beelzebul Controversy," in *The Synoptic Problem 2022: Proceedings of the Loyola University Conference*, ed. Olegs Andrejevs et al., BTS 44 (Leuven: Peeters, 2023), 257.

have them involved with Jesus at the temple in Jerusalem. I propose, then, that Luke 11 derives from Matthew and Mark. It would have been cumbersome to include all the possible instigators of the Beelzebul controversy and the saying about the sign of Jonah; also, some characters would appear out of place. Luke does not simply copy Mark as the only source text. Instead, being bombarded with options, Luke generalized that "some of those people" made the Beelzebul accusation (11:15), while "other tempters" asked for a sign (11:16).

Woes against Scribes and Pharisees

In each of the Synoptics, Jesus insults scribes or Pharisees for the clothes they wore, where they preferred to sit, and how they liked to be greeted. As shown in figure 3.1, Mark has one such saying about scribes; Matthew has one such saying about scribes and Pharisees; and Luke has one saying for scribes and a separate saying for Pharisees.

Matt 23:2b, 5b–8a	Mark 12:38b–39	Luke 20:46	Luke 11:43
The scribes and the Pharisees sat on Moses's seat. . . . For they broaden their phylacteries and lengthen their tassels. They like the prime positions at the dinners, the prime seats in the synagogues, the greetings in the markets, and to be called "rabbi" by people. You are not to be called "rabbi."	Watch out for the scribes who want to walk around in robes and greetings in the markets, prime seats in the synagogues, and prime positions at the dinners.	Beware of the scribes who want to walk around in robes and like greetings in the markets, prime seats in the synagogues, and prime positions at the dinners.	Woe to you Pharisees, because you love the prime seat in the synagogues and the greetings in the markets.

Figure 3.1. Insulting scribes and Pharisees

Luke 20:46 matches Mark 12:38b–39 verbatim except for two verbs: Luke's "beware of" (*prosechō*) is synonymous with Mark's "watch out" (*blepō*); Luke also adds the verb "like" (*phileō*), a minor agreement with Matthew, since Mark omitted a verb at that point. Luke 11:43 does not agree verbatim with Matthew 23:6–7; as opposed to Mark, though, Matthew and Luke have in common the order of synagogue seating and marketplace greetings.

According to the two-source hypothesis, Mark and Q must have overlapped here as well. If so, then in this case, Luke carefully preserved each source at different points,[37] while Matthew combined similar sayings from different

---

37. E.g., Joseph A. Fitzmyer, *The Gospel according to Luke*, AB 28–28A (New York: Doubleday, 1970–1985), 2:943, 1316.

sources.[38] The Matthean posteriority hypothesis works similarly here, since Matthew would have conflated the two similar Lukan sayings.[39]

In defense of the Farrer hypothesis, I offer an alternative explanation for why Luke would have created separate sayings for Pharisees and scribes: Luke isn't keeping his sources separate; he's keeping his characters separate.[40] As I see it, Matthew added Pharisees to Mark's short denunciation of scribes as part of an extended excoriation of both groups (Matt 23). By contrast, Luke doubled the saying not only to separate the Pharisees but also to reposition their denunciation earlier in the narrative when Jesus was still on his way to Jerusalem.

Luke's doubling and repositioning fits withing a broader schema of exculpating the Pharisees in the plot against Jesus. Very early in the Synoptics, Matthew (12:14) and Mark (3:6) have the Pharisees planning to destroy (apollymi) Jesus. The Lukan parallel rewrites the sentence so that the Pharisees are just trying to decide "what to do to Jesus" (6:11). When Jesus gets to Jerusalem, the Pharisees make one last appearance in Luke's Gospel. They tell Jesus's disciples to stop calling him a king when he enters the city (19:38–39), but that could be a sign of concern. That warning coheres with an earlier story, told only by Luke, where Pharisees warn Jesus that Herod Antipas wanted to kill him (13:31).

Matthew and Mark cast the Pharisees in Jesus's temple controversies leading up to the crucifixion. Specifically, Pharisees asked Jesus whether people should pay their taxes to the emperor.[41] The same question arises at the same point in Luke's narrative, but he alters his sources so that "spies from the chief priests and scribes" ask the question (Luke 20:19). In Luke's Gospel, then, it makes sense for Jesus to denounce scribes in Jerusalem during passion week, because they would soon be part of the plot to kill Jesus (22:2).[42] Similarly, in Matthew's Gospel, it is sensible for Jesus to add Pharisees to the denunciation during passion week, because the Pharisees had already tried to arrest Jesus

---

38. E.g., W. D. Davies and Dale C. Allison Jr., *The Gospel according to Saint Matthew*, ICC (1988–1997), 3:265.

39. Robert K. MacEwen (*Matthean Posteriority: An Exploration of Matthew's Use of Mark and Luke as a Solution to the Synoptic Problem*, LNTS 501 [London: Bloomsbury T&T Clark, 2015]) inconsistently describes Luke's purported gathering of Matthean material "implausibly complex" (184), while elsewhere claiming that Matthew's purported gathering of Lukan material "seems more plausible" (194).

40. Goulder (*Luke*, 2:520) says that Luke divides the woes so that lawyers receive material pertaining to them while Pharisees are condemned for being legalistic, but it's unclear why legalistic material wouldn't apply to lawyers as well.

41. Matt 22:15–17 // Mark 12:13–15; Mark joins Herodians with the Pharisees here.

42. Jesus implicated the scribes in his first passion prediction according to all three Synoptics: Matt 16:21 // Mark 8:31 // Luke 9:22.

(21:45–46), and they continued to oppose the Jesus movement even after his death (27:62).

To summarize, Luke kept Mark's insult against scribes in place. There was no need for Luke to include a nearly identical insult against Pharisees anywhere. But Matthew had combined scribes and Pharisees in the insult about their clothing, marketplace greetings, and seating preferences in synagogues and at dinner parties. So Luke separated the Pharisees out of Matthew's saying and placed the doublet long before the arrival at Jerusalem (11:43). Luke went a step farther and cleverly orchestrated a dinner party with Pharisees so that Jesus could insult them for their seating preferences at such gatherings (11:37).

LUKE'S FRAMING OF THE PARALYSIS HEALING

In all three Synoptics, Jesus heals a paralyzed person, and this has long been my go-to text for teaching the Synoptic problem. The main goal is to spot similarities and differences and to resist the urge simply to say that all three gospels tell basically the same story. There are small differences, such as Mark's earthen roof that must be dug through (2:4), as opposed to Luke's tiles that are removed (5:19). And there is a huge difference insofar as Matthew has no roof at all, because there isn't even a house full of people. Presumably Jesus and the disciples remain outdoors, since they just got out of a boat (Matt 9:1).[43]

Luke's opening sentence sets the scene: "And it happened on one of the days he also was teaching, and sitting there were Pharisees and torah-teachers who had come from every village of Galilee and Judea and Jerusalem; and the power of the Lord was unto him to heal" (5:17). The reference to healing lets readers know that the content of Jesus's teaching is not the point of this story.[44] And in film terms, mentioning Pharisees and torah-teachers would be a master shot (Luke 5:17), where main characters are shown on screen before any of them say anything. This is the only reference to "torah-teachers" (*nomodidaskaloi*) in Luke's Gospel, but they are synonymous with scribes (v. 21).[45]

Both Matthew (9:3) and Mark (2:6) have scribes object to Jesus's forgiveness of sins later in this story. So Luke makes sure to introduce them from the

43. In that regard, the Augustinian and Griesbach hypotheses can make a decent case for Matthean priority: Jesus merely sees people carrying a paralyzed person, but somehow he sees their faith; Mark and Luke add the elaborate roof removal to demonstrate how Jesus saw the people's faith.

44. Similar to the earlier story of the exorcism in the Capernaum synagogue (4:31–36), Luke may say that Jesus was teaching, but the teaching is just a setup for a miracle.

45. Luke's "lawyers" (νομικοί) are also synonymous with scribes (7:30; 10:25; 11:45, 46, 52; 14:3).

beginning. Luke's addition of Pharisees may appear out of place, since neither Matthew nor Mark mentions them in this episode. However, their presence makes sense in light of the ensuing story. All three Synoptics proceed from the paralysis healing to Jesus's call of the tax collector Levi (aka Matthew), and then Jesus and the disciples eat with tax collectors and sinners.[46] At that point, Matthew (9:11) says that Pharisees asked why Jesus would eat with those people, but according to Mark (2:16) and Luke (5:30), both Pharisees and scribes ask the question. Again thinking in film terms, Luke combines these two scenes with a tracking shot: the formerly paralyzed person has exited the scene, but the camera would follow Jesus and his disciples along with scribes and Pharisees out of one house, by a tax table, and back into a house for dinner.

Luke also shows a touch of fatigue in the middle of this story. As Mark Goodacre explains,

> Editorial fatigue is a phenomenon that will inevitably occur when a writer is heavily dependent on another's work. In telling the same story as his predecessor, a writer makes changes in the early stages which he is unable to sustain throughout. Like continuity errors in film and television, examples of fatigue will be unconscious mistakes, small errors of detail which naturally arise in the course of constructing a narrative. They are interesting because they can betray an author's hand, most particularly in revealing to us the identity of his sources.[47]

As shown in figure 3.2, it is odd for Luke (5:22) to have Jesus ask why his adversaries are debating in their hearts.

Matthew	Mark	Luke
And look, some of the scribes said in themselves, "This one blasphemes." And Jesus, seeing their thoughts, said, "Why do you think evil in your hearts?"	Some of the scribes were there sitting and debating in their hearts, "Why is this one talking like this? He blasphemes. Who is able to forgive sins except one, God?" And immediately Jesus, knowing in his spirit that they were debating in themselves like this, says to them, "Why are you debating these things in your hearts?"	And the scribes and the Pharisees started to debate saying, "Who is this who talks blasphemy? Who is able to forgive sins except God alone?" Jesus, knowing their debatings, answering said toward them, "Why are you debating in your hearts?"

Figure 3.2. Synopsis of Matt 9:3–4 // Mark 2:6–8 // Luke 5:21–22

46. Matt 9:9–13 // Mark 2:13–17 // Luke 5:27–32.
47. Mark Goodacre, "Fatigue in the Synoptics," *NTS* 44 (1998): 46.

Mark states most clearly that scribes were "debating in their hearts" but that Jesus knew it "in his spirit," so he asked why they were debating in their hearts. Matthew says that scribes said "in themselves" (*en heautois*), perhaps in their minds, that Jesus was blaspheming. That could also be translated "among themselves," in which case they would be speaking aloud. However, Matthew clarifies that Jesus saw their thoughts, not that he heard their words, so he asks why they thought evil in their hearts. Luke says that the scribes and Pharisees were debating why Jesus would talk blasphemy, and Luke adds that Jesus knew what they were debating. If Luke's narrative is taken in isolation, it doesn't make much sense why he would ask the scribes and Pharisees about debating in their hearts, since up to this point they have been speaking openly.[48] Luke's "in your hearts" makes sense, however, if Luke has in mind Matthew (9:4) or Mark (2:8).[49]

Finally, there is a trove of so-called minor agreements in this short story. At the beginning, the narrators of Matthew (9:2) and Luke (5:18) not only say "and look" (*kai idou*) but also use the word "bed" (*klinē*) rather than "pallet" (*krabbatos*) as in Mark 2:4. In the middle, Jesus's rhetorical question is to "get up and walk around" in Matthew (9:5) and Luke (5:23); Mark (2:9) had already added "pick up your pallet" at that point. Then Jesus commanded the paralyzed person to get up, to pick up what he was lying on, and to go to his house.[50] Mark (2:12) says that the person got up, took his pallet, and left, but readers can't be certain where the person went. Matthew (9:7) says that the person got up and went to his house, so readers know where he went but might wonder whether he had neglected to pick up his bed. Luke (5:25) clarifies that the formerly paralyzed person did everything Jesus commanded: the person stood up, picked up what he was lying on, "and went away into his house."[51] And just for good measure, the one who had been healed joined the crowd in glorifying God. Finally, when the crowd witnessed the miracle, Mark says that they were amazed (2:12), whereas Matthew says that they were afraid

48. Cf. the disciples' debating "in themselves" who is greater in Luke 9:46, and then Jesus knows "the debating of their hearts" (v. 47). In that case, Luke emphasizes the disciples' inner thoughts, since Mark (9:34) had them debating openly "toward one another"; Mark's disciples seem embarrassed that Jesus had overheard them. The point is that Luke could have added "in themselves" or "in their hearts" earlier in the paralysis healing if he had thought of it.

49. Goodacre, "Fatigue in the Synoptics," 50.

50. Matt 9:6 // Mark 2:11 // Luke 5:24.

51. The phrase ἀπῆλθεν εἰς τὸν οἶκον αὐτοῦ is verbatim in Matt 9:7 // Luke 5:25; the verb choice is important since Mark gave the command to "go away" (ὑπάγω) in 2:11 and then reported that the person "went out" (ἐξέρχομαι) in v. 12.

(9:8); Luke combines both accounts so that the crowd was both stunned and filled with fear (5:26). Luke's rendition straightforwardly combines aspects of Matthew's and Mark's.

Luke's Crowd of Disciples

Except in one notable instance, which I will address in the next chapter, Luke loves a crowd. By contrast, in the Gospels of Matthew and Mark, Jesus regularly interacts with crowds, but without exception the disciples are separated out. The reason is that the crowds turn out to be fickle in Matthew and Mark. No matter how much they admire Jesus's teachings, marvel at his miracles, and hail his entry into Jerusalem, the crowds ultimately turn on him at his arrest and at his condemnation by Pilate.[52]

Mark (4:10) vaguely refers to "the ones around him with the disciples," who are told the purpose of parables. At that point, a minor agreement between Matthew (13:10) and Luke (8:9) is that "the disciples" alone have been given "the mystery of the kingdom."[53] Luke is synthesizing Matthew and Mark to create the largest group of Jesus's disciples.

Luke's intent appears most clearly for the setting of the Sermon on the Plain, when Jesus stands with "a great crowd of his disciples" (6:17). It was from this crowd that Jesus had just appointed the twelve apostles (6:13), a classic example of Luke "moving things ahead."[54] Yet the larger group of disciples never goes away in the Gospel of Luke.

Matthew's audience for the Sermon on the Mount is a bit confusing. Matthew's placement of the sermon depends on Mark, where people "were amazed at (Jesus's) teaching, for he was teaching them like someone having authority and not like the scribes" (1:22). The problem is that Jesus has only preached a sentence or two (Mark 1:15), so Matthew found a natural place to elaborate Jesus's teaching. To begin the sermon, though, Jesus leaves the crowds and preaches to the disciples who come to him (4:25–5:2). An incongruity arises

52. Regarding the crowds in Matthew, see Matthias Konradt, *Israel, Church, and the Gentiles in the Gospel of Matthew*, trans. Kathleen Ess, BMSEC (Waco, TX: Baylor University Press, 2014). I disagree with John P. Meier's (*A Marginal Jew*, vol. 3, *Companions and Competitors*, ABRL [New York: Doubleday, 2001], 33) conclusion that the crowds are ambivalent and distinguished from the disciples in Luke's Gospel.

53. Matt 13:11 // Mark 4:11 // Luke 8:10.

54. Greg Carey, "Moving Things Ahead: A Lukan Redactional Technique and Its Implications for Gospel Origins," *BibInt* 21 (2013): 302–19; Matthew does not appoint apostles until the mission discourse (10:2–4).

when Matthew says that somehow the crowds overheard the sermon and were amazed (7:28–29).[55] This is another case of Matthew becoming fatigued (7:29) and copying Mark (1:22) verbatim.

From Mark's parables discourse and from Matthew's Sermon on the Mount, Luke is picking up on his predecessors' fleeting and undeveloped references to a larger group of insiders. Luke's "great crowd of (Jesus's) disciples" foreshadows the mission of the seventy (10:1),[56] who preach and heal (v. 9) just as the Twelve had already done (9:1–2). By increasing the number of Jesus's disciples, Luke blurs the line between the crowds and the disciples. Luke codes all of these crowds positively, and they are true disciples of Jesus.

"I AM LUKE'S COMPLETE LACK OF SURPRISE"[57]

Luke claims in his preface (1:3) to have written an "orderly" (*kathexēs*) narrative about Jesus. One aspect of orderliness is eliminating surprises, a telltale sign of Lukan redaction. I imagine Luke asking himself questions as he reads his sources and then rewriting the stories to be less jarring at certain points.

Who Are the Women at the Crucifixion?

Moments after Jesus's death, Mark (15:40–41) introduced a group of women who witnessed the crucifixion from a distance. Three are named: Mary Magdalene, Mary of Jacob and Joses, and Salome. Come to find out, they were not only followers of Jesus in Galilee, but they ministered to him (the verbal form of the word "deacon"), and a lot of other women had also accompanied Jesus from Galilee to Jerusalem.

Matthew (27:54–55) introduced the women at the same moment as in Mark, but Matthew made slight edits. Many women who followed and served Jesus in Galilee were witnessing the crucifixion. After naming Mary Magdalene, Matthew clarifies that the other Mary was the mother of Jacob and Joseph (spelled differently than Joses). Matthew did not name Salome, but she might be the mother of the sons of Zebedee, whom Matthew did mention.

55. Davies and Allison (*Gospel according to Saint Matthew*, 1:421–22) interpret that Jesus did leave the crowds but that they overheard the sermon. Ulrich Luz (*Matthew*, trans. James E. Crouch, Hermeneia [Minneapolis: Fortress, 2001–2007], 1:182) interprets Matthew's concluding statement to mean that Jesus clearly taught the crowds.

56. The number is seventy-two in some manuscripts.

57. Cf. the narrator's (Edward Norton's) line, "I am Jack's complete lack of surprise," in David Fincher, dir., *Fight Club*, 20th Century Fox, 1999.

At the crucifixion, Luke (23:49) mentions women who followed Jesus from Galilee, but some of them had been named long before. In chapter 2, I discussed the woman who anoints Jesus, yet another example of Luke moving things ahead.[58] Jesus appears to be in Galilee at this time,[59] and immediately following the anointing scene (7:36–50), Luke adduces that many women were ministering to Jesus and the Twelve (8:1–3). Mary Magdalene is given the backstory of having been demon possessed (v. 2). Although hers is the only name in common with Matthew's and Luke's crucifixion witnesses, Luke's readers would not be surprised to find a large group of women who followed from Galilee and witnessed the crucifixion (23:49).

How Many People Did Jesus Feed?

With the addition of subject headings to the biblical text, readers often find something like "Feeding the Five Thousand" before the story is told in any of the four canonical gospels.[60] Without a subject heading, however, the number of people would surprise ancient readers, depending on which gospel they were reading. According to Mark (6:39–40), Jesus orders the disciples to have the crowds lie down, and the crowds apparently sort themselves into symposia of hundreds and fifties. Multiple hundreds and multiple fifties yield a minimum of three hundred people who were miraculously fed by Jesus's multiplication of five loaves and two fish. But three hundred turns out to be a tiny fraction of the total, since five thousand men are numbered at the end of the story (v. 44).

Matthew accentuates the element of surprise, since he omits altogether any sorting into hundreds or fifties. Readers simply know that a "big crowd" was there (Matt 14:14), and Matthew reveals more than five thousand people like a punch line (v. 21).[61] Luke spoils the joke. Similar to Mark (6:40), Luke (9:15) separates the crowd into groups of fifties, but Luke has already informed readers that "there were about five thousand men" (v. 14a).[62]

58. Carey, "Moving Things Ahead," 310–12.
59. Jesus healed the centurion's slave in Capernaum (Luke 7:1–10), and he raised the widow's son at Nain (vv. 11–17). Both are Galilean cities, and soon thereafter is the anointing at a Pharisee's home.
60. Matt 14:13–21 // Mark 6:32–44 // Luke 9:10b–17 // John 6:1–15.
61. Mark had said five thousand men (6:44), but Matthew (14:21) qualifies that additional women and children were present.
62. Fitzmyer (*Luke*, 1:767) attributes the move to "Luke's better sense of storytelling," and I agree that Luke would have seen it this way; conversely, Matthew seems to have preferred the element of surprise.

How Frequently Was Jesus Teaching in the Temple?

At Jesus's arrest, he asked why all of a sudden he was being treated like an in-surrectionist (*lēstēs*), since he'd been teaching "day by day" (*kath' hēmeran*) in the temple without being seized.[63] In Matthew and Mark, day-by-day teaching can mean only "two days in a row, several days ago."

When Jesus disrupts the commerce in the temple, he quotes Isaiah 56:7b regarding the temple being called a house of prayer. Mark (11:17–18) explicitly identifies Jesus's biblical quotation with the verb for teaching (*didaskō*), and the crowd was impressed by the noun for teaching (*didachē*). On the following day, there was a whole lot of teaching and debating at the temple,[64] but then Jesus left and was never said to return. The next temporal marker placed Passover and the Feast of Unleavened Bread two days away,[65] and the Last Supper and arrest occurred on the first night of the feast.[66] Matthew does not expressly refer to the Isaiah quotation as teaching, but Matthew has the same teaching block on the following day. In Matthew and Mark, then, it should be puzzling that Jesus claims to have been teaching every day in the temple.

Luke noticed the incongruity and smoothed it out. When narrating Jesus's disruption of the temple commerce and quotation of Isaiah (Luke 19:45–46), Luke states explicitly that Jesus "was teaching day by day in the temple" (v. 47). Luke relays much of the same teaching and debating as in Matthew and Mark, but Luke specifies that those things happened "on one of the days of his teach-ing the people in the temple" (20:1), thereby implying that there were other unrecorded days of teaching. And unlike Matthew and Mark, Luke locates the apocalyptic discourse at the temple, not outside its walls.[67] At the conclusion of that discourse, Luke reiterates that "through the days (Jesus) was in the temple teaching" (21:37) and that "all the people got up early to hear him in the temple" (v. 38).[68] These are subtle changes, but Luke ensures that it rings true when Jesus says at his arrest that he had been teaching day by day in the temple (22:53).

---

63. Matt 26:55 // Mark 14:49 // Luke 22:52–53; Luke has Jesus say more generally that every day he had been "with" the ones who were arresting him.

64. Matt 21:23–23:39 // Mark 11:27–12:44.

65. Matt 26:1 // Mark 14:1; cf. Luke 22:1, where the feast was approaching.

66. Matt 26:17 // Mark 14:12 // Luke 22:7.

67. In Matthew (24:1) and Mark (13:1), the apocalyptic discourse begins when Jesus leaves the temple, but Luke (21:5) does not mention an exit from the temple.

68. Contra Fitzmyer (*Luke*, 2:1357), there is no need to suppose these verses come from a lost L source.

Who's Carrying Swords?

A memorable element of Jesus's arrest scene comes when one of the disciples chops off a guy's ear.[69] Compared to the other synoptists, Luke adds a short phrase to clean up the mess by having Jesus reattach the ear (22:51c). Besides that piece of Lukan redaction, Luke foreshadowed the swordplay, since the weapon literally comes out of nowhere in the other gospels.[70] At the conclusion of the Last Supper, Luke has Jesus command his disciples to sell their clothes and buy swords; they replied that two swords were on hand, and Jesus said that would be enough (22:35–38). The command to take up two swords propelled centuries of interpretation regarding Christians wielding political power.[71] I see it much more simply: Luke was stuck with a swordfight, and he just didn't want readers to be caught completely off guard when someone got an ear cut off.

Who's Pilate, and Why Does He Call Jesus the King of the Jews?

After Jesus's arrest and questioning by the Sanhedrin, they send him to Pilate (Mark 15:1). This is Pilate's first appearance in the Gospel of Mark. Uninformed readers might wonder who Pilate is, especially since his term as governor had ended decades before the Gospels were written. From the narrative, Pilate clearly has authority to issue the death sentence (15:13–15), and he commands soldiers who are stationed at the *praetorium* (15:16), the Latin term for the governor's house. Eventually, then, Pilate's imperial rank can be inferred, but Mark never names it explicitly. By contrast, in the Gospel of Matthew (27:2), Jesus is handed over to Pilate the governor (*hēgemōn*), a title Matthew uses repeatedly throughout the questioning.[72] Luke (3:1) leaves no doubt about Pilate's position, for he was said to be governing (*hēgemoneuō*) Judea at the outset of Jesus's ministry.

Luke clarifies another aspect of Pilate's interaction with Jesus. As soon as Pilate meets Jesus in the Gospel of Mark (15:2), Pilate asks, "Are you the king

---

69. Matt 26:51 // Mark 14:47 // Luke 22:49–50 // John 18:10.

70. Raymond E. Brown (*The Death of the Messiah: From Gethsemane to the Grave*, ABRL [New York: Doubleday, 1994], 1:269) rightly sees that Luke has "considered the problem" of where the swords came from, but contra Brown there is no need to think that Luke was using a lost source text.

71. For an overview, see François Bovon, *Luke*, trans. Christine M. Thomas, Donald S. Deer, and James Crouch, Hermeneia (Minneapolis: Fortress, 2002–2013), 3:185–88.

72. Matt 27:11, 14, 15, 21.

of the Jews?" The same thing happens in Matthew's Gospel (27:11). Pilate asks an important question, but readers may wonder where it comes from. Earlier in Mark (11:10), many people screamed, "Blessed is the coming kingdom of our father David" when Jesus entered Jerusalem; perhaps Pilate heard about the uproar. Matthew had the crowds call Jesus "Son of David," but there was no reference to a kingdom, so Pilate's question makes even less sense in Matthew's rendition; here, too, Matthew shows fatigue in his use of Mark. Luke clears up any confusion by adding a line of dialogue. Just before Pilate asks Jesus whether he is the king of the Jews in Luke (23:3), a bunch of accusers tell Pilate that Jesus has called himself a king (v. 2).

All of these details can be easily passed over, especially by readers who are familiar with the other gospels. Back when Jesus was primarily in Galilee, Luke tells about his female followers who ministered to him; Matthew and Mark wait until the very end to tell readers that women had been among Jesus's followers all along. The feeding of the five thousand is such a widely known miracle that the number hardly sounds surprising. Upon closer inspection, though, the total number comes as a shock in Matthew and Mark, so Luke adduces the sum much earlier than his fellow synoptists. When Jesus was arrested, he claims to have been teaching daily in the temple, but that's not at all clear in Matthew and Mark, so Luke adds multiple references to Jesus's daily temple teaching. And when a disciple cuts off a slave's ear, Luke has foreshadowed the swordplay: as the Last Supper drew to a close, Jesus told the disciples to be ready to draw their swords. Luke has also established Pilate's role at the beginning of Jesus's ministry, and Pilate was explicitly told that Jesus was called "king of the Jews," so it makes more sense for Pilate to ask Jesus whether that was true. Taking all of these examples together, the elimination of any element of surprise emerges as a discernible tendency of Luke's redaction of Matthew and Mark.

Luke's (Further) Delay of the Parousia

Matthew (25:14–30) tells the parable of the talents, which has many parallels to Luke's parable of the minas (19:11–37).[73] Both stories are vehicles for final judgment: a person goes away after leaving money with those who were enslaved to him; when the master returns, profitable slaves are rewarded, while

---

73. The exact weight of a Greek talent is difficult to determine, but it was usually gold or silver that was worth sixty minas. A mina was a Latin monetary sum worth one hundred denarii; one denarius was a day's pay for a day laborer (Matt 20:1–16).

an unprofitable slave is punished. The differences between the parables automatically present a problem for the two-source hypothesis. The International Q Project concluded that Luke preserved the wording of Q, which was "ten minas" per slave; however, the editors grant that Q could have had the slaves receive ten, five, and two talents as in Matthew.[74] According to the two-source hypothesis, either Matthew or Luke had to rewrite Q's parable extensively. Those who are Q skeptics think that either Luke rewrote Matthew (Farrer, Griesbach, and Augustinian hypotheses) or that Matthew rewrote Luke (Matthean posteriority hypothesis).

I have already cited Mark Goodacre's classic article "Fatigue in the Synoptics," in which he makes an excellent argument for Luke's use of Matthew in this parable. The key insight is that in the beginning, Matthew has three slaves as compared with Luke's ten slaves; yet when the master returns, only three slaves are mentioned in Luke.[75] Similarly, Matthew's moneymaking slaves are rewarded with even more money, but Luke's two productive slaves are placed in charge of cities; yet Luke's unproductive slave has his money taken away and given to the most productive slave—the same thing that happened to Matthew's unprosperous slave.[76] Goodacre's insight is that Luke became fatigued by the rewriting process and slipped into a Matthean mode toward the end.

Goodacre's presentation is as succinct and compelling an argument for Luke's use of Matthew that I know of. I would add that these parables also reveal a direction of dependence from Mark to Matthew to Luke. The parable of the talents is part of the apocalyptic discourse, where Matthew found a foothold in Mark. In Mark 13, Jesus talks about the end times and says that "this generation will not pass away until all these things happen" (v. 30), but God alone knows exactly when the end will come (v. 32). As the discourse comes to a close, Mark has Jesus say in passing, "Like a person traveling away leaving his house and giving his slaves authority, to each one his work, and to the doorkeeper he commanded that he should be on the lookout. So be on the lookout: you don't know when the master of the house comes, whether late, at midnight, at the cockcrow, or early" (vv. 34–35). The word "late" (*opse*) can also mean "after a long time," although that's not Mark's meaning.

---

74. James M. Robinson, Paul Hoffmann, and John S. Kloppenborg, eds., *The Critical Edition of Q*, Hermeneia (Minneapolis: Fortress, 2000), 526–27.

75. Goodacre, "Fatigue in the Synoptics," 55; Tobias Hägerland ("Editorial Fatigue and the Existence of Q," *NTS* 65 [2019]: 194–97) challenges Goodacre's methodology but is unable to refute the clear case Goodacre makes for the parable of the talents/minas.

76. Goodacre, "Fatigue in the Synoptics," 55–56; Matt 25:28 // Luke 19:24.

Matthew expands Mark's short analogy into a long parable. Mark's point was that the end could come at any point in that generation, but Matthew could be picking up on the alternate meaning of *opse*, since he says explicitly that the master would return "after a long time" (25:19).[77] To be sure, when the end comes, it will come suddenly, but everyone should keep working in the meantime. In particular, Mark had said that all the gentiles must be evangelized (13:10), and Matthew will conclude his gospel with that command (28:19). Jesus definitely wants his disciples to stay on guard, but Matthew shows slightly less urgency than Mark. "Parousia" is the Greek term for coming or arrival, but it became a technical term for Jesus's second coming and final judgment. Matthew's apocalypticism exemplifies "the delay of the parousia," a phrase typically applied to the Gospel of Luke.

Hans Conzelmann's *The Theology of St. Luke* was a foundational work of redaction criticism. Conzelmann's section "Luke's Eschatology" explains numerous editorial interventions to alleviate the early church's pressing question of precisely when the end would come. Luke constructs "a timeless conception" of God's kingdom, one that counterintuitively enables the church to realize its mission by casting the parousia farther into the unknowable future.[78] There is much to commend in Conzelmann's analysis even now. As I see it, though, Matthew had already delayed the parousia. Luke just delayed it further.

As yet another example of Luke's tendency to move things ahead, the minas parable is removed from the apocalyptic discourse and placed before Jesus's entry into Jerusalem. Luke explicitly states the purpose of the parable: people thought that the kingdom of God was about to appear immediately (19:11). Luke's slave owner goes away to a faraway land to receive a kingdom (v. 12), so—given the distance—no one should expect him to return too soon. The departing–slave owner motif forms a neat trajectory across the Synoptics. In Mark's short analogy, the slave owner was supposed to return in that generation—maybe tonight or as late as tomorrow morning. At the same place as in Mark's narrative, Matthew expanded the story into a parable where the slave owner will be gone for a long time. Luke further delayed the parousia by instructing readers not to expect the kingdom to appear immediately. These stories are best explained by Matthew's use of Mark and then by Luke's use of Matthew.

77. μετὰ δὲ πολὺν χρόνον ἔρχεται ὁ κύριος (Matt 25:19).
78. Hans Conzelmann, *The Theology of St. Luke*, trans. Geoffrey Buswell (Philadelphia: Fortress, 1961), 95–136, esp. 108, 123.

Conclusion

This chapter has covered a wide range of material related to the Synoptic problem. In dialogue with recent scholarship on the Gospel of Mark's identification as a notebook, I showed that in antiquity such a designation could still refer to a finished, published, and quoted book. Mark's Gospel definitely does not have to be read as incomplete. Even though Matthew and Luke supplemented the First Gospel, Mark could stand on its own, and early readers clearly identified the Synoptics as separate books—albeit closely related ones.

Regarding Matthew's and Luke's supplementation of Mark, that is where the explanatory power of the Farrer hypothesis is at its strongest. To the beginning of Mark, Matthew added the nativity story from Joseph's perspective. Luke supplemented Matthew by giving Mary's perspective and by adding a birth story for John the Baptist. When it comes to the end of the gospel, Mark had added a story of an empty tomb to Paul's limited information about Jesus's resurrection. Compared to Mark, Matthew then added a resurrection appearance by Jesus and his promise to remain with the disciples until the end of time. Lest there be any confusion about Jesus's whereabouts, Luke added to Matthew the ascension narrative as a way of clarifying that Jesus would remain with the disciples in spirit, although he had definitely risen in the flesh.

In the middle of his Gospel, sometimes Luke conflated material from Matthew and Mark. At other times, Luke created doublets by dividing Matthean and Markan materials into separate locations. And if Matthew and Mark left too many characters to choose from, Luke tended to leave some characters unidentified. No author is perfectly consistent, but I have highlighted rhetorical reasons why Luke might have made different editorial decisions depending on the situation. The crowd of disciples emerged as a distinctive feature of Luke's Gospel, although it is easy to miss. Also, along the same lines as Luke's redactional tendency to move things ahead, I have shown numerous instances where Luke eliminates surprising elements from Matthew and Mark.

In the end, Luke's delay of the parousia was a foundational piece of redaction criticism. I simply qualify that Matthew had already delayed the parousia, particularly in the long parable of the talents, which expanded a brief analogy in Mark's apocalyptic discourse. Luke furthered Matthew's idea by rewriting the parable and by moving it ahead in the narrative. Luke also added a preface to the parable, dispelling the notion that the kingdom of God would appear on earth anytime soon.

Taken as a whole, these features support the Farrer hypothesis. Against the Augustinian and Griesbach hypotheses, too many aspects of Mark show it to be the first written gospel. Against the two-source hypothesis, there is no need to appeal to a lost Q source for the material common to Matthew and Luke but absent from Mark, especially given the preponderance of minor agreements between Matthew and Luke in material that is present in Mark—the healing of paralysis, for example. And against the Matthean posteriority hypothesis, there are too many places where Luke's use of Matthew is more likely than the reverse.

As I mentioned at the outset, there is no way to solve the Synoptic problem conclusively in a single chapter. Nevertheless, I hope to have collected key points from prior scholarship and offered new insights of my own to bolster the Farrer hypothesis, which may ultimately overturn the waning hegemony of the two-source hypothesis.

Chapter 3

JOHANNINE TRAJECTORIES

IN THE PREVIOUS CHAPTER, I showed how particular events snowball from Mark to Matthew to Luke. I see the Synoptic Gospels written in that order and with each subsequent evangelist using every preceding gospel. This chapter extends the same kind of snowballing trajectories to the Fourth Gospel. John used all three Synoptic Gospels as sources.

The same disclaimers from the previous chapter apply here. Scholars have debated John's relation to the Synoptics for centuries, and others have already written excellent histories of the question.[1] I cannot conclusively settle this perennial problem in just one chapter, but I can highlight what I consider the strongest examples of John's rewriting of the Synoptics.

More than three-fourths of John is unparalleled in the Synoptics. So where there are no parallels, it would be futile to draw many connections to the Fourth Gospel. John must simply be granted a great deal of authorial prerogative. Where there are parallels, however, John can be fruitfully compared.[2] And even when John diverges from the Synoptics in a given episode, I maintain that intentional rewriting best explains John's writing process. At times, John's storytelling exemplifies *oppositio in imitando*, a modern term to describe an ancient technique of imitating a classic story while turning many elements inside out.

I begin with the extent of Jesus's ministry, which John expands in both time and space. I then look at how the Gospel of John recasts the character of John the Baptist, particularly his self-awareness and knowledge of Jesus's identity.

---

1. D. Moody Smith, *John among the Gospels*, 2nd ed. (Columbia: University of South Carolina Press, 2001); Harold W. Attridge, "John and Other Gospels," in *The Oxford Handbook of Johannine Studies*, ed. Judith M. Lieu and Martinus C. de Boer (Oxford: Oxford University Press, 2018), 44–62.

2. By way of analogy, approximately half of the Gospel of Thomas has no parallels with the Synoptics; where there are parallels, though, Thomas used all three Synoptics as source texts. See Mark Goodacre, Thomas *and the Gospels: The Case for* Thomas's *Familiarity with the Synoptics* (Grand Rapids: Eerdmans, 2012).

I next align with previous scholarship that sees John's use of Matthew for Jesus's dialogue with Nicodemus in John 3 and Jesus's healing of an imperial official's son in John 4. John 4 also takes readers to Samaria, where the Samaritans become some of the earliest believers in Jesus—a surprising counternarrative to all three Synoptics. The paralysis healing in John 5 provides a quintessential example of *oppositio in imitando*, since nearly every element of the synoptic paralysis healing is reversed. For the feeding of the five thousand, I align with previous scholarship that shows John's use of all three Synoptics.

The raising of Lazarus provides another example of *oppositio in imitando*, specifically that a character in one of Luke's parables becomes a real person who dies and comes back from the dead. There are several elements of the Johannine passion narrative that reflect and refract the synoptic renditions, but trajectories from Mark to Matthew to Luke to John can often be discerned. Finally, I argue that the Gospel of John presupposes and approves of sacraments commemorating Jesus's death—certainly baptism and the Eucharist and perhaps also ritual anointing.

THE EXTENT OF JESUS'S MINISTRY

For the Synoptic Gospels, there is no easy answer to the simple question of how long Jesus's ministry lasted. Encompassing five Sabbath days, the forty-day temptation is the longest specified duration of a single episode. Including the moments leading up to Jesus's burial, Luke explicitly mentioned seven Sabbath days,[3] a greater number than in Matthew or Mark.[4] Also, Luke's reference to eight days leading up to the transfiguration implies yet another Sabbath day.[5] Since Easter Sunday was two days after the Sabbath, the minimum span from Jesus's baptism to ascension could be less than one hundred days.

The Sabbath days are significant time markers, because the spatial markers reveal that Jesus never traveled very far. By mapping the cities mentioned in the Gospel of Mark, for example, Jesus and the disciples needed just over a month for their journeys. By estimating fifteen miles per day on foot and truncating half days of travel (see figure 4.1), Jesus needed approximately thirty-five days to cover less than five hundred miles.[6]

3. Luke 4:16, 31; 6:1, 6; 13:10; 14:1; 23:54.
4. Sometimes the Synoptics use plural "Sabbaths" but intend just one Sabbath day (e.g., Matt 28:1; Mark 1:21; 2:23; Luke 4:31); this was not unprecedented (e.g., Josephus, *Life* 279; see BDAG, 909).
5. Luke 9:28; cf. six days according to Matt 17:1 and Mark 9:2.
6. For these approximations, I have used Adrian Curtis, *Oxford Bible Atlas*, 4th ed.

Start and End Points	km	mi	number of days
Nazareth to the Jordan River	35	22	1.5
Jordan River to Capernaum	30	19	1.3
Capernaum to Nazareth	45	28	2
apparently back near Capernaum	45	28	2
Capernaum to Bethsaida by boat	12	7.5	0.5
Bethsaida to Gennesaret by boat	17	10.5	1
Gennesaret to Tyre	80	50	4
Tyre to Sidon	40	25	2
Sidon to the Decapolis border	140	87	6
Decapolis border to Bethsaida	20	12.5	1
Bethsaida to Caesarea Philippi	50	31	2
Caesarea Philippi to Capernaum	55	34	2
Capernaum to Jericho	150	93	6
Jericho to Jerusalem	36	22	1.5
Minimum Travel Distance and Time	755	469.5	35

Figure 4.1. Jesus's journeys according to Mark

Jesus's ministry must have lasted longer than the thirty-five travel days or the thirteen or so Sabbath days. The reason is that the Synoptics give summary statements of Jesus's and the disciples' preaching and healing. In film terms, these would be montages of numerous events at various times and places. All three Synoptics say that Jesus preached in multiple Galilean synagogues.[7] There is another reference to Jesus preaching in the synagogues of the villages surrounding Nazareth (Mark 6:6). Matthew says more generally that Jesus was preaching in all the cities and villages (9:35),[8] including his disciples' cities (11:1). Luke even adds that Jesus "was preaching inside the synagogues of Judea" (4:44),[9] something he never explicitly does according to Matthew or Mark. There is no way to know how many days, weeks, or months to count for Jesus's preaching tours; the same applies to the mission work by Jesus's disciples.[10]

(Oxford: Oxford University Press, 2007); Google Maps, www.google.com/maps; and OR-BIS: The Stanford Geospatial Network Model of the Roman World, https://orbis.stanford.edu. ORBIS estimates between fifteen and twenty miles per day on foot, and I have used the lower estimate based on my own experience of backpacking when I became an Eagle Scout as a teenager.

7. Matt 4:23 // Mark 1:39 // Luke 4:14–15.

8. Similarly, Luke later tells that Jesus was teaching by city and by village (8:1) after returning to Galilee (7:1).

9. Among others, Byzantine manuscripts, Codex Alexandrinus, and Codex Bezae find this odd and change Judea to Galilee in Luke 4:44; however, Judea is the reading in Papyrus 75, Codex Vaticanus, and Old Syriac Sinaiticus.

10. For the mission of the Twelve, see Matt 10:1–16 // Mark 6:7–11 // Luke 9:1–5; see also the mission of the Seventy in Luke 10:1–12.

The overarching point here is that the Synoptics show no interest in specifying how long Jesus's ministry lasted. Nevertheless, accounting for the preaching and healing montages, there is no strong indication that the ministry lasted longer than a year. Luke may even envision a one-year ministry. Luke relocates Jesus's preaching in the synagogue at Nazareth very early (4:16–30). There Jesus read from a scroll of Isaiah (61:2) "to preach the year of the Lord's favor" (Luke 4:19). The Greek word *eniautos* can mean an unspecified long period, but it can also mean "year," and Isaiah specifically used the Hebrew word for "year" (*shanah*). Luke also begins Jesus's ministry "in the fifteenth year of the reign of Tiberius Caesar" (3:1), which is most likely 29 CE,[11] and 30 CE is the likeliest date for the crucifixion.[12]

Since the patristic era, scholars have noted just how sharply John's geography and chronology diverge from the Synoptics. More than one week passes in John 1:19–2:12, but the precise duration is unspecified. For three consecutive days, Jesus was around John the Baptist in Bethany across the Jordan.[13] But in the Fourth Gospel, Jesus was neither baptized by John nor tempted by the devil for forty days. Instead, Jesus departed for Galilee with his first disciples, and three days later they attended the wedding in Cana along with Jesus's mother (John 2:1–2).[14] After returning to Cana, Jesus, his family, and his disciples stayed in Capernaum for "many days" (2:12). Since John mentions days rather than weeks or months, "many days" likely means less than a month.

Just over three weeks elapse in John 2:13–4:54. When Passover was near (2:13), Jesus needed six or seven days to travel the ninety-nine miles (160 km) from Capernaum to Jerusalem.[15] Presumably Jesus spent a week in Jerusalem "at the Passover, at the festival" (v. 23), and the discourse with Nicodemus (ch. 3) would have occurred somewhere in there. The trip from Jerusalem to Sychar in Samaria was approximately sixty miles (100 km) and would have taken around four days (4:3–5). Jesus stayed there for two days before de-

---

11. See John P. Meier, *A Marginal Jew*, vol. 1, *The Roots of the Problem and the Person*, ABRL (New York: Doubleday, 1991), 385–86, for dating the fifteenth year of Tiberius (Luke 3:1) to 27, 28, or 29 CE.

12. Meier, *Marginal Jew*, 1:402.

13. John 1:29, 35, 43.

14. Cana was approximately eighty-one miles (130 km) from Bethany, so it would be very difficult to cover this much ground on foot in so few days. Yet the return from Cana to Capernaum was only twenty miles (35 km), a trip that could have taken just one day.

15. Josephus (*Life* 52) needed three days to travel from Galilee to Jerusalem, straight through Samaria, but he was traveling on horseback (51), which doubles or triples the distance a person could travel in one day. The Synoptics presuppose foot travel, either with (Mark 6:8) or without (Matt 10:10 // Luke 9:3) a walking stick.

parting for Galilee (v. 43). Jesus ends up in Cana, another twenty-eight miles (45 km) away, which required another two days of travel on foot.

That was the first of three Passovers in the Gospel of John, so Jesus's entire ministry lasted just over two years, and he repeatedly traveled back and forth between Galilee and Jerusalem (see figure 4.2).

John	Festival	Season
2:13	Passover 1	Spring
5:1	unnamed	?
6:4	Passover 2	Spring
7:2	Sukkoth	Fall
10:22	Hanukkah	Winter
11:55	Passover 3	Spring

Figure 4.2. Jesus's journeys according to John

In film terms, editors would use long fades out and back in to signify the passage of time between most of John's long scenes. The unnamed festival in John 5 would have occurred sometime after the healing of the imperial official's son (4:46–54). John 6:1 begins with the general phrase "after these things," and Jesus had made his way back to Galilee. When John says that Passover was near (6:4), it might be surprising that a full year has passed since the events of chapters 2–4. John 7:1 also begins with "after these things," but the feast of Sukkoth (v. 2) means that approximately five months have passed since the feeding of the five thousand. Another three months have passed when John announces Hanukkah in winter (10:22). John does not specify when Jesus raised Lazarus (ch. 11), but the anointing at Bethany was six days before the third and final Passover (12:1),[16] about four months after Hanukkah in chapter 10. Overall, the Fourth Gospel narrates far fewer days of Jesus's life, yet John doubled the length of Jesus's ministry, as compared to the Synoptics.

One glaring discrepancy emerges from John's alternate timeline. Jesus's disruption of the commerce in the Jerusalem temple (2:14–16) occurred two years

16. In the Synoptics, it comes as a surprise that Jesus is in Jerusalem at the time of Passover. Jesus had spoken repeatedly about going to Jerusalem with the disciples, and they finally arrived there (Matt 21:10 // Mark 11:11 // Luke 19:45). Much later, readers discover that Passover was near (Matt 26:2 // Mark 14:1 // Luke 22:1). By contrast, John's Gospel habitually notes which festival was upcoming, so readers know the occasion for Jesus's trips to Jerusalem. One argument against Luke's use of John is Luke's disdain for surprises, as noted in the previous chapter. In other words, if Luke had read John, then Luke might not have waited until the last minute—as did Matthew and Mark—to mention Passover.

before the crucifixion. Readers of the Synoptics expect the temple incident at the Passover coinciding with Jesus's death.[17] In the late second century, Tatian's Diatessaron split the difference by placing the temple incident at the second of three Passovers.[18] At the turn of the fifth century, Augustine surmised that Jesus must have caused a disturbance on two separate occasions, the earlier incident narrated by John and the later one found in the Synoptics.[19] I prefer the path paved by Origen in the early third century. Origen carefully observed such discrepancies and stated frankly that someone would become dizzy if they tried to reconcile all the historical disharmony among the Gospels. Yet Origen chose not to begrudge the four evangelists for telling "something at this time as happening at another."[20]

John's alternate timeline nevertheless proves fitting as the last attempt to understand Jesus's disturbance in Jerusalem. The temple used local currency, and pilgrims traveled long distances for Passover, so there was nothing unseemly about changing money and buying a sacrificial animal on site. According to Mark, Jesus's actions were premeditated, since he arrived in Jerusalem and saw what was happening (11:11) the day before he disrupted the commerce (v. 15). Matthew narrates spontaneous action, whereby Jesus stopped the buying, selling, and changing money as soon as he arrived in Jerusalem (21:12). Luke reinterprets that Jesus acted out of deep sadness, since he was weeping about the inevitable destruction of Jerusalem as he entered the city (19:41–44) and then he wouldn't let anyone sell anything (v. 45). Subsequent synoptists were trying to make sense of Jesus's actions, but in all three Synoptics, the temple incident emerges as a probable factor in the priests' plot against Jesus. The Fourth Gospel's relocation is striking. By moving the event two years ahead, John significantly downplays the temple incident, which became just one of many controversies in Jerusalem.

JOHN THE BAPTIST AND JESUS

"The beginning of the gospel of Jesus Christ" (Mark 1:1) is actually an introduction to John the Baptist as someone predicted centuries earlier: "Just as it has been written by Isaiah the prophet, 'Look, I am sending forth my angel

17. This episode is often referred to as the cleansing of the temple, something of a misnomer since apparently Jesus made quite a mess.

18. Arabic Diatessaron 32.1–6; see James W. Barker, "The Narrative Chronology of Tatian's Diatessaron," *NTS* 66 (2020): 288–98.

19. Augustine, *Cons.* 2.129.

20. Origen, *Comm. Jo.* 10.3, 5.

before your face who will prepare your way. A voice shouting in the desert, 'Prepare the way of the Lord; make his paths straight'" (vv. 2–3). The problem with Mark's opening is that the first part of the scriptural quotation comes from Malachi: "Look, I am sending out my angel, and he will attend to a road before my face" (3:1). Mark's ensuing phrases do quote Isaiah (40:3), however. Matthew and Luke noticed the problem with Mark's conflated quotation, so they extracted the Malachi material. Matthew (3:3) simply quotes Isaiah 40:3, whereas Luke (3:4–6) lengthens the quotation to include Isaiah 40:3–5.[21]

The Isaiah prophecy recurs in the Fourth Gospel. However, rather than having the narrator quote Scripture as in all three Synoptics, John's Gospel gives John the Baptist a speaking part: "I am a voice shouting in the desert: 'Straighten the road of the Lord,' just as Isaiah the prophet said" (John 1:23). All of this forms a snowballing trajectory beginning with Mark's conflated quotation. Matthew excised Mark's Malachi material so that the prophecy is exclusively Isaiah's. Luke followed suit while adding the ensuing lines from Isaiah's prophecy. John's Gospel most closely aligns with Matthew's as far as the Scripture quotation goes, but John rewrites all the Synoptics when it comes to John the Baptist's first-person self-understanding as the one preparing the way of the Lord.

Mark follows the prophecy by narrating that John the Baptist was "preaching a baptism of repentance unto forgiveness of sins" (1:4), and soon thereafter Jesus came to be baptized by John (1:9). That sounds like Jesus wanted forgiveness for his sins, so Matthew rewrote the story. When Jesus came to John the Baptist, John said that he needed to be baptized by Jesus (3:14). Luke doesn't even describe the baptism, but he mentions in passing that Jesus had been baptized or perhaps that he had baptized himself (3:21).[22] The Gospel of John does not say that Jesus was baptized at all, and Jesus never says a word to John the Baptist in the Fourth Gospel. In this way, there is a discernible trajectory whereby Jesus is increasingly distanced from, and superior to, John the Baptist. In the Fourth Gospel, John the Baptist even says about Jesus, "It is necessary for that one to increase but for me to decrease" (John 3:30).

John's Gospel also provides an answer to a question that Luke alone had raised. According to Luke (3:15), all the people were "debating in their hearts concerning John [the Baptist], whether he might be the Christ."[23] In the Gos-

---

21. Later in their gospels, Matthew (11:10) and Luke (7:27) have Jesus quote Mark's (1:2) rendition of Malachi (3:1) to inform the crowds that the prophet was predicting the coming of John the Baptist.

22. Luke's participle βαπτισθέντος could be interpreted as either passive or reflexive (3:21).

23. John the Baptist doesn't answer directly, but he does say that someone stronger is coming (v. 16), a saying paralleled in Matthew (3:11) and Mark (1:7).

pel of John, priests and Levites from Jerusalem directly ask John the Baptist who he is (1:19), and he answers in the first-person, "I am not the Christ" (1:20b). Twice in proximity, then, the Fourth Gospel lifts ideas from the Synoptics and has John the Baptist speak for himself, thereby leaving no doubt about his identity: he wasn't the Messiah, but John was the one preparing the way.

The Fourth Evangelist also uses John the Baptist to rewrite a crucial scene that occurs much later in the Synoptics. The exact midpoint of Mark's Gospel is the transfiguration (9:2–8).[24] The transfiguration is literally Jesus's metamorphosis, when he spoke with Moses and Elijah and when God declared Jesus to be his son. All of this was witnessed by the apostles Peter, Jacob (aka James), and John. Just before this transformative event, Jesus had asked his disciples who people thought he was.[25] Some reportedly thought of Jesus as John the Baptist resurrected from the dead,[26] others said Elijah, and still others thought Jesus was one of the prophets. When Jesus asked who the disciples thought he was, Simon Peter declared him to be the Messiah.

The Fourth Gospel extensively rewrote this scene and had John the Baptist do all the work at the outset of the story. It's hardly an accident that John the Baptist says that he is neither the Messiah, Elijah, nor the prophet (John 1:20–21)—the very people Jesus was mistaken for in the Synoptics. The Gospel of John had already elevated Jesus above John the Baptist in the prologue (1:6–8), and John the Baptist himself declared Jesus to be "the lamb of God who takes away the sin of the world" (1:29) as well as "the Son of God" (v. 34). In other words, characters do not gradually recognize Jesus's identity in the Gospel of John. Everything is firmly established from the start.

I do not find it problematic that Matthew (11:14; 17:10–14) has Jesus say that John the Baptist was Elijah, while John's Gospel (1:21) says that he wasn't. The issue was how literally to interpret the identification. Mark (1:2) began with Malachi's (3:1) prophecy about the Lord sending his angel or messenger to prepare the way; Malachi (4:5) adds that Elijah the prophet will return before the day of the Lord.[27] Matthew wanted that prophecy to be fulfilled so that

24. By my count of Mark according to Codex Vaticanus, the transfiguration comprises letters 27,002–27,581; the gospel's total letter count is 54,637; the parallels are Matt 17:1–9 // Luke 9:28–36.

25. Matt 16:13–20 // Mark 8:27–30 // Luke 9:18–21.

26. Matt 14:10 // Mark 6:27. Mark foreshadows the discussion at Caesarea Philippi by adding that Herod Antipas was one person who thought that Jesus was the resurrected John the Baptist (6:16); some people were saying that (6:14), while others thought Jesus was Elijah or one of the prophets (6:15).

27. Mal 4:5 is the English reference; it's Mal 3:22 in the Septuagint and Mal 3:23 in the Tanak.

Jesus could be the Messiah. Therefore Jesus associated John the Baptist with Elijah (Matt 17:12–13) to clarify that the disciples didn't need to wait on anyone else. Elijah had come and gone, the Messiah was right there, and the kingdom of God was coming soon.

Luke 16:16 parallels Matthew (11:12–13) but lacks the part about Elijah having returned (Matt 11:14). Long before, Luke had narrated the annunciation and birth of John the Baptist (1:5–25, 57–80), lest anyone think the ancient prophet Elijah the Tishbite had ridden his chariot of fire in a whirlwind back down to earth (2 Kgs 2:11). In the literal sense, then, John's Gospel agrees with Luke that John the Baptist wasn't the biological Elijah, but the fourfold gospel unanimously considers Jesus the Messiah whose Elijah-type forerunner had come and gone.

These and other parallels between John and the Synoptics have long been observed, and they have sometimes been chalked up to oral tradition, since the differences outnumber the similarities.[28] Yet it is problematic to assume that John would have followed the Synoptics as closely as they follow each other, especially when John's differences often look like deliberate reinterpretations of the Synoptics' portrayals of John the Baptist.

Nicodemus and the Imperial Official

M.-É. Boismard developed an extravagant hypothesis for the composition of the Gospel of John.[29] He posited multiple sources and compositional layers for each gospel, and ultimately Boismard concluded that the final edition of the Gospel of John made use of all three Synoptics.[30] The theory as a whole was far too complicated and speculative to gain acceptance,[31] and Raymond Brown famously said that a chart of Boismard's model "looks like a twelve-man football team with a lot of motion in the backfield."[32] Yet if Boismard's hypothetical sources and redactional layers are set aside, he deserves credit for

28. E.g., C. H. Dodd, *Historical Tradition in the Fourth Gospel* (Cambridge: Cambridge University Press, 1963), 260; see also Percival Gardner-Smith's (*Saint John and the Synoptic Gospels* [Cambridge: Cambridge University Press, 1938], 10) conclusion that if John the Evangelist did in fact read the synoptic accounts of John the Baptist, then John held the Synoptics "in very low esteem."

29. M.-É. Boismard, Pierre Benoit, and A. Lamouille, *Synopse des quatre Évangiles en français*, 3 vols. (Paris: Cerf, 1965–1977).

30. For a summary of the theory, see Smith, *John among the Gospels*, 141–47.

31. For a book-length refutation, see Frans Neirynck et al., *Jean et les synoptiques: Examen critique de l'exégèse de M.-É. Boismard*, BETL 49 (Leuven: Leuven University Press, 1979).

32. Raymond Brown, review of *L'Évangile de Jean* (*Synopse des quatre Évangiles en français*, vol. 3), by M.-É. Boismard and A. Lamouille, *CBQ* 40 (1978): 625.

many keen insights into the relationship between John and the Synoptics. Two brief examples come respectively from John chapters 3 and 4.

In John 3, Jesus converses at length with a Pharisee named Nicodemus. The first thing Jesus says to him is that to see the kingdom of God, one must be either born "from above" or born "again" (John 3:3); John uses the Greek word *anōthen*, which carries both meanings.[33] Nicodemus thinks in terms of being born "again," so he asks how such a thing could be biologically possible (v. 4), and Jesus replies that Nicodemus lacks spiritual understanding (vv. 5–8).

As shown in figure 4.3, John 3:3 has a close parallel in Matthew (18:3). The narrative contexts have nothing in common, since John is the only canonical gospel that features Nicodemus. The similarity in sayings is striking nonetheless, and Boismard pointed out that the Aramaic word "turn" (*tuv* = Hebrew *shuv*) signifies repetitive action when it's joined with another verb. So Matthew's "turn and become like children" (18:3) could very well mean to become again like children. Boismard surmised that John picked up on this meaning and derived his "born again" saying directly from Matthew.[34]

And (Jesus) said, "Amen I say to you [pl.], unless you turn and become like the children, you will not at all enter into the kingdom of the heavens" (Matt 18:3).	Jesus answered and said to (Nicodemus), "Amen, amen I say to you [sg.], unless someone be born again, it is not possible to see the kingdom of God" (John 3:3).

Figure 4.3. Synopsis of Matt 18:3 and John 3:3

There is a long-standing notion that John's saying was a piece of oral tradition used in early baptism rituals.[35] The main reason was that the saying is quoted in slightly different forms by several early Christian authors in the second, third, and fourth centuries. As I have demonstrated elsewhere,[36] the main problem with this argument is that every one of the patristic texts undeniably quotes the Gospel of John elsewhere, so there has never been any firm basis for an orally transmitted "born again" baptismal saying. A related idea is

33. Given the double meaning, Francis J. Moloney (*The Gospel of John*, SP 4 [Collegeville, MN: Liturgical Press, 1998], 88) translates, "born again, from above."

34. Boismard, Benoit, and Lamouille, *Synopse*, 3:118.

35. E.g., Helmut Koester, *Ancient Christian Gospels: Their History and Development* (Philadelphia: Trinity International, 1990), 257–58. I will discuss baptism in the Fourth Gospel at the end of this chapter.

36. James W. Barker, "Written Gospel or Oral Tradition? Patristic Parallels to John 3:3, 5," *EC* 6 (2015): 543–58.

that Matthew 18:3 and John 3:3 arose independently via oral tradition.[37] Since I have found numerous other instances of John's use of Matthew,[38] I am inclined to agree with Boismard in this case: John not only liked Matthew's saying but also created a compelling character and an elaborate dialogue to ponder the meaning of being born again.

The short healing narrative at the end of John 4 (vv. 46b–54) has numerous parallels with a story in Matthew (8:5–13) and Luke (7:1–10). I am convinced that Matthew and Luke are interrelated, but the question has always been whether John is independent. All three stories are set in Capernaum. Matthew and Luke talk about a centurion (*hekatontarchos*) as opposed to John's imperial official (*basilikos*). According to John, the man first requests healing for "his son [*huios*], for he was about to die" (4:47); later he's called a "little boy" (v. 49b), but he's distinguished from the slaves (*douloi*) who report on his condition. Matthew (8:8) and Luke (7:7) have the man request healing for his "boy" (*pais*), which could mean his child or his slave; Luke definitely means "slave," since he uses the term *doulos* at the end of the story (v. 10). In all three versions, Jesus performs the healing remotely rather than going to the man's house. Also, Matthew (8:13b) and John (4:52a) call attention to "the hour" (*hōra*) when the boy was healed.

For some interpreters, John's differences outnumber the similarities, and so the story is thought to be a piece of oral tradition.[39] For others, John's similarities are striking enough that John more likely used Matthew and Luke.[40] Boismard made the strongest case for John's use of the Synoptics simply by reading across to the next story in Matthew. By doing so, Boismard could account for a key difference among the three stories. Matthew says the boy was paralyzed (8:6), Luke simply says that he'd taken sick and was about to be done in (7:2), but John (4:52) reports in the end that "the fever left him" (*aphēken auton ho pyretos*). According to Matthew (8:15), after the healing of the centurion's boy, Jesus healed Peter's mother-in-law, and "the fever left her" (*aphēken autēn ho pyretos*). I agree with Boismard that John most likely caught the boy's fever not by hearing oral tradition but by knowing the narrative sequence of Matthew's written gospel.[41]

---

37. E.g., Rudolf Bultmann, *The Gospel of John: A Commentary*, trans. G. R. Beasley-Murray, R. W. N. Hoare, and J. K. Riches (Philadelphia: Westminster, 1971), 135 n. 4; Dodd, *Historical Tradition*, 358–59.

38. James W. Barker, *John's Use of Matthew*, Emerging Scholars (Minneapolis: Fortress, 2015; repr., Eugene, OR: Wipf & Stock, 2021).

39. E.g., Gardner-Smith, *Saint John*, 23–24; Dodd, *Historical Tradition*, 195.

40. E.g., Ulrich Wilckens, *Das Evangelium nach Johannes*, NTD 4 (Göttingen: Vandenhoeck & Ruprecht, 2000), 89.

41. Boismard, Benoit, and Lamouille, *Synopse*, 3:149.

Answering the Samaritan Question

The Gospels give conflicting answers to the question whether the Samaritans were included in Jesus's mission.[42] Samaria was the region between Galilee in the north and Judea in the south. In rabbinic literature and in the New Testament, Jewish people often referred to themselves as "Israelites," for example, when Jesus meets Nathaniel in John 1:47. It can be confusing that Samaritans were the descendants of the ancient, northern kingdom of Israel, and yet Samaritans are distinguished from Israelites in the Gospels and in rabbinic literature (e.g., m. Ber. 8:8). A long-standing point of contention had been the Samaritans' cultic center at Mount Gerizim in Samaria, rather than the Jewish temple in Jerusalem. Nevertheless, both groups descended from Abraham and adhered to the torah of Moses. In terms of religious observance, then, Jews and Samaritans had much more in common with one another than with anyone who worshiped Greek or Roman gods and goddesses in pagan temples. Also, rabbinic literature describes amicable interactions such as Jews visiting Samaria (e.g., Gen. Rab. 32.10) and Jews eating with Samaritans (m. Ber. 7:1).

There was animosity at times, however. According to Josephus, "It was the custom among the Galileans coming to the festivals in the holy city to travel via the region of Samaria" (*Ant.* 20.6.1), but then he describes a Samaritan attack on Galilean pilgrims in 52 CE. By the time the Gospels were written, some Jews would have avoided Samaria when traveling between Galilee and Judea. Reading between the lines, Jesus and his followers appear to have done so on their way to Jerusalem for Passover in the Gospel of Mark. Mark never mentions Samaria or Samaritans, but after leaving Capernaum (9:33), Jesus travels in the Transjordan (10:1), and later he and disciples are on the road to Jerusalem (v. 32) via Jericho (v. 46). Jesus explicitly crossed the Jordan River early in the journey (10:1). The implication is that Jesus and the disciples traveled southward on the eastern side of the Jordan River, so they would have literally gone out of their way to avoid Samaria. They later arrive at Jericho (10:46), Bethpage and Bethany (11:1), as well as Jerusalem (11:11), all of which are on the west side of the Jordan, so they must have crossed back over the river at some point.

Compared to Mark, Matthew has a similar travel itinerary for the Passover journey. Jesus left Galilee for the Transjordan (19:1), and later he is on the way to Jerusalem (20:17) via Jericho (v. 29). Matthew doesn't mention Samaria as

---

42. I looked at this question in *John's Use of Matthew*, 93–106 (ch. 5); however, I paid little attention to Luke's Gospel, which adds important context for John's reconceptualization of a Samaritan mission.

part of the journey, but earlier in the gospel, Jesus expressly commanded the Twelve not to evangelize Samaritans: "Into a road of gentiles do not depart, and into a city of Samaritans do not enter; go instead toward the lost sheep of the house of Israel" (10:5b–6). After the resurrection, Jesus instructed his remaining followers to "disciple all the gentiles" (28:19). Samaritans are neither Israelites nor gentiles, so they are left out of the disciples' initial mission in chapter 10, and they are not included in the Great Commission at the end of the gospel. According to Matthew, Jesus intentionally excludes Samaritans from being evangelized and discipled.

Compared to Mark and Matthew, Luke moves Jesus closer to Samaria and Samaritans. When Jesus first set out for Jerusalem with his disciples, he wanted to stay in a Samaritan village (9:51–52), but "they did not receive him," since he was headed toward Jerusalem (v. 53). That was a subtle way for Luke to rewrite Matthew: Jesus didn't exactly reject the Samaritans; instead, there was one Samaritan village whose inhabitants rejected him. Jesus didn't begrudge them, for he scolded his disciples Jacob and John when they asked to burn up the Samaritan village with fire from heaven (vv. 54–55). Soon thereafter, Jesus told the so-called parable of the good Samaritan (10:30–37). Farther along the trip to Jerusalem, Jesus remained in "the middle of Samaria and Galilee" (17:11). At a village in that area, he cured ten men with leprosy (vv. 12–14), one of whom was a Samaritan (v. 16b). Jesus called him a foreigner (v. 18), literally "this one of a different tribe" (*ho allogenēs houtos*), but he was the only one who thanked Jesus for curing him.

According to Luke, then, one Samaritan village rejected Jesus, but a Samaritan was the moral exemplar in a parable, and Jesus healed a grateful Samaritan of his leprosy. The Gospel of Luke never has the Samaritans evangelized, and eventually the risen Jesus commands his disciples to preach "unto all the gentiles" (24:47). However, the Acts of the Apostles presents itself as a sequel to Luke's Gospel, and the resurrected Jesus told the apostles that they would be his witnesses in Samaria (Acts 1:8). That commandment was fulfilled when Philip preached in a city of Samaria (8:5). The inhabitants became believers, and Philip baptized women and men (v. 12). Soon thereafter Peter and John "evangelized many villages of Samaritans" (8:25). The book of Acts recognized the problem of Samaritans being excluded, so they were intentionally included in the early apostolic church. According to Luke-Acts, though, Jesus himself never evangelized Samaritans.

The Gospel of John thoroughly reinterpreted Jesus's relationship with Samaritans. After he had gone to Jerusalem during Passover (ch. 2) and talked with Nicodemus (ch. 3), "he left Judea and went away again into Galilee; it was necessary for him to go through Samaria" (4:3–4), specifically the city of Sychar (v. 5). There Jesus spoke to a Samaritan woman by a well (vv. 7–17). Jesus somehow knew that she'd had five previous husbands and currently had a man who was not her husband (v. 18). She then recognized him as a prophet (v. 19) and inquired about Samaritans' and Jews' respective cultic centers (v. 20). Jesus replied that neither would be a place of worship in the future (v. 21), and the Samaritan woman told Jesus that she was awaiting the Messiah (v. 25). Jesus told her that he was the Messiah (v. 26), and she left to tell the city people that the Messiah could be in their midst. They came to see (vv. 29–30), and many Samaritans believed in Jesus because of the woman's testimony (v. 39). Many others believed in Jesus as "the Savior of the world," and he stayed with them for two days (vv. 40–42).

John's expanded geography and chronology made room for a Samaritan mission. Matthew, Mark, and Luke narrate just one pilgrimage from Galilee to Judea for Passover, and there was no Samaritan mission along the way. John harmonizes particularly well with Luke's Samaritans' rejection of Jesus (9:53). That could have happened on the way to Jerusalem at the Passover when Jesus disrupted the temple commerce. Upon leaving Jerusalem, Jesus went some-where in Samaria, and he told the Samaritan woman that the proper place of worship was neither here nor there.

John can also harmonize with both Matthew and Luke, since all three have a harvest saying that functions as a metaphor for evangelism. Matthew and Luke say verbatim, "The harvest is a lot, but the workers few; ask therefore the lord of the harvest how he can send out workers into his harvest."[43] In Matthew, Jesus then tells the disciples not to go near the Samaritans when they preach and heal. Yet if Matthew is read in light of John, then Jesus himself can spend two days revealing himself as the Messiah and Savior in Samaria while the disciples went elsewhere to preach. Similarly, Luke's harvest saying occurs not long after some Samaritans had refused hospitality to Jesus. But unlike Matthew and Mark, Luke has Jesus remain in the vicinity of Samaria for an unspecified time. So at that time and place, Jesus could liken evangelism to a harvest. If John is read in light of Luke, then it was a short step for John to place the saying in a Samaritan city.

According to John, while the Samaritan woman has left to bring the city people to Jesus, he tells his disciples,

---

43. Matt 9:37b–38 // Luke 10:2bc. The words are all the same in Greek, but Luke trans-poses the verb and direct object; also, in the Coptic Gospel of Thomas, saying 73 has the verbatim harvest saying using Matthew's word order.

"Don't you say that there's still four months and then comes the harvest? Look, I say to you, lift up your eyes and see the fields, that they are white for harvest. Already the harvester receives a wage and gathers together fruit unto eternal life, so that the sower should rejoice together with the harvester. For in this way, the saying is true: one is the sower, and another the harvester. I sent you to harvest what you have not labored; others have labored, and you have entered into their fruit." (John 4:35–38)

John's harvest saying can be read as a reinterpretation of Matthew's and Luke's. Jesus is not rejecting the Samaritans, as it sounds like in Matthew (10:5b–6). And even though Luke's Samaritan village refused hospitality for one night on the way to Jerusalem (9:51–53),[44] the Samaritan village of Sychar hosted Jesus for two nights and proclaimed him the Messiah and Savior of the world. To be sure, Matthew and Luke intended to exclude Samaritans from Jesus's ministry. Nevertheless, John cleverly constructed a story of Samaritan inclusion—a story that can be complementary rather than contradictory as long as John is the lens through which one rereads Matthew and Luke.

John's Paralysis Healing

In the previous chapter, I looked at the healing of paralysis in the Synoptics, and there is a related paralysis healing in John 5, which I find to be a textbook case of *oppositio in imitando*. A core element connects to the Synoptics, while numerous aspects of John's story are the exact opposite of its synoptic counterparts. The differences are so striking that they betray John's intentional rewriting of his predecessors' story. According to Matthew, Mark, and Luke,[45] the paralyzed person was in Galilee; he had friends to carry him; readers do not know how long the person had been paralyzed; a crowd witnessed the healing; yet the story does not create a Sabbath controversy. By contrast, according to John (5:1–16), the paralyzed person was in Judea; he had no one to carry him; readers learn that his ailment had lasted thirty-eight years; a crowd does not witness the healing; yet the healing created a Sabbath controversy. Despite so many differences, John and Mark have one nearly verbatim sentence. Mark has Jesus say to the paralyzed person, "Get up and pick up your bed and walk

---

44. If Luke were reading John, as some have proposed, then the Gospels cannot harmonize nearly as well. That is, Luke would be erasing John's Samaritan mission and delegating it to the disciples after the ascension. I think it makes much more sense to see John reinterpreting Luke so that all four canonical gospels can be read harmoniously.

45. Matt 9:9–13 // Mark 2:13–17 // Luke 5:27–32.

around" (2:9c).[46] John simply deletes the first "and" when Jesus commands the sick person, "Get up, pick up your bed, and walk around" (John 5:8b).[47]

There are also elements of fatigue in John's version. The Synoptics clearly identify the person as paralyzed from the outset.[48] John simply says that the person was one of many who were sick, blind, disabled, or withered (5:3). They all wanted to be healed miraculously whenever the water was stirred in the pool by the Sheep Gate (vv. 2, 7). John twice refers to the person as "sick" (vv. 5, 7), and he is said to by lying down when Jesus asked, "Do you want to be healthy?" (v. 6). The person replies that someone else always gets to the pool before him, so he never gets healed. Then Jesus gives the command to get up, pick up the bed, and walk around (v. 8). At this point, readers might simply think that Jesus is saying to get a head start and go to the pool, since his infirmity has not yet been indicated. But then, "the person immediately became healthy and picked up his bed and was walking around" (v. 9a). John never says that the person was paralyzed, but under the influence of the Synoptics, John surprisingly discloses that the sickness was an inability to walk for thirty-eight years.

A similar phenomenon pertains to the forgiveness of sins. In the Synoptics, before saying anything about the paralyzed person's potential to walk, Jesus declares his sins forgiven.[49] That declaration causes controversy, and the healing miracle is supposed to prove Jesus's authority to forgive sins. In the Gospel of John, Jesus heals the person so that he can walk, and nothing has been said about sin or forgiveness. But later a controversy arose, since the man was carrying his bed—as Jesus commanded—on what turns out to be a Sabbath day (John 5:9b–12). Jesus had disappeared for a moment (v. 13), but then he meets the person in the temple and tells him, "Look, you have been made healthy; sin no more, so that nothing worse should happen to you" (v. 14b). John's reference to sin makes the most sense if he has in mind the synoptic story.

Some have claimed John's use of, or familiarity with, Mark in this passage.[50] Others have at least acknowledged such a possibility.[51] Many others

---

46. Cf. "Get up and walk around" (Matt 9:5c // Luke 5:23c).

47. ἔγειρε καὶ περιπάτει (Matt 9:5c // Luke 5:23c); ἔγειρε καὶ ἆρον τὸν κράβαττόν σου καὶ περιπάτει (Mark 2:9c); ἔγειρε ἆρον τὸν κράβαττόν σου καὶ περιπάτει (John 5:8b).

48. παραλυτικόν (Matt 9:2 // Mark 2:3); ἄνθρωπον ὃς ἦν παραλελυμένος (Luke 5:18).

49. Matt 9:2c // Mark 2:5b // Luke 5:20b.

50. For John's direct use of Mark, see, e.g., Wendy E. S. North, *What John Knew and What John Wrote: A Study in John and the Synoptics* (Lanham, MD: Lexington Books/Fortress Academic, 2020), 54–55; for John's familiarity with Mark, see, e.g., Andrew T. Lincoln, *The Gospel according to Saint John*, BNTC (London: Continuum, 2005), 198.

51. E.g., C. K. Barrett, *The Gospel according to St. John*, 2nd ed. (Philadelphia: Westminster, 1978), 249, 254.

have claimed that the differences outnumber the similarities, so John simply knows oral tradition.[52] Yet if *oppositio in imitando* is taken seriously as a Greco-Roman compositional practice, then it seems increasingly likely that John intentionally rewrote the synoptic paralysis healing.

FEEDING THE FIVE THOUSAND

Steven Hunt has written a thoroughgoing demonstration of John's use of all three Synoptics in the feeding of the five thousand story.[53] Hunt's study is especially commendable for its methodology, which isolates John's knowledge of the synoptists' individual compositions or redactions. This method has long been the strictest test for determining literary dependence among the Gospels.[54] Simply put, there's not just a free-floating story of Jesus feeding a multitude that was told and retold here and there. John not only knows details that are unique to Mark but also reuses specific alterations that Matthew and Luke had made to Mark's original version.[55]

I highly recommend Hunt's book as a whole, since it is such a fine piece of scholarship—so much so that I see no need to reinvent the wheel in discussing the feeding miracle. Here, then, I'll highlight a few of Hunt's insights. Like Mark (6:37), John (6:7) mentions two hundred denarii as the cost of feeding so many people, although John questions whether that precise amount would be enough. In Matthew (14:19) and Mark (6:39), the narrator says that Jesus arranged for the crowd to be seated. John (6:10) follows Luke (9:14), so that via direct speech, Jesus commands the crowds. At that point, John (6:10) refers to

---

52. Regarding oral tradition, see Gardner-Smith, *Saint John*, 26–27; see also René Kieffer, "Jean et Marc: Convergences dans la structure et dans les détails," in *John and the Synoptics*, ed. Adelbert Denaux, BETL 101 (Leuven: Leuven University Press, 1992), 118–19. For claims that John knew synoptic material or traditional material, see Dodd, *Historical Tradition*, 178; see also Rudolf Schnackenburg, *The Gospel according to St. John*, trans. Kevin Smyth et al., HThKNT 4 (repr., New York: Crossroad, 1990), 2:96.

53. Steven A. Hunt, *Rewriting the Feeding of Five Thousand: John 6.1–15 as a Test Case for Johannine Dependence on the Synoptic Gospels*, StBibLit 125 (New York: Lang, 2011).

54. E.g., Helmut Koester, "Written Gospels or Oral Tradition?," *JBL* 113 (1994): 293–97; Andrew F. Gregory and Christopher M. Tuckett, "Reflections on Method: What Constitutes the Use of the Writings That Later Formed the New Testament in the Apostolic Fathers?," in *The Reception of the New Testament in the Apostolic Fathers*, ed. Andrew F. Gregory and Christopher M. Tuckett (Oxford: Oxford University Press, 2005), 75–76.

55. For John's use of Mark in the feeding miracle, see also Christopher W. Skinner, "ἐγώ εἰμι in Mark and John: Exploring the Johannine Trajectory of a Received Memory of Jesus," *BR* 69 (forthcoming 2024).

the people (*anthrōpoi*), whereas Luke (9:14) specified men (*andres*), since Mark (6:44) concluded with five thousand men. John's "people" reflects knowledge of Matthew's (14:21) addendum to Mark, that there were "about five thousand men, apart from women and children."[56] Moreover, John (6:9) invents one character who is a boy (*paidarion*), not a man, and his lunch was requisitioned to multiply for the crowd.

I've taken just one example of John's use of each synoptic gospel. There are many more that Hunt discusses in detail, and I agree with his conclusion that the case for John's use of the Synoptics is "cumulative."[57] Hunt's eye for synoptic redaction is highly impressive, but so too are the ways he shows John's deliberate rewriting of the Synoptics at the same time. As I see it, John can be an independent thinker even though his gospel is literarily dependent on the Synoptics.

JOHN'S ENLIVENING LAZARUS

In the entire Bible, the name Lazarus appears only as a character in one of Luke's parables (16:19–31) and as the brother of Mary and Martha in John (chs. 11–12).[58] Both men are named Lazarus, they both die, and each story entertains the possibility of Lazarus coming back to life. That pretty much sums up the stories' similarities. As glaring differences, John's Lazarus is a not only a real person, but he actually does come back from the dead. On account of the differences, many scholars have appealed to oral traditions that mutated into disparate accounts.[59] However, I join the handful of scholars who think John has rewritten Luke for the story of Lazarus.[60]

---

56. Hunt, *Rewriting*, 251, 257, 259.

57. Hunt, *Rewriting*, 280.

58. Luke does not explicitly call this story a parable, but interpreters have done so at least since Clement of Alexandria's *Miscellanies* (*Strom.* 4.6.30) around the turn of the third century. I think that John simply drew Mary and Martha from Luke 10:38–42; cf. Philip F. Esler and Ronald A. Piper (*Lazarus, Mary and Martha: Social-Scientific Approaches to the Gospel of John* [Minneapolis: Fortress, 2006]), who are not convinced that John read Luke or vice versa.

59. E.g., Ernst Haenchen, *John*, trans. Robert W. Funk, Hermeneia (Philadelphia: Fortress, 1984), 2:69. For "cross-influence" between Luke's and John's oral traditions, see Joseph A. Fitzmyer, *The Gospel according to Luke*, AB 28–28A (New York: Doubleday, 1981–1983), 1:88. For John's oral traditions influencing Luke's oral traditions, see Raymond E. Brown, *The Gospel according to John*, AB 29–29A (Garden City, NY: Doubleday, 1966–1970), 1:xlvii, 429; see also Paul N. Anderson, *The Fourth Gospel and the Quest for Jesus: Modern Foundations Reconsidered*, LNTS 321 (London: T&T Clark, 2006), 113.

60. E.g., Alan Richardson, *The Gospel according to Saint John*, TBC (London: SCM, 1959),

According to Luke 16, Lazarus lay sick and poor outside a rich man's gate (vv. 19–21). Both men died, and there is a simple reversal of fortune in the hereafter: father Abraham comforted Lazarus while the rich man was tormented in flames on the other side of a great chasm (vv. 22–26). Come to find out, the rich man had five brothers, and he asked Abraham to send Lazarus back to warn them about the afterlife (vv. 27–28). Abraham refused, since the brothers could simply follow Moses and the prophets (v. 29). The rich man insisted that his brothers would repent if they saw someone come back from the dead (v. 30), but Abraham persisted that Moses and the prophets were sufficient: "If they are not listening to Moses and the prophets, nor will they be persuaded if someone should resurrect from the dead" (v. 31).

In chapter 1, I paired Luke's Lazarus story with an elaborate scene from the Acts of Thomas, where a brother does come back from the dead. That story ended happily ever after, since both brothers repented. That was an exemplar of *oppositio in imitando*, since Luke's parable seems rather pessimistic that resurrection would lead to repentance (16:31). Fitting neatly in between Thomas's optimism and Luke's pessimism, the raising of Lazarus in John leads some people—but not all—to belief in Jesus. John (11:45) tells that "many of the Jews . . . believed in (Jesus)," and Jesus had stated expressly that the point of the miracle was for the crowd standing around to believe that the Father is the one who sent him (vv. 41–42). Not everyone was pleased, for the Pharisees and priests feared that "everyone will believe in (Jesus)" and that the Romans would intervene; that's when the priest Caiaphas said it was necessary for Jesus to die (vv. 47–51).

The typical objection to John's use of Luke is that the two stories are just too different.[61] But that type of reasoning does not take into account the literary conventions of rewriting and *oppositio in imitando*. Plus, there are good reasons why John would have altered or omitted some of Luke's prominent features.[62] Luke develops repentance as a central theme, but it is entirely lacking from the

---

139; Hartmut Thyen, "Die Erzählung von den bethanischen Geschwistern (Joh 11,1–12,19) als 'Palimpsest' über synoptischen Texten," in *The Four Gospels: Festschrift Frans Neirynck*, ed. Frans van Segbroeck et al., BETL 100 (Leuven: Leuven University Press, 1992), 3:2021–50; Ulrich Busse, "Johannes und Lukas: Die Lazarusperikope, Frucht eines Kommunikationsprozesses," in *John and the Synoptics*, ed. Adelbert Denaux, BETL 101 (Leuven: Leuven University Press, 1992), 304.

61. E.g., Fitzmyer, *Luke*, 1:88; D. A. Carson, *The Gospel according to John*, PNTC (Grand Rapids: Eerdmans, 1991), 404; John P. Meier, *A Marginal Jew*, vol. 2, *Mentor, Message, and Miracles*, ABRL (New York: Doubleday, 1994), 824.

62. One could argue that Luke has read John, since Luke (13:6–9) elsewhere took an actual event, namely, the cursing of the fig tree (Mark 11:11–14, 19–21 // Matt 21:18–20), and turned it into a parable. I think that John's supersessionism makes it far more likely that the trajectory runs from Luke to John.

Gospel of John; there are no *metanoia* or *metanoeō* "repenting" nouns, verbs, or participles anywhere in the Fourth Gospel. Instead, all through the gospel— including the Lazarus story—John emphasizes "believing" (*pisteuō*) in Jesus and the one who "sent" him (*apostellō*). Furthermore, compared to Luke's Gospel, there is much more supersessionism in John. To be sure, John says that people should believe in him if they truly believe Moses (5:46). Yet Luke's parable simply presumes that Moses and the prophets suffice for repentance and salvation (16:29, 31). According to John, the law and the prophets are insufficient on their own: they must find their fulfillment in Jesus (e.g., John 1:17, 45).

Once again, if *oppositio in imitando* is taken seriously as a biblical and classical rhetorical strategy, then John's narrative can simultaneously be deeply indebted to, and significantly different from, Luke's parable. I find this kind of creative rewriting far more convincing than appeals to hypothetical source texts or mutating oral tradition,[63] both of which sidestep the all-important questions of who changed whose story and why. In general, John exercised artistic freedom in turning Lazarus into a real person, the brother of Mary and Martha. And the particular elements that John added and subtracted fit within the broader context of the gospel. Most importantly, John used the raising of Lazarus to transition to the passion narrative. There had already been plots to kill Jesus at the unnamed festival (ch. 5) and at Sukkoth (chs. 7–8). But the plan to kill Jesus after the raising of Lazarus (11:53) came to fruition at John's third and final Passover, which was soon approaching (v. 55).

REWRITING THE PASSION NARRATIVE

Having arrived at the passion narrative, John rewrote numerous elements from the Synoptics. Here I highlight John's characterization of Judas, the figures who arrested Jesus, the presence of Jesus's mother at the crucifixion, and the functionality of Jesus's resurrected body.

Why Did Judas Betray Jesus?

Judas Iscariot is a classic Johannine snowman, since his characterization rolls from Mark to Matthew to Luke to John. Mark (3:19) introduces Judas last in the list of twelve apostles: "Judas Iscariot, who also betrayed (Jesus)." Mark

---

63. For the theory that John found a ready-made Lazarus story in a long-lost signs source, see Bultmann, *John*, 395; see also Robert T. Fortna, *The Gospel of Signs: A Reconstruction of the Narrative Source Underlying the Fourth Gospel*, SNTSMS 11 (Cambridge: Cambridge University Press, 1970).

does not mention Judas again until the passion narrative, when Judas went to the chief priests to betray Jesus (14:10). They rejoiced and promised him money (v. 11), and later Judas led them to Jesus to arrest him (v. 43). According to Mark, readers have absolutely no idea why Judas betrayed Jesus. He wasn't motivated by money, because the promise of money came later, and Mark never says whether Judas got paid.

Following Mark closely, Matthew (10:4) introduces Judas at the end of the list of the Twelve: "Judas Iscariot the one who also betrayed (Jesus)." Judas is not referenced again until the passion narrative. There Matthew reversed Mark's sequence so that Judas asked the chief priests for money up front, and they indeed give him thirty silver coins (26:14–15), maybe as little as a thousand dollars in contemporary currency. Whereas Mark mentioned money as an afterthought, Matthew turned money into Judas's motivation for betraying Jesus.

Luke follows his predecessors part of the way and then makes a surprising turn. Yet again Judas is introduced as the last of the twelve apostles, "Judas Iscariot, who became a traitor" (6:6). Judas is not mentioned again until he conspires to betray Jesus. At that point, though, Luke presents an entirely different motivation: the devil made him do it. Luke says that "Satan entered into Judas," who then plotted the betrayal with the chief priests (22:3–4). The priests rejoiced and "agreed" (*syntithēmi*) to give Judas money. Similar to Mark, the priests' rejoicing and the prospect of money are mentioned after Judas instigates the betrayal. Yet Luke also aligns with Matthew, since the priests' agreement about payment may imply that Judas bargained for a price and received the money. Most importantly, Luke added the new element of Satan's power over Judas.

John had plenty of precedents for what to do with Judas. Similar to the Synoptics, John has Jesus say that he has chosen the Twelve, "and one of you is a devil" (6:70). John then introduces Judas of Simon Iscariot as follows: "for this one, one of the Twelve, was about to betray (Jesus)" (6:71), even though the betrayal would occur two years later. When the time comes, though, John adds a speaking part for Judas. In all four canonical gospels, a woman anoints Jesus with expensive perfume,[64] and someone usually complains that it could have been sold and given to the poor. Mark (14:4) says vaguely that some people were complaining, while Matthew (26:8) says that the disciples made the complaint.[65] John sometimes assigns individual speaking parts where other gospels

64. Matt 26:6–13 // Mark 14:3–9 // Luke 7:36–50 // John 12:1–8.
65. In Luke (7:39), the Pharisees complain that the woman was a sinner, but they say nothing about the cost of the ointment.

have a group seemingly speaking in unison.[66] At this point, John specifies the one complaining that the expensive perfume could have been sold and given to the poor: "Judas Iscariot, one of (Jesus's) disciples, who was about to betray him" (12:4–5). John adds that Judas "said this not because it mattered to him concerning the poor but because he was a thief, and having the moneybag, he was removing what was thrown in" (12:6).

John (12:3, 5) agrees verbatim with Mark (14:3, 5) that the woman used "expensive genuine nard" that was worth "three hundred denarii." And while John does not say that Judas betrayed Jesus for money, the reference to Judas's greed recalls Matthew's motivation for the betrayal.[67] John relies on Luke as well, for after Judas complains about the anointing, John (13:2) says that "the devil had already put into the heart that Judas of Simon Iscariot should betray (Jesus)." And it wasn't just the idea the devil put in Judas's heart, because John adds that the devil possessed Judas. That is, "Satan entered into him" (John 13:27), just as Luke had said (22:3). John's characterization of Judas carefully combines distinct elements from each of the three Synoptics.

Who Arrested Jesus?

All four canonical gospels introduce Judas Iscariot as Jesus's eventual betrayer. When the time comes in the Synoptics, Judas always shows up leading a crowd (*ochlos*) to arrest Jesus,[68] and everyone on the scene appears to be Jewish. According to Mark, Judas brings a crowd "from" (*para*) the chief priests, scribes, and elders (14:43). Soon thereafter (v. 53), Jesus is taken to the chief priests, elders, and scribes (v. 53)—the very groups he had predicted would put him to death (8:31). Matthew's presentation is similar. Judas comes with a large crowd "from" (*apo*) the chief priests and elders (26:47). Mark's preposition (*para*) means that the crowd came on behalf of the authorities. Matthew's preposition (*apo*) could mean the same thing, or it could mean that the crowd was actually made up of chief priests and elders. In the latter case, some of the priests

66. For example, in the feeding of the five thousand, the Synoptics have the disciples ask Jesus to dismiss the crowd so that they can buy food in the surrounding villages (Matt 14:15 // Mark 6:35–36 // Luke 9:12), but John (6:5) has Jesus ask Philip where to buy food; in Mark (6:37), the disciples mention the sum of two hundred denarii, but John (6:8) assigns that line to Philip; in the Synoptics (Matt 14:17 // Mark 6:38 // Luke 9:13b), the disciples mention five loaves and two fish, whereas John (6:8) gives Andrew that line.

67. Also, according to John (13:26) and Matthew (26:25), Jesus indicates Judas as the betrayer.

68. Matt 26:47 // Mark 14:43 // Luke 22:47.

and elders would have arrested Jesus, and then they would have taken him to the full group of chief priests, scribes, and elders (26:57)—the ones Jesus first predicted would have him killed (16:21).

Luke rewrites aspects of the arrest scene. As I mentioned in the previous chapter, Luke typically loves a crowd. Unlike Matthew and Mark, throughout Luke's Gospel a crowd is usually a large group of true disciples. The exception comes at Jesus's arrest, but Luke differentiates this crowd from all the ones that have come before. At first, Judas leads a nondescript crowd to Jesus (22:47). But when Jesus addresses them, they turn out to be chief priests, temple captains (*stratēgoi tou hierou*),[69] and elders carrying swords and clubs (22:52).[70] Luke has added officers (*stratēgoi*), so that there are authority figures and not simply a mob out to get Jesus.

According to Luke, then, only at Jesus's arrest (22:47, 52) and at the questioning by Pilate (23:4) are crowds coded negatively. However, that bad crowd should not at all be confused with the large crowds of Jesus's disciples found in the rest of Luke's Gospel. Nor is Luke's bad crowd to be confused with Matthew's and Mark's fickle crowds who have suddenly turned against Jesus.[71] By extension, unlike Matthew (27:10) and Mark (15:11), Luke does not need the priests to stir up the crowd and cry out for Jesus's crucifixion before Pilate. Instead, priests are always already part of Luke's crowd at the arrest. The same goes for Jesus's hearings, since priests and other authorities remain on the scene when Jesus is questioned by Herod Antipas (23:10) and Pontius Pilate (23:4, 13). The point is that the bad crowds in Luke 22–23 are the very opponents Jesus warned about in his first passion prediction (9:22). When Jesus is condemned in Luke's Gospel, the proceedings do not even appear open to the public. The crucifixion itself is, of course, a public spectacle, and there Luke mentions one final crowd (23:48). Yet that good crowd grieves at what they see

69. Luke had adduced the priests and temple captains when Judas plotted the betrayal (22:4). They are usually interpreted as "guards" (φύλακες), who reported to a singular "captain" (στρατηγός) as described by Josephus (*J. W.* 6.5.3 [294]).

70. Luke tends to use the preposition ἀπό as Matthew does, and Luke likely got the idea from Matthew that priests and elders were on the scene at the arrest. For example, in Luke 16:30, "someone from the dead" could come back to warn the rich man's brothers, and the dead person was not just coming from the place of the dead; the person was in fact one of the dead. Similarly, in Luke 19:39, the Pharisees "from" the crowd are necessarily part of the crowd.

71. Regarding the crowds in Matthew, see Matthias Konradt, *Israel, Church, and the Gentiles in the Gospel of Matthew*, trans. Kathleen Ess, BMSEC (Waco, TX: Baylor University Press, 2014).

and are thus differentiated from the leaders (*archontes*) and soldiers (*stratiōtai*) who were taunting Jesus while he was on the cross (23:35–36).

The cast of characters is markedly different in the Fourth Gospel. In John 18:3, "Judas comes there bringing the cohort and underlings of the chief priests and the Pharisees with lamps, lanterns, and weapons." A couple of terms stand out in sharp relief. One is *hypēretai*, which is translated as "police" in the NRSV, "officials" in the NIV, and "officers" in the ESV. I suspect that these translations are influenced by Luke's "captains," and I think that John is also influenced by Luke here. The problem is that John has demoted Luke's captains to mere underlings, assistants, or even slaves.[72] John definitely has authorities on the scene, but John's authorities are a cohort (*speira*), the technical term for one thousand Roman soldiers. Scholars sometimes deny that John understands this technical term,[73] but he clearly does, since he places a chiliarch in command—a tribune in Latin (v. 11).[74]

John most likely derived the *speira* from Matthew 27:27 // Mark 15:16, where "the entire cohort" joins the soldiers (*stratiōtai*) in the praetorium to mock Jesus with a crown of thorns right before the crucifixion commences.[75] John likewise has soldiers mock Jesus with a crown of thorns (19:2) just before Jesus is handed over to be crucified (19:16), but the soldiers have been there ever since the arrest. The cohort is present at the betrayal and arrest (18:3), and they tie Jesus up (18:12).

At the arrest, one of Jesus's disciples always cuts off the chief priest's slave's ear,[76] and John identifies Peter as the perpetrator and Malchus as the victim (18:10). As in Matthew (26:52), John (18:11b) has Jesus command the sword to be put away. Luke (22:51b) adds that Jesus miraculously reattached the severed ear, but John omits that detail, since Jesus's miracles in John are always followed by a long, theological discourse; there was no time for that, now that Jesus's long-awaited hour had finally come. Instead of Jesus's disciples deserting him as in Matthew (26:56b) and Mark (14:50), John's Jesus knew that they

---

72. John (18:18) groups slaves and underlings around the fire outside the house of Annas.

73. E.g., Brown, *John*, 2:813; Craig Keener, *The Gospel of John: A Commentary* (Peabody, MA: Hendrickson, 2003), 2:1079; Lincoln, *John*, 443.

74. Schnackenburg, *John*, 3:222; Urban C. von Wahlde, *The Gospel and Letters of John*, ECC (Grand Rapids: Eerdmans, 2010), 2:745–46. For comparison, in the US Army, a lieutenant colonel commands a battalion of one thousand soldiers ("Military Units: Army," U.S. Department of Defense, https://www.defense.gov/Multimedia/Experience/Military-Units /Army/).

75. Matt 27:31 // Mark 15:20.

76. Matt 26:51 // Mark 14:47 // Luke 22:50 // John 18:10.

would be scattered (16:32), but he commanded that they go free (18:8). And in all three Synoptics, Jesus had prayed to the Father and asked whether it was possible for "the cup" (i.e., the passion) not to happen after all.[77] John omits that plea and instead presents Jesus as ready and willing to drink the Father's cup (18:11c).[78]

Jesus remains in the cohort's custody all along the circuitous Johannine path from Annas (18:13) to Caiaphas (18:24) and to Pilate (19:2). When Pilate begins questioning Jesus, Pilate calls him the king of the Jews (18:33), to which Jesus replies, "Are you saying this by yourself, or did others speak to you about me?" (v. 34). In this way, John lets readers connect the dots across Synoptics. Pilate always asks whether Jesus is a king,[79] but Luke—characteristically eliminating any element of surprise—clarifies that the Sanhedrin told Pilate that Jesus had called himself a king (23:2). Depending on which other gospel is in view, Pilate could be speaking on his own or repeating what he'd just been told.[80]

The cohort also leads Jesus to the place of the skull for the crucifixion (19:23–24).[81] The overkill of having one thousand Roman soldiers all along the way fits perfectly in John. All four canonical gospels make the chief priests and others conspire to kill Jesus.[82] John (11:48) alone has the Sanhedrin expressly raise the specter of the Romans taking over Judea if something isn't done about Jesus. And John alone gives Caiaphas a speaking part, where he

77. Matt 26:39 // Mark 14:36 // Luke 22:42; John (12:27) earlier had Jesus say flat out that he would not ask God "to save me from this hour."

78. Later Jesus carries his own cross (John 19:17) with no assistance from Simon of Cyrene as in the Synoptics (Matt 27:32 // Mark 15:21 // Luke 23:26). In those instances, John thoroughly rewrote and tacitly critiqued the Synoptics' portrayal of Jesus appearing to be weak. Yet I maintain that John expected his gospel to be read alongside the Synoptics, not instead of them. For example, what is known of the Greek Epic Cycle reveals that derivative works could contradict Homer at times, even as the works were being studied side by side.

79. Matt 27:2 // Mark 15:2 // Luke 23:3.

80. A similar thing happens when John has a crowd debate whether the Messiah would come from Bethlehem or Galilee (7:40–43). As I have pointed out elsewhere (*John's Use of Matthew*, 112), readers of Matthew would know that Jesus is the Messiah and that he comes from both places: Matthew says that Jesus's birthplace in Bethlehem fulfills a prophecy of Micah (5:2; cf. Matt 2:4–6), and his eventual residence in Galilee fulfills a prophecy of Isaiah (8:23–9:1; cf. Matt 4:12–16).

81. The "Jews' underlings" are clearly involved in the arrest and binding (18:12), but some of them remain fireside at Annas's (18:18), while at least one goes inside and slaps Jesus (18:22). However, the underlings' remaining role is simply to cry out for the crucifixion (19:6), not to carry it out. In other words, they're involved, but they're not in charge.

82. Matt 26:3–4 // Mark 14:1 // Luke 22:2 // John 11:47–48.

famously prefers having one man die to save the entire Jewish *ethnos* (11:50). The implication in the Fourth Gospel is that Caiaphas could have requested a large number of Roman soldiers to assist in handling Jesus from his arrest to his crucifixion.

How Did Jesus's Mother Find Her Way to the Crucifixion?

In Mark 6:3, Jesus is called the son of Mary and the brother of Jacob and Joses. When Mark narrates the crucifixion, Mary of Jacob and Joses stands at a distance with Mary Magdalene and Salome (15:40). Two of the twelve apostles were named Jacob,[83] so that's a fairly common name in the Synoptics. But in the entire Old and New Testaments, the name Joses (*Iōsēs*) occurs only in Mark 6:3; 15:40, 47.[84] And of the Four Gospels, John is the only one to place Jesus's mother Mary and Mary Magdalene along with Mary of Clopas near the cross (19:25). The simplest explanation is that John knew the names of Jesus's brothers from Mark. John then made explicit what was implicit in Mark, that Jesus's mother witnessed the crucifixion.[85]

What Was Jesus's Resurrected Body Like?

Paul and the evangelists attest Jesus's resurrection, but the (super)natural question arises about what a resurrected body could do. In 1 Corinthians 15, Paul passes on the tradition of Jesus's death, burial, and resurrection (vv. 1–4). For the resurrection, Paul sharply distinguishes between Jesus's mortal, physical body and his immortal, oxymoronic "spiritual body" (v. 44). The point is to say

---

83. Matt 10:2–3 // Mark 3:17–18 // Luke 6:14–15.

84. All three times, the name appears in the genitive form Ἰωσῆτος.

85. Raymond E. Brown (*The Death of the Messiah: From Gethsemane to the Grave*, ABRL [New York: Doubleday, 1994], 2:1019) denies John's use of Mark here. Although patristic and medieval scholars weren't making modern source-critical arguments, it wasn't uncommon to identify Mark's "Mary of Jacob and Joses" with Jesus's mother witnessing the crucifixion in John. For example, a catena on John 19:25 attributed to Cyril of Jerusalem (J. A. Cramer, *Catenae in Evangelia* [Oxford, 1841], 2:393) identifies Mary the Mother of God (θεοτόκος) with the one called Mary mother of Jacob and Joses in the Gospels of Matthew and Mark; this catena also calls Mary the adoptive mother of Jacob and Joses. In the eleventh century, the Byzantine archbishop Theophylactus of Ochrida observes, "The disciples flee, but the women remain steadfast: Mary, mother of Jacob and Joses, is called mother of God [θεοτόκος]. For Jacob and Joses were children of Joseph from his previous wife. Therefore, since the mother of God was said to be wife of Joseph, naturally the stepmother of those was also called mother of his children" (*Commentary on Matthew* 27 [PG 123:473]).

that the resurrected Jesus had not simply been resuscitated, in which case he might die again. The risen Jesus had an imperishable body, and believers will someday turn into the same kind of spiritual being (vv. 50–53).

Nothing in 1 Corinthians 15 necessarily entails an empty tomb story, so Mark adds that scene. Mary Magdalene, another Mary, and Salome came to the tomb on Easter Sunday (Mark 16:1–2). The stone had been rolled away, and Jesus's body was gone, but a young man in a white robe told them that Jesus was risen and that they should tell the disciples that Jesus would meet them in Galilee (vv. 3–7). However, they left and "said nothing to nobody, for they were afraid" (v. 8). That is the original ending to the gospel, but Mark at least qualified that Jesus's physical body was not decomposing in a tomb.

Matthew rewrote Mark's Easter scene. As two Marys went to the tomb, Matthew adds that an earthquake and an angel dressed in white caused the stone to be rolled away (Matt 28:1–2). This time the women actually carried out the angel's instructions to tell the disciples that Jesus would meet them in Galilee (vv. 7–8). Along the way, the two Marys encountered the risen Jesus, who had a tangible body, for they could grab his feet and worship him (v. 9). Jesus reiterated the message about meeting in Galilee (v. 10), and there Jesus appeared to his disciples and gave the Great Commission at the conclusion of the gospel (vv. 16–20).

Luke enhanced both the physical and spiritual aspects of Jesus's resurrected body. Spiritually, the risen Jesus spent time with two people, who did not recognize him at first, but when they did recognize him, he "became invisible" (24:31). When those two returned to Jerusalem and told the disciples what they had witnessed (vv. 33–35), Jesus materialized in their midst, and they thought he was a ghost (vv. 36–37). Physically, Jesus then showed them his flesh and bones, specifically his hands and feet, and he ate a piece of fish (vv. 38–43).

John combined and clarified aspects of Matthew and Luke. Readers were not told that Mary Magdalene had grabbed Jesus (cf. Matt 28:9), yet he told her to stop touching him (John 20:17).[86] Similar to the scene in Luke, Jesus could materialize in a locked room (v. 19), and he showed them his hands and side (v. 20). Thomas had not witnessed this resurrection appearance, and he told the disciples that he'd have to put his hand in the nail marks of Jesus's hands and side (vv. 24–25). The next week, Jesus materialized again, and he

---

86. The parallel Matt 28:9 // John 20:17 was Frans Neirynck's quintessential case for John's use of Matthean redaction; see, e.g., Frans Neirynck, "Les femmes au tombeau: Étude de la rédaction matthéenne," *NTS* 15 (1968–1969): 168–90; Neirynck, "Note on Mt 28,9–10," *ETL* 71 (1995): 161–65.

gave Thomas the opportunity to touch his wounds (vv. 26–27); Jesus's wounds were implicit in Luke, but John makes them explicit. Finally, John 21 adds a resurrection appearance in Galilee, and Jesus served bread and fish to the disciples (v. 13). John says that "they ate breakfast" (v. 15), which could refer to the disciples alone or to Jesus as well. For readers of Luke, John 21 can harmonize with Jesus's eating fish, but John could also be dodging the question whether a resurrected body needs food. More importantly, the bread and fish can be read as though the risen Jesus presided over the first Eucharist.

JOHANNINE SACRAMENTS

Worship of Jesus and ritual commemorations of his death commenced incredibly early. The Gospels attribute the institution of sacraments to Jesus himself. In the Synoptics, on the first day of the Feast of Unleavened Bread,[87] Jesus celebrated the Passover with his disciples, and he equated his body and blood with bread and wine;[88] Luke (22:19c) added Jesus's explicit commandment, "Do this for my remembrance."[89] In the Fourth Gospel, Jesus shared a final meal with the disciples, but the Johannine last supper was not a Seder, since it took place "before the feast of Passover" (13:1). Moreover, there were no words of institution for the Eucharist. Instead, Jesus washed the disciples' feet (13:1–11), which would eventually become ritualized annually on Maundy Thursday.

The Fourth Gospel neither ignores nor replaces the Eucharist, however. John simply moves it forward to Jesus's Bread of Life Discourse following the feeding of the five thousand, which John alone places at the time of Passover (6:4), the second of three in the gospel.

> "I am the bread of life that came from Heaven. If anyone should eat from this bread, they will live into the aeon, and the bread that I will give is my flesh on behalf of the life of the cosmos." Therefore the Jews were disputing against one another saying, "How can this one give us flesh to eat?" Therefore Jesus said to them, "Amen, amen I say to you, if you should not eat the flesh of the Son of Man and drink his blood, you will not have life in yourselves. The one who chews my flesh and drinks my blood has eternal life, and I will resurrect them on the last day. For my flesh is true meat, and my blood is true drink. The one who chews my flesh and drinks my blood

---

87. Matt 26:17 // Mark 14:12 // Luke 22:7; Luke omits "first."
88. Matt 26:26–28 // Mark 14:22–24 // Luke 22:19–24.
89. The same wording appears in 1 Cor 11:24–25.

remains in me and I in them. Just like the living Father sent me, I also live via the Father, and the one who chews me, that one also will live via me. This is the bread that came down from heaven, not the same way the fathers ate and died. The one who eats this bread will live into the aeon." (John 6:51–58)

This passage has been interpreted by some as an allusion to the Eucharist,[90] where the sacrament could lurk or hover behind the discourse.[91] Others see this portion of the discourse more clearly as sacramental but as something a later editor has written and inserted.[92] And some contend that the passage is altogether nonsacramental.[93] Despite the prevalence of ambiguity in the Gospel of John, I read the flesh and blood portion of the Bread of Life Discourse as intentionally sacramental.[94] John uses the word "Eucharist" (6:11), says that Jesus "gave thanks" for the bread,[95] and would have taken for granted that the ritual was already a fixture among believers in Jesus. John also would have known that eating Jesus's flesh and drinking his blood would have been a difficult saying that some people found offensive (6:60–61). There is also a strong sense of supersessionism here in John's Gospel, whereby the Eucharist replaces Passover.

Just as John didn't need to wait until the Last Supper to adduce the Eucharist, baptism comes much earlier as well. During John's first Passover, in the dialogue with Nicodemus, Jesus says, "Amen, amen I say to you, unless someone is born of water and Spirit, it is not possible to enter into the kingdom of God" (3:5b). Earlier I dispelled the notion that this was an orally transmitted baptismal saying. I do consider it to be a baptismal saying, nonetheless. It's simply an example of John rewriting one of Matthew's sayings and developing a long discourse pertaining to baptism.

The baptismal connection is clear, for at the conclusion of the dialogue (3:21), John says that "after these things" Jesus was baptizing (v. 22) at the same

90. E.g., Barrett, *John*, 297; cf. Paul N. Anderson (*The Christology of the Fourth Gospel*, 2nd ed. [Eugene, OR: Cascade, 2010], 114) sees an allusion to a sacrament in the broad sense of the term, but Anderson also thinks that John de-emphasizes the institution of rituals.

91. E.g., D. Moody Smith, *The Theology of the Gospel of John*, NTTh (Cambridge: Cambridge University Press, 1995), 159; Moloney, *John*, 223.

92. E.g., Bultmann, *John*, 234–37; von Wahlde, *John*, 2:321.

93. E.g., Meredith J. C. Warren, *My Flesh Is Meat Indeed: A Nonsacramental Reading of John 6:51–58* (Minneapolis: Fortress, 2015); for a helpful bibliography of the debate, see p. 33 n. 29.

94. Similarly, see Schnackenburg, *John*, 2:61.

95. John could have borrowed the Eucharist verb (εὐχαριστέω) from the feeding of the four thousand in Matthew (15:36) and Mark (8:6).

time as John the Baptist (v. 23). John the Baptist was told that Jesus was baptizing (v. 26), and the Pharisees heard that Jesus was baptizing more than John
the Baptist was (4:1). Then the gospel awkwardly clarifies that "Jesus himself
wasn't baptizing, but his disciples" were baptizing (4:2). For the interrelation
of John and the Synoptics, the crucial point is that the Fourth Gospel has
Jesus's disciples performing ritual baptisms two years before the crucifixion
and resurrection.

According to the Fourth Gospel, John the Baptist was merely baptizing with
water (1:26), and—unlike Mark 1:4—John's baptism was not said to forgive
sins. Also, John the Baptist explicitly identified Jesus as "the one who baptizes
with the Holy Spirit" (John 1:33).[96] In the Gospel of Matthew, Jesus does not
command his disciples to baptize anyone until after the resurrection (28:19).[97]
The Gospel of John does not contradict Matthew here, but John does make the
point that Jesus's disciples had been baptizing long before the passion. Here I
am in full agreement with Raymond Brown, who sees John clearly placing the
sacraments of baptism and the Eucharist "in scenes throughout the ministry,"[98]
rather than waiting until the end of the story.

I would also suggest anointing as a final possibility for Johannine sacraments. There are synoptic and Pauline parallels at some of the following points,
but John clusters more elements than can be found in any single source. When
Jesus is anointed at Bethany six days before Passover (John 12:1), John uses the
verb to "anoint" (*aleiphō*; 11:2; 12:3).[99] Jesus explicitly connects his anointing
with his impending burial (12:7),[100] and there is a similar Pauline notion of
believers' baptisms as participating in the death of Christ.[101] The location of

96. The superiority of Jesus's baptism of the Holy Spirit, as compared to John the Baptist's
water baptism, recurs in the book of Acts (e.g., 1:5; 11:16; 19:1–7).

97. The ascension in the Gospel of Luke does not mention baptism, but in the book of
Acts (1:5) Jesus promises the disciples that they will be baptized with the Holy Spirit; when
that occurs at Pentecost, Peter preaches repentance, baptism in the name of Jesus Christ,
forgiveness of sins, and receiving the gift of the Holy Spirit (2:38). The rendition of the Great
Commission in the longer ending of Mark juxtaposes preaching the gospel with the ritual
of baptism (16:15–16).

98. Raymond E. Brown, *An Introduction to the Gospel of John*, ed. Francis J. Moloney,
ABRL (New York: Doubleday, 2003), 234.

99. Luke (7:38, 46) also uses this verb; conversely, in Matthew (26:7) and Mark (14:3),
the woman "pours out" (καταχέω) ointment.

100. Matthew (26:12) and Mark (14:8) also connect the anointing to Jesus's burial.

101. Romans (6:3–5) describes baptism as mystically participating in the death of Christ,
so that one day believers will be resurrected; the deutero-Pauline letter of Colossians (2:12)
reframes baptism as already participating in Jesus's burial and resurrection.

Bethany may be unsurprising for the anointing,[102] yet the Fourth Gospel is the only one to locate John the Baptist's activity in Bethany (1:28). In other words, the Fourth Gospel implies a connection between baptism and anointing. Also, baptism and anointing were closely associated rituals very early on, particularly in the apocryphal Acts.[103] Finally, the subsequent epistle 1 John (2:20, 27) refers to receiving the chrism of the Holy One, which may very well be a sacrament.[104] Ultimately this is a chicken-and-egg question: perhaps the Gospel of John contributed to the development of an anointing ritual, or maybe John reflects a practice that was already established. I am convinced that John presupposed and intentionally alluded to the rituals of baptism and Eucharist. I at least want to raise the possibility that John might also have known an anointing ritual.

Conclusion

The Synoptics seem uninterested in answering the question of how long Jesus's ministry lasted, but it is difficult to extend it beyond a year. By contrast, John has Jesus's ministry last a bit longer than two years, since there are three Passovers. In the Fourth Gospel, John the Baptist has more speaking parts, and he shows deep self-awareness that he is the one preparing the way of the Lord. Besides that, John the Baptist declares Jesus to be the Son of God (John 1:34). Also, John the Baptist forestalls the confusion in the Synoptics that Jesus might be John the Baptist, Elijah, or one of the prophets.

As previous scholarship has pointed out, John reflects knowledge of Matthew not only for the "born again" saying in Jesus's dialogue with Nicodemus but also for Jesus's remote healing of the imperial official's son. John's Gospel cleverly asserts itself as the answer to whether Jesus's ministry included Samaritans: Mark doesn't mention them; Matthew says that Jesus prohibited evangelism to them; and Luke says that some Samaritans rejected Jesus. John, however, creates space for Jesus to stay in Samaria, where Samaritans believe him to be the Messiah and Savior of the world.

The previous chapter looked at the healing of paralysis as it pertains to the Synoptic problem. This chapter showed how John rewrote nearly every ele-

---

102. Matthew (26:6) and Mark (14:3) also place the anointing in Bethany in connection with the passion.

103. For example, baptism and anointing are juxtaposed in Acts of Thomas 25 and 157.

104. Judith M. Lieu (*I, II, and III John: A Commentary*, NTL [Louisville: Westminster John Knox, 2008], 103) raises the possibility of ritual anointing in 1 John 2:20, 27. Elsewhere I have argued that 1 John is dependent on the Gospel of John; see *John's Use of Matthew*, 58–60.

ment of the story—so much so that John's account can hardly be independent of the Synoptics. With many more similarities that have been pointed out in previous scholarship, John's account of the feeding of the five thousand also relies on all three Synoptics. John's Lazarus story is another example of *oppositio in imitando*, a Lazarus account so different from Luke's that John's must counterintuitively be an intentional rewriting.

The Johannine passion narrative has numerous similarities and differences compared to the Synoptics, but John repeatedly ties together different strands of the synoptic accounts. The motivation of Judas's betrayal, the characters who arrested Jesus, the presence of Jesus's mother at the crucifixion, and the functionality of Jesus's resurrected body are all examples of trajectories running from Mark to Matthew to Luke and to John. Thereafter, Jesus's death and resurrection were commemorated by sacraments. The Gospel of John has been characterized as ambiguous regarding sacraments or even as antisacramental, but I read John as clearly sacramental—not only presupposing the rituals of baptism and the Eucharist but perhaps anointing as well.

Chapter 4

Johannine Christology in Context

IN THE FILM *MONTY PYTHON'S LIFE OF Brian*, Brian's mother (Terry Jones) pointedly informs a large crowd of his followers: "He's not the Messiah. He's a very naughty boy."[1] One version of Campus Crusade for Christ's film *Jesus* equated the Messiah with the Son of God, but "in a spiritual, not a physical sense."[2] In *The Last Temptation of Christ*, Satan reminds Jesus of his childhood prayer to God, "Make me God," and the temptation is to believe that he really is the only Son of God.[3] In different ways, these modern artistic portrayals are wrestling with the fundamental theological question of what "Son of God" even means.

"Christology" is the term for the doctrine about Jesus, particularly how he is regarded as both human and divine. Since humanity and divinity are typically considered opposites, it has always been difficult to explain the union of both natures in the person of Jesus. Emphasizing his divinity produces a relatively higher Christology, whereas emphasizing his humanity results in a relatively lower Christology. In time, the early church set limits: denying Jesus's actual humanity was too high, while denying his divinity was too low.

Any kind of Christology has a bearing on Jewish-Christian relations. The Jewish Scriptures literally refer to angels as sons of God (Gen 6:2, 4). "Angels of God" appears as the Greek translation for "sons of God" in Hebrew when God and Satan agree to torment Job (1:6; 2:1). The singular "angel of God" is the Greek translation of the Aramaic phrase "a son of the gods," who accompanies Daniel's friends in the fiery furnace (Dan 3:25). In the New Testament, Jesus's

1. Terry Jones, dir., *Monty Python's Life of Brian*, Orion Pictures, 1979 (1:05).

2. John Heyman, prod., *Jesus*, Warner Brothers, 1979, 2:02; see also 0:06; the current version of the film at www.jesusfilm.org has removed the earlier references to the physical-spiritual dichotomy.

3. Martin Scorsese, dir., *The Last Temptation of Christ*, Universal Studios, 1988 (0:59); Nikos Kazantzakis, *The Last Temptation of Christ*, trans. P. A. Bien (New York: Bantam Books, 1961), 256–57.

identity as God's Son means that he is above the angels, but such a claim could be blasphemous in the context of early Judaism.[4]

Since Christology is so complicated, this chapter plots several trajectories within early Christian literature. I cover a wider range of material than in previous chapters, but that is necessary if we are to contextualize Johannine Christology. I begin with the Pauline corpus, since I am convinced that at least some of the material in Paul's letters influenced every one of the evangelists. Also, various theological positions pop up in different epistles, so I highlight places where Pauline Christology creeps higher. Turning to the canonical gospels, I find that their Christologies steadily ascend. Jesus's divinity in Matthew and Luke is higher than in Mark, and John has the highest Christology within the fourfold gospel. Yet striking similarities emerge between Johannine Christology and some of the latest letters associated with Paul.

Gospel writing did not end with the fourfold gospel, and later gospels wrote contesting Christologies. Some asserted an even higher Christology than the earlier gospels, while others attempted to bring Jesus back down to earth. Accordingly, the early church fathers made decisions about what to read and what to discard as well as which christological statements should be believed and which ones might be condemned. In that regard, I extend my analysis to the late fourth century, when the Fourth Gospel became the key to discerning early Trinitarian dogma. On the one hand, John could not have foreseen all the disputations that would arise hundreds of years after the gospel was written. On the other hand, I conclude that the christological and Trinitarian formulations of the first two ecumenical councils surprisingly cohere with John's original intentions.

PAULINE CHRISTOLOGY

Years before any gospel was written, the apostle Paul laid a foundation for beliefs about Jesus as the Son of God. Modern scholarship debates whether Paul actually wrote all the letters attributed to him, so I will consider core statements about Jesus's divinity found in some of the undisputed letters before I address data from disputed epistles. In some cases, later writings presuppose and enhance the christological claims found in earlier letters.

Modern editions of the New Testament conclude the Letter to the Romans with a doxology referencing Paul's "preaching Jesus Christ according to the

---

4. For example, in John 10:33, 36, Jesus is accused of blasphemy for making himself God or calling himself Son of God.

revelation of the mystery that had been silenced for eternal times but is now shown via prophetic Scriptures" (Rom 16:25–26).[5] The language of "mystery" is significant, for Paul was acknowledging just how incredible it would seem for the one and only God of Israel to have a Son—unlike the Greek gods who often sired demigods through women.[6]

Paul clearly believed Jesus was somehow not only the son of a human mother but also the Son of the God of Israel. Paul says nothing about Jesus having a human father, but Paul does refer to the Jewish God as the "Father of our Lord Jesus Christ" (e.g., Rom 15:6; 2 Cor 1:3). Paul never names Mary, but he does affirm Jesus's human birth: "When the fullness of time came, God sent forth his Son, born from a woman, born under the law" (Gal 4:4). Putting the two claims together, Paul identifies "Jesus Christ our Lord" as "(God's) Son, born from David's seed according to the flesh, designated Son of God in power according to the spirit of holiness by means of resurrection from the dead" (Rom 1:3–4).

Romans 1:3–4 alone sounds like Jesus transformed into something new by virtue of the resurrection.[7] Indeed, Paul thought that a resurrected body was a substantially different kind of thing (1 Cor 15:44), an oxymoronic "spiritual body" (*sōma pneumatikon*) as opposed to a "physical body" (*sōma psychikon*). Conversely, the earlier statement that God *sent* his Son (Gal 4:4) could imply that God mysteriously had a Son all along. Paul says so explicitly in the Letter to the Philippians. Jesus was "in the form of God" and even "equal to God" (Phil 2:6); then came kenosis, the "emptying" by which Jesus was born like a human and eventually died on the cross (vv. 7–8); yet God exalted Jesus (v. 9). Elsewhere Paul describes the exaltation as God's raising Jesus from the dead (1 Thess 1:10). In other words, Jesus's imperishable resurrected body has to be different from the mortal body that was crucified and died, but Jesus did not

5. These verses do not appear in every manuscript. For example, Rom 16:25–27 is missing in the ninth-century Codex Augiensis (f. 31; sigla F and 010), a Greek-Latin manuscript of Paul's letters. Also, the verses sometimes appear earlier in Romans. For example, in Papyrus 46, the oldest extant collection of Paul's letters, these verses appear at the end of our modern chapter 15.

6. For example, Herakles was the son of Zeus and Alkmene, and Asclepius was the son of Apollo and Coronis.

7. Adela Yarbro Collins ("Paul and His Legacy to Trinitarian Theology," in *The Bible and Early Trinitarian Theology*, ed. Christopher A. Beeley and Mark E. Weedman, CUASEC [Washington, DC: Catholic University of America Press, 2018], 165) interprets Rom 1:3–4 to mean that Jesus's earthly Messiahship rested solely on his Davidic genealogy and that he reached his full potential "only on the occasion of his resurrection from the dead." Yet Yarbro Collins acknowledges that Paul thinks of Jesus as preexistent in Phil 2:6 (163).

originate as God's Son merely by means of resurrection. Instead, via the resurrection, Jesus reattained the status of divine sonship that he held before he was born. The crucial point is that Philippians affirms Jesus's preexistence.

The notion of preexistence raises the question of just how old the Son of God is, and the Letter to the Colossians affirms what I call Creator Christology. This letter is attributed to Paul, but modern scholars debate whether he actually wrote it. Regardless, my purpose is simply to show an intentionally higher Christology than is found in the undisputed letters. Colossians 1:15–17 declares Jesus to be the "image of the unseen God, firstborn of all creation, because in him was created everything in the heavens and on the earth, things seen and things unseen—whether thrones, dominions, or rulers: everything via him and unto him was created. And he himself is prior to everything, and everything consists in him." Here we find the claim that Jesus did not merely exist before he entered the world: the Son of God participated in the creation of the very world he would someday enter.[8]

The Epistle to the Hebrews does not claim to be written by Paul, but for centuries it was included among Paul's letters.[9] Hebrews also claims Creator Christology: via the Son, God "made the aeons" (Heb 1:2). I mentioned earlier that angels are literally called "sons of God" in the Old Testament, so the question arises where the angels come from. The easy answer is that God created them. Another question immediately arises: *when* were angels created? We can infer that God's angels were made sometime before the creation story in Genesis 1. For one thing, birds with wings were created on the fifth day (Gen 1:20–23), whereas land animals and humans were created on the sixth

8. Larry W. Hurtado (*Lord Jesus Christ: Devotion to Jesus in Earliest Christianity* [Grand Rapids: Eerdmans, 2003], 119) considers 1 Cor 8:6 a reference to Jesus as an agent in creation. In a discussion of food sacrificed to Greek gods, Paul insists on monotheism—that "no one [is] God except one" (v. 4), "although there are so-called gods" (v. 5). Paul goes on, "But for us [there is] one God the Father, from whom [is] the everything, and we [are] unto him; and [for us there is] one Lord Jesus Christ through whom [is] the everything, and we [are] through him" (v. 6). In my opinion, Paul claims there that everything comes *from* (ἐκ) the one Creator God, and now the Corinthians are related to the one Creator God *through* (διά) the Lord Jesus Christ. I grant, though, that 1 Cor 8:6 is open to the interpretation of Christ's role in creation, and it might very well have influenced the Creator Christology of Colossians and Hebrews, which explicitly add verbs for Christ's creating or making everything.

9. For example, Papyrus 46 places Hebrews in second position, between Romans and 1 Corinthians. For a compelling argument that Hebrews was always intended as a Pauline imitation and accompaniment, see Claire K. Rothschild, *Hebrews as Pseudepigraphon: The History and Significance of the Pauline Attribution of Hebrews*, WUNT 235 (Tübingen: Mohr Siebeck, 2009).

day (vv. 24–25). However, some angelic creatures transcend the framework of Genesis 1. For example, the prophet Ezekiel had a vision of humanlike creatures that were nonetheless composed of calves' feet, human hands, and multiple faces of a human, lion, ox, and eagle—not to mention that they could fly with two pairs of wings (Ezek 1:5–12). For another thing, there is already an angelic council to whom God speaks in the plural, "Let us make humanity in our image" (Gen 1:26).[10]

The creation of angels is important because the book of Hebrews explicitly differentiates Jesus's divine sonship from that of the angels. As Son of God, Jesus is "better than the angels" (Heb 1:4), because he was "begotten" (*gennaō*) by God (v. 5). As God's "firstborn," Jesus is to be worshiped by the angels (v. 6). Since angels are immortal, they are considered divine beings, who are superior to human beings.[11] Yet Jesus's human experience necessitated his morality, so in that regard he had to be temporarily "diminished vis-à-vis the angels" (Heb 2:9). The overarching point of Creator Christology, though, is that even the angels and aeons were created via the Son of God (Col 1:16; Heb 1:2). Creator Christology is as high as we climb in the New Testament. It is not found in the Synoptic Gospels, but we will encounter it again as a key facet of Johannine Christology.

Synoptic Christology

Paul's letters preceded the Gospels, and to varying extents Paul's teachings influenced the Gospels. The Christology of the Synoptics develops from one gospel to the next, so I will begin with Mark and then show how Matthew's and Luke's additions produce a higher Christology. Overall, I find the Christology of the Synoptic Gospels to be compatible with the Christology found in Paul's undisputed letters.

Possible Adoption at Jesus's Baptism

Mark's opening sentence identifies Jesus as the Messiah (1:1),[12] and Mark immediately introduces John the Baptizer. John appears at the Jordan River

---

10. To be sure, Christians have long interpreted Gen 1 as referring to the Trinity, and I will discuss Trinitarianism later in this chapter. At this point, suffice it to say that the book of Genesis was originally written by Jews and for Jews, who do not believe in the Christian Trinity.

11. Similarly, the Neoplatonist philosopher Porphyry referred to angels as gods simply because they were immortal and had an incorruptible nature (*Apocr.* 4.21).

12. The Gospel of Mark undoubtedly refers to Jesus as the Son of God, but there is a

preaching repentance, baptizing the penitent, and already predicting a successor (vv. 4–8). Then John baptizes Jesus (1:9), who receives the Spirit (v. 10); the Spirit literally "came down into [*eis*]" Jesus (v. 10). Jesus also heard a voice from the heavens declaring, "You are my beloved son; I am delighted with you" (v. 11).

The heavenly voice—the *bat qol* in Hebrew—carries strong resonances of Psalm 2:7, where Yahweh says to his anointed one, "You are my son; today I have begotten you." This term "anointed one" is "Messiah" in Hebrew or "Christ" in Greek, but in this case, the psalm references a king (v. 6).[13] Nevertheless, the begotten messiah of Psalm 2 was associated with Jesus very early. According to Acts 13:33, Paul explicitly cites "the second psalm" and quotes, "You are my beloved son; today I have begotten you." In that context, Jesus was begotten as God's Son via the resurrection, as discussed earlier in connection with Romans 1:3–4.[14] However, in the mid-second century, Justin Martyr twice quotes "You are my son; today I have begotten you" in connection with Jesus's baptism (*Dial.* 88.8; 103.6).[15]

If Mark's *bat qol* echoes Psalm 2, and if "today" is emphasized, then Jesus's baptism can be interpreted as a transformative religious experience. Jesus receives the Spirit (Mark 1:10), who then "throws him out into the desert" (v. 12), where Jesus withstands temptation (v. 13). Thereafter he begins preaching and working miracles. Jesus's miracles appear to be a new superpower activated by the Spirit. This line of thinking is called Adoptionist Christology, that Jesus was a lowly human being until he was adopted and elevated to God's Son via a baptismal transformation.[16]

According to Mark, some people were soon saying that Jesus had begun acting completely differently or perhaps that he had gone out of his mind (3:21b);[17] scribes said that Jesus was demon possessed (v. 22). Yet there is an

---

long-standing text-critical question whether the opening sentence did so. For example, in Mark 1:1, Codex Sinaiticus initially omitted "Son of God" after "Jesus Christ," whereas "Son of God" is added at that point in the majority of manuscripts, including Codices Vaticanus and Bezae as well as a corrector of Sinaiticus.

13. The referent is usually interpreted as King David, which is made explicit by the Vulgate's inscription "a psalm of David" before Ps 2.

14. Ps 2:7 is also quoted in Heb 1:5 and 5:5 to differentiate Jesus from the angels.

15. The Greek text of Codex Bezae revised the Lukan baptism scene (3:22) so that the heavenly voice quotes Ps 2:7 verbatim.

16. The category and terminology of "Adoptionism" has recently been challenged by Jeremiah Coogan, "Rethinking Adoptionism: An Argument for Dismantling a Dubious Category," *SJT* 76 (2023): 31–43.

17. The Greek verb ἐξίστημι could be translated either way.

Old Testament parallel to such a change in behavior. The prophet Samuel anointed Saul as ruler over the Israelites (1 Sam 10:1). Samuel then predicted that Saul would meet a group of prophets, be seized by the Spirit, and "be transformed into a different man" (vv. 5–6). These things came to pass, thereby engendering the proverb, "Is Saul also among the prophets?" (vv. 9–13). The point is that Jesus's religious experience at his baptism can be interpreted as transformational. Even if Jesus were merely human prior to receiving the Spirit, he could become the Son of God by adoption at the baptism. That is not how early orthodox and catholic tradition carried, but baptismal Adoptionism would still be a higher Christology than believing that Jesus became the Son of God by virtue of the resurrection.

From the outset of Mark's Gospel, Jesus is said to come from Nazareth (1:9). Later his mother and brothers appear (3:31), and later still he is said to have had sisters (6:3). The presence of Jesus's siblings alongside his mother could imply that he had a human father, but Mark nowhere says so explicitly.[18] The opening baptism scene instead identifies Jesus as God's Son (1:11b). Right in the middle of the gospel, Jesus undergoes some sort of metamorphosis (Greek) or transfiguration (Latin), which was visible to others.[19] The apostles Peter, Jacob (aka James), and John had accompanied Jesus, and they not only saw the transformation but also heard the *bat qol* say, "This is my beloved son; listen to him" (9:7). Toward the end of the gospel, Jesus prays to God as "Abba, Father" (14:36).[20] Throughout Mark's Gospel, Jesus has a human mother, but Jesus is the Son of God. In the Gospel of Mark, then, Jesus has a similar type of generation as in Paul's undisputed letters.

The Addition of Nativity Stories

The Gospel of Mark leaves itself open to an Adoptionist interpretation. By contrast, Matthew and Luke each added nativity stories, which explicitly identify Jesus as the Son of God, who was miraculously conceived by the Virgin Mary.

The Gospel of Matthew opens with Jesus's genealogy, beginning with the Israelite patriarch Abraham and ending with Joseph, who was the husband of

18. Some manuscripts, even an early one like Papyrus 45, say "carpenter's son" rather than "carpenter" in Mark 6:3, but that is a harmonistic variant drawn from Matt 13:55.

19. Mark does not describe how his physical appearance might have changed (9:2b), but his clothes became "super dazzling white" (v. 3).

20. Contrary to popular belief, in Aramaic "Abba" is a formal address like "O, Father," not baby talk like "Dada" or "Daddy"; see James Barr, "'Abbā Isn't 'Daddy,'" *JTS* 39 (1988): 28–47.

Mary but not the biological father of Jesus (1:1–17). Readers learn that Mary is pregnant, not by Joseph but from the Holy Spirit (v. 18), and an angel of the Lord reports this news to Joseph (v. 20). Matthew reiterates that Joseph could not have been Jesus's biological father (vv. 24–25), and on multiple occasions both the narrator and an angel of the Lord refer to Jesus as the son of Mary but not the son of Joseph (2:13–14, 20–21). After Jesus has escaped Herod the Great's slaughter of the innocents, the narrator quotes a prophecy from Hosea (11:1b) to call Jesus the Son of God (Matt 2:15c). Thereafter Jesus grew up in Nazareth, where he was considered "the carpenter's son" (13:55).

The Gospel of Luke narrates Mary's perspective. When her relative Elizabeth was six months pregnant with John the Baptist, God sent the angel Gabriel to Nazareth (1:26–27). The angel informed Mary that she would conceive Jesus (v. 31). Mary questioned how that could be, since she was a virgin (v. 34), and Gabriel explained that the Holy Spirit would come to her and that God's power would overshadow her (v. 35). Here at the annunciation, Gabriel told Mary that Jesus would be called "Son of the Most High" (v. 32) and "Son of God" (v. 35b). Luke's readers therefore know that Jesus was not the biological son of Joseph, "as was believed" by others (3:23).

If Mark were our only gospel, then Jesus's association with the Spirit and Jesus's relation to God as Father could have originated at the baptism. To be sure, Matthew and Luke join Mark in narrating the *bat qol*'s identification of Jesus the Son of God at his baptism and at the transfiguration.[21] Yet, by adding complementary nativity stories, Matthew and Luke designate Jesus as the Son of God decades earlier than his baptism, since Jesus was approximately thirty years old at that time.[22] The virginal conception thereby espouses a higher Christology than we find in Mark: God is declared Jesus's father through the work of the Holy Spirit at the beginning of Mary's miraculous pregnancy. For Matthew and Luke, then, the baptismal manifestation of God the Father, God's Son, and the Holy Spirit was in some way the continuation—rather than the beginning—of a lifelong relationship.

---

21. For the baptism, see Matt 3:17b // Mark 1:11b // Luke 3:22b; for the transfiguration, see Matt 17:5b // Mark 9:7b // Luke 9:35b. Matthew and Luke also say that the Spirit descended *upon* (ἐπί) Jesus at his baptism (Matt 3:16b // Luke 3:22a), not that the Spirit came *into* (εἰς) him (Mark 1:10).

22. Mark nowhere indicates Jesus's age. Matthew says that Jesus was born prior to the death of Herod the Great (ch. 2) and that Jesus died during the governorship of Pontius Pilate (ch. 27); accordingly, ancient and modern historians can deduce that Jesus probably did not reach the age of forty. Luke states explicitly that Jesus was "around thirty years" old at his baptism (3:23).

Matthew's and Luke's nativity stories also flesh out the Christology found in the undisputed Pauline epistles. Paul wrote that Jesus had God for a father (Rom 15:6; 2 Cor 1:3) along with a human mother: "When the fullness of time came, God sent forth his Son, born from a woman, born under the law" (Gal 4:4). Regarding Jesus's being "born under the law," Luke emphasizes the holy family's fulfillment of torah commandments, since Jesus was circumcised on the eighth day (2:21) and Mary was purified on the fortieth day (vv. 22–24; Lev 12). The virginal conception attempts to explain how and when God sent forth his Son into the world.

Jesus's Exorcisms and Possible Preexistence

The undisputed Letter to the Philippians adduced the notion of preexistence, that Jesus was "in the form of God" even before he was born like a human (Phil 2:6–7). There is always a risk of reading too much into a text, but I do think we can reasonably infer Jesus's preexistence from the Synoptics. The clue here is that angels and demons call Jesus the Son of God, and we have already seen that angelic beings are themselves called sons of God in the Old Testament. Simply put, it takes one to know one.

After the baptism and temptation stories in the Gospel of Mark, Jesus calls Simon (Peter), Andrew, Jacob (aka James), and John as his first disciples. Then they enter Capernaum, where Jesus teaches in a synagogue on the Sabbath. One man had an unclean spirit, who screams at Jesus, "I know who you are: the Holy One of God" (Mark 1:23–24); then Jesus exorcises the unclean spirit (vv. 25–26). Luke follows Mark closely by telling the same story nearly verbatim at the same point in the narrative (4:31–37).[23] Mark also makes a summary statement about many healings and exorcisms, and on these occasions unclean spirits would fall before Jesus and scream, "You are the Son of God" (3:11). Luke similarly narrates that at Simon's house, Jesus performed many healings and exorcisms, and the exorcised demons screamed that Jesus was the Son of God (4:41). On all these occasions, Jesus shushes the demons so that they do not continue proclaiming his divine status.[24]

Matthew omits the aforementioned demonic professions, but one such episode is common to all three Synoptics. Matthew refers to the region of the Gadarenes (8:28), as opposed to the Gerasenes (Mark 5:1; Luke 8:26).[25] And

23. Luke had brought forward the story of Jesus's rejection at Nazareth (4:16–30), but otherwise Luke follows Mark's sequence for this early part of Jesus's ministry.

24. Mark 1:25b; 3:12; Luke 4:35a, 41b.

25. The region of Gergesenes is yet another name appearing as a textual variant. For

Matthew has two demon-possessed people (Matt 8:28) instead of just one (Mark 5:2; Luke 8:27). Yet the synoptists at least agree that this one or these two demon-possessed person(s) came from the local tombs and recognized Jesus as "Son of God" (Matt 8:29) or "Son of the Most High God" (Mark 5:7 // Luke 8:28). Although Jesus is not the only exorcist in the Synoptics,[26] he is the only one whom demons address as Son of God.[27]

Matthew's and Luke's temptation story has the devil ask Jesus to prove *whether* he is a Son of God.[28] The devil even thinks himself Jesus's superior, since one of the temptations was for Jesus to worship him (Matt 4:9b // Luke 4:7). By contrast, the demons are clearly subject to Jesus's commands, and the demons profess that Jesus *is* Son of God. Not only that, one demon thinks Jesus has come to destroy him (Mark 1:24c // Luke 4:34b), and Matthew's demons assert that it is too early for Jesus to be torturing them (8:29c).[29] Presumably that shouldn't happen until Jesus would preside over judgment day.

A simple question arises about how demons comprehend Jesus's superior, divine status. An Adoptionist interpretation of Mark could say that the demons are responding to the Holy Spirit. That is, "holy" is the opposite of "unclean," so if Jesus underwent a baptismal transformation, then his newfound indwelling of the Holy Spirit could be overpowering the unclean spirits. Conversely, Matthew's and Luke's nativity stories relate Jesus to the Holy Spirit from the moment of his conception. From there, it is a short step to read Matthew and Luke in light of Philippians (2:6–8). In that case, the angelic annunciations could imply Jesus's being the preexistent Son of God who was about to be born into the world. In other words, Jesus could be the Son of God before his birth. Demons are divine beings themselves, and the exorcisms show them to be inferior to Jesus. Most importantly, these demons—along with God and God's angels—are the characters who most frequently recognize Jesus as Son of God throughout the Synoptics.

---

example, this reading is found in the main text of Luke 8:26 in Codex Sinaiticus, and a later corrector of Sinaiticus harmonized Matt 8:28 and Mark 5:1 to read Gergesenes as well.

26. Jesus gave his disciples and apostles the authority to cast out demons and unclean spirits (Matt 10:1, 8; Mark 3:15; 6:7, 13; Luke 9:1; 10:17). At one point, Jesus's disciples met a stranger who was performing exorcisms in Jesus's name (Mark 9:38 // Luke 9:49), and Jesus said not to stop the outsider exorcist. Jesus stated elsewhere that some people would be rejected on judgment day, even though they had cast out demons in his name (Matt 7:21–23). Jesus even acknowledged that Pharisees could perform exorcisms (Matt 12:27); the parallel in Luke 11:19 does not specify Pharisees but does refer generally to other successful exorcists.

27. The angel Gabriel had predicted that Jesus would be called Son of God (Luke 1:35b).

28. Matt 4:3b, 6b // Luke 4:3b, 9b. Other questions on whether Jesus is the Son of God are found in the trial before the Sanhedrin (Matt 26:63b // Mark 14:61b // Luke 22:66, 70).

29. Cf. Mark 5:7c // Luke 8:28c, where the demons beg Jesus not to torture them.

JOHANNINE CHRISTOLOGY

I have emphasized instances where divine beings acknowledge Jesus as Son of God in the Synoptics. On rare occasions, though, humans come to the same conclusion. Mark (15:39), followed by Matthew (27:54), has the centurion at the crucifixion call Jesus Son of God.[30] Matthew adds two key moments where Jesus's disciples profess his divine nature. After Jesus walks on water, the disciples in the boat worship Jesus and call him Son of God (14:33).[31] Later at Caesarea Philippi, Simon Peter declares Jesus "the Christ, the Son of the living God" (Matt 16:16).[32] Jesus replies that Peter must have received a revelation of Jesus's divinity (v. 17), one that is soon confirmed when Peter—along with Jacob and John—hears the *bat qol* call Jesus "my beloved Son" at the transfiguration (Matt 17:5).

Unlike Mark and Luke, Matthew and John have disciples declare Jesus to be the Son of God or the Holy One of God. Simon Peter does so in both of these gospels (Matt 16:16; John 6:69), and Matthew has one other place where a group of disciples collectively acclaim Jesus Son of God (14:43). John runs with this idea and creates numerous occasions for particular disciples to profess their belief in Jesus's divinity.[33] Compared to the Synoptics, John transfers the professions of Jesus as Son of God from demons to the disciples. Instead of having a demon call Jesus "the Holy One of God" (Mark 1:24 // Luke 4:34), John assigns this profession to Simon Peter. By nearly eradicating angels and demons from the gospel,[34] John enhances Jesus's divinity: angels and demons need not affirm Jesus's divine identity; it is plainly perceived by numerous humans.

In John's Gospel, Jesus never stops anyone from proclaiming his identity, and John intentionally multiplies the human characters who know Jesus to be the Son of God. When he first saw Jesus, John the Baptizer said, "Even I have seen and have testified that this one is the Son of God" (John 1:34). Jesus immediately attracts followers. Philip is the fourth disciple whom Jesus calls (v. 43), and Philip brings Nathanael along (v. 45). Although Philip had intro-

---

30. Luke's centurion merely declares Jesus righteous or innocent (23:47).

31. At this point, Mark (6:51) says only that the disciples were astonished.

32. Cf. Mark 8:29c // Luke 9:29d, where Jesus is called Christ, but not Son of God.

33. As we saw in the previous chapter, this is another example of John's tendency to assign speaking parts to individual disciples where the Synoptics had them say something in unison.

34. At the end of the gospel, two angels appear to Mary Magdalene at the empty tomb (John 20:12), but nowhere else do angels, demons, or the devil appear as characters in John's narrative.

duced "Jesus, son of Joseph, who is from Nazareth" (v. 45b), Nathanael instead addressed Jesus as "the Son of God" (v. 49b). Simon Peter had already become a disciple, and he later declares on behalf of the disciples, "We have believed and we have known that you are the Holy One of God" (6:69). Jesus himself will say, "I am the Son of God" (10:36).[35] And just before Jesus raises Lazarus from the dead, his sister Martha professes, "I have believed that you are the Christ, the Son of God who is coming into the world" (11:27).

At the end of the gospel, the risen Jesus had appeared to other disciples, but not to Thomas. When told about the resurrection, Thomas said that he would not believe unless he could see and touch the risen Jesus (20:19–25). A week later Jesus appeared to Thomas (vv. 26–29), who expressly equated Jesus with God by professing, "my Lord and my God" (v. 28b). In the beginning of the gospel, the Logos is equal to God (1:1). In the middle of the gospel, to be the Son of God is to be one with the Father, since Jesus makes himself God (10:30–36). In the end, the narrator summarizes that the entire point of the gospel is for readers to believe that "Jesus is the Christ, the Son of God" (20:31).

A distinct aspect of Johannine Christology is Jesus's unique relation to God as the "only begotten" (*monogenēs*). John presses this christological point in the gospel's prologue: Jesus has "glory as an only begotten from the Father" (1:14), and Jesus is the "only begotten God, who is inside the bosom of the Father" (v. 18b). After Jesus's discourse with the Pharisee Nicodemus, readers learn that God "gave the only begotten Son" (3:16) and that people should believe "in the name of the only begotten Son of God" to avoid condemnation (v. 18).[36]

In Greek Jewish Scriptures, the term *monogenēs* typically refers to an only child.[37] Jepthah's daughter was an only child (*monogenēs*), "and there was not to him a son or daughter besides her" (Judg 11:34). Also, Sarah was the only child (*monogenēs*) of Raguel (Tob 3:15; 6:11), and she married Tobias, son of Tobit (3:17; 6:13); it turns out that both Sarah and Tobias were only children (8:17). In the New Testament, Luke uses the term in the same way: Jesus resuscitates the only begotten son of the widow at Nain (7:12) along with the only begotten daughter of the synagogue leader (8:42), and Jesus exorcises a man's only begotten son (9:38).[38]

---

35. Jesus had said, "I and the Father are one" (10:30), and "the Jews" were ready to stone him. They said that "you, being a person, are making yourself God" (v. 33), an accusation that recurs just before the crucifixion (19:7).

36. The claim that "God has sent his only begotten Son into the world" recurs in 1 John 4:9.

37. In the Psalms (22:20; 25:16; 35:17—using English versification), μονογενής more generally means "the only one" or "all alone."

38. Heb 11:7 describes Abraham's willingness to sacrifice Isaac, "the only begotten"; Abra-

There is one crucial reference to *monogenēs* as a divine personification in Greek Jewish Scriptures. The term "only begotten" refers to Wisdom's role in creation in the book known as the Wisdom of Solomon. Wisdom is a feminine noun in Greek (Sophia), and she is personified as "the craftswoman of all things";[39] she is further described as having a spirit that is holy and unique (*monogenēs*) along with other attributes (Wis 7:21–22).

In the deuterocanonical Wisdom of Solomon, the use of "only begotten" for Wisdom appears unprecedented, and yet the author inherited the notion of Wisdom's role in creation from the canonical book of Proverbs. Wisdom is a feminine noun in Hebrew as well, and the personified Wisdom says that Yahweh "acquired" (*qanah*) her at the beginning of his activity, "eternally interwoven from the beginning, earlier than the earth" (Prov 8:22–23). Instead of acquiring or taking on Wisdom as an attribute, as in the Hebrew text, the Greek translation of Proverbs 8:22–23 says that the Lord "created" (*ktizō*) Wisdom at the beginning and that Wisdom was founded "before the aeons."

The word "wisdom" does not appear at all in the Gospel of John, but Jesus is associated with divine, only begotten, creative power. Among the canonical gospels, John alone attests Creator Christology. John's description has much in common with the Wisdom (Sophia) motif found in Proverbs and in Wisdom of Solomon, but John uses the Greek term "Logos" instead. In its simplest form, the word "Logos" means "word," something someone says, but it can also mean "reason," rational thought that can go unspoken.

The Logos developed into *divine* reason in ancient Greek philosophy. Stoics taught that the passive, material world could not exist without the active Logos, which is in fact the eternal god responsible for the creation of every single thing; this "generative Logos" (*spermatikos logos*) of the world existed unto itself from the beginning and then produced the primordial elements, fire, water, air, and earth.[40] The early Jewish philosopher Philo of Alexandria found much of this explanation compatible with the book of Genesis. In particular, God separated air from water on the second day of creation (Gen 1:6–8), and Philo considered the created world like a shadow that allows us to comprehend the Logos of the uncreated God.[41] Elsewhere Philo reflected

---

ham had another son, Ishmael, of course. From the perspective of Hebrews, though, the point may be that Isaac was the only one who counts, since he was to be the patriarch and father of Jacob/Israel.

39. ἡ . . . πάντων τεχνῖτις (Wis 7:21).
40. Diogenes Laertius, *Lives* 7.134, 136.
41. Philo, *Leg.* 3.23/100.

on the "beginning" of all things and extolled the "invisible, generative, crafty, divine Logos."[42]

John took up a similar line of reasoning and associated God's Logos with Jesus: "In the beginning was the Logos, and the Logos was in relation to [*pros*] the God,[43] and God was [*ēn*] the Logos. This one was in the beginning equal to God. Everything came into being via (the Logos), and apart from him not one thing came into being" (1:1–3). John adds that "the Logos became flesh" (1:14), which is traditionally interpreted as the incarnation when Jesus became human and took on Mary's flesh.

Jewish Scriptures had already entertained the notion of a preexistent, only begotten, divine entity who participated in creation. And at least one early Jewish thinker connected those ideas to Stoic teachings about the divine Logos. The prologue to John's Gospel ties together the same threads to espouse Creator Christology, very similar to what we observed in Colossians and Hebrews.[44] As one "begotten" of God (Heb 1:5) or the "only begotten" of God (John 1:14, 18; 3:16, 18), Jesus is not only differentiated from but also elevated above angels, demons, and the devil. If all things came into existence through Jesus, then he is greater than everything he himself worked to create. Even if the Logos created immortal beings, the preexistent Logos must be superior to them. Following the prologue, John's Christology remains elevated and straightforward throughout the narrative, for it is never a secret that Jesus is the Son of God. Human characters repeatedly profess Jesus's divine status, and Jesus never shushes anyone who does so.

---

42. Philo, *Her.* 119.

43. Translations of John 1:1 customarily say that the Logos was "with" God, similar to the definition of πρός as "by, at, near" (BDAG 3.g [p. 874]), which would work well with an object in the dative case. However, in the accusative case, πρός typically means "toward," so I commend Francis J. Moloney (*The Gospel of John*, SP 4 [Collegeville, MN: Liturgical Press, 1998], 33, 35) for his literal translation, "the Word was turned toward God," and his explanation that the Word was "in a relationship with God" (35). Building on the relational sense, I am considering the definition of πρός as "*in proportion or relation to, in comparison with*" (LSJ C.III.4), one aspect being the value of one thing in comparison to another. As I see it, John 1:1 (a) asserts the preexistence of the Logos, (b) adduces some proportionality between Logos and God, and (c) declares the Logos equal to God.

44. I make no attempt to solve the chicken-and-egg question of which of these books might have come first. However, I think it unlikely that Colossians, Hebrews, and the Gospel of John derived Creator Christology independently. Whichever one came first most likely influenced the others, and I find it beneficial to cluster and compare these books, given their highly similar high Christologies.

CHAPTER 4

LATER CHRISTOLOGIES, LOWER AND HIGHER

I have plotted relatively lower and higher Christologies, which can be envisioned at various points on a staircase. Adoptionism via the resurrection occupies the lowest step, and Jesus's adoption via the baptism is a step higher. Another step up would be the nativity stories of Matthew and Luke, whereby Jesus was the Son of God from the moment of his miraculous conception. Philippians ascends farther by adducing Jesus's preexistence; that is, the conception of his human flesh was not his actual beginning. The highest step we have climbed thus far is Creator Christology, according to which Jesus did not merely exist before his conception but actually participated in the creation of all things.

At the risk of oversimplification, I contend that there is some degree of correlation between chronology and Christology. I have no intention of pinpointing dates for all of the texts under consideration. However, for the Pauline corpus, I accept that Colossians and Hebrews are later works written by someone other than Paul, and their Creator Christology elevates Jesus's divine nature above any explicit statement found in the earlier, authentic letters of Galatians, Romans, and Philippians. Also in chronological arrangement, successive gospels correlate with relative Christologies, beginning with Mark and proceeding in order to Matthew to Luke and to John. Each subsequent evangelist knew the work of his predecessor(s), so the Gospels' increasingly higher Christologies reveal intentional pieces of supplementation.

To be sure, there are many other early Christian texts and traditions, which reveal early christological speculation to have been far more complicated than I can fully address in this one chapter. Standing on the staircase metaphor, any theologian at any time could hold fast to a low Christology, while other theologians could ascend even higher than I have described thus far. And when a higher Christology gained traction, another thinker might descend the staircase to reassert a lower Christology. On the lower end of the spectrum, for example, the so-called Ebionites purportedly read a harmony of the Synoptic Gospels and taught that Jesus was the biological son of Joseph and Mary; the Ebionites equated the divine Spirit with Christ, a separate entity who first came to Jesus at his baptism.[45] This group is dated to the mid-second century, and the excerpts from the Ebionite gospel harmony are clearly dependent on the Synoptic Gospels; yet the nativity stories were excised, since their gospel

---

45. See Epiphanius, *Pan.* 30 for the fullest description of these alleged heretics.

began with the baptism.[46] The fundamental point is that some later Christians knew but rejected higher Christologies, thereby settling on a lower one.

Along these lines, Christine Jacobi has elucidated the Gospel of Philip,[47] which was discovered among the Nag Hammadi codices and is typically classified as gnostic. The Gospel of Philip can affirm that Jesus was not only the biological son of Joseph and Mary but also the Son of God. Most incisively, Jacobi demonstrates that the Gospel of Philip can subsume and reinterpret the Gospel of John. Yes, the Logos became flesh (John 1:14), but that could simply mean that the Logos/Christ descended upon Jesus at his baptism.

To avoid Adoptionism, one could fill in the gaps of Matthew's and Luke's nativity stories. Protevangelium Jacobi claims to have been written by Joseph's son Jacob (25.1). In this supplemental gospel, Joseph was an old widower, and his prior marriage had produced Jacob and Jesus's other siblings who appear in the canonical gospels (chs. 8–9). Although Mary is said to be the "wife" of Joseph (8.8), he is told "to take into his safe-keeping the virgin of the Lord" (9.7). Joseph is never expected to consummate the marriage, because after the twelve-year-old Mary goes to live in Joseph's house, the priests rightly presume that she has remained undefiled (10.2). When she is later found to be pregnant, Joseph stands accused of wrongdoing, but a priestly ritual proves that Joseph was not the father and that Mary remained a virgin (chs. 13–16). Finally, this text surpasses the virginal conception and attests the virgin birth, since Mary's postpartum virginity is proven by a gynecological examination performed by a doubting midwife (chs. 19–20). Protevangelium Jacobi supplements the canonical nativity stories and amplifies the meaning of "the Virgin Mary" by constructing multiple characters outside the holy family who knew of Jesus's virginal conception and virgin birth.

The Infancy Gospel of Thomas is another extracanonical text that dispels Adoptionism by filling in gaps from the canonical gospels. The Gospel of Luke tells one story of Jesus when he was twelve years old (2:41–52), but there is nothing else about Jesus's childhood. So the Infancy Gospel of Thomas tells numerous stories of Jesus publicly working miracles as early as age five (ch. 2). This text often surprises modern readers when Jesus strikes a couple of children dead (chs. 3–4), but he does plenty of good miracles too. And at one

---

46. Epiphanius, *Pan.* 30.13.6.

47. Christine Jacobi, "Jesus' Body: Christology and Soteriology in the Body-Metaphors of the *Gospel of Philip*," in *Connecting Gospels: Beyond the Canonical/Non-canonical Divide*, ed. Francis Watson and Sarah Parkhouse (Oxford: Oxford University Press, 2018), 77–94, esp. 80–82, 91.

point, in conversation with his teacher Zacchaeus, Jesus declares that he was present when the world was created (6.10). Zacchaeus believes him and soon tells Joseph that Jesus was not a child who had been born but that he might have been born before the world was made (7.4). The overarching christological point of the Infancy Gospel of Thomas is that Jesus publicly proved his divine nature even when he was a child.

Later Christologies could climb higher still. The main question was always how Jesus's humanity and divinity might have been united. But what if Jesus was so divine that he wasn't human at all? Perhaps it just *seemed* like he was human. That is the view known as docetism, derived from the Greek word *dokeō*, which means, "seems like, but isn't really." The extracanonical Acts of John presents itself as a sequel to John's Gospel, and chapters 87–105 of the Acts are widely regarded as a gnostic interpolation.[48] In this section, a polymorphous Jesus alternates between appearances as a child and adult (ch. 88), elderly and pubescent (ch. 89), flabby and muscular (ch. 89), as well as exceedingly tall and short (ch. 90). These depictions allegedly verge on docetism, since polymorphy "clearly reduces the bodiliness and the humanity of the earthly Jesus."[49]

Conversely, these episodes from the Acts of John do not radically depart from canonical miracle stories. Jesus's hovering just above the earth and leaving no footprints (ch. 93) complements Jesus's walking on water in the Gospel of John (6:16–21), and the glorified Jesus of the Fourth Gospel could suddenly materialize out of nowhere and appear in a locked room, but then he could prove himself to be tangible (20:26–27). Inspired by the synoptic account of the transfiguration, which is retold in chapter 90, the Acts of John multiplies examples of Jesus revealing his glory to John prior to the resurrection. Jesus paradoxically claims that on the cross, he suffered but did not suffer. This

48. There is only one extant manuscript of this episode, namely, Vienna hist. gr. 63; Janet Spittler ("Is Vienna hist. gr. 63, fol. 51v–55v a 'Fragment'?," *Ancient Jew Review*, 6 May 2019, https://www.ancientjewreview.com/read/2019/4/30/is-vienna-hist-gr-63-fol-51v-55v-a-fragment?rq=spittler) has rightly questioned whether the text should be considered a fragment, since it "works on its own" and may best be seen "as an independently circulating episode." This paragraph and the next one are adapted from James W. Barker, "The Acts of John within the Johannine Corpus," in *Studies on the Intersection of Text, Paratext, and Reception: A Festschrift in Honor of Charles E. Hill*, ed. Gregory R. Lanier and J. Nicholas Reid, TENTS 15 (Leiden: Brill, 2021), 367–68.

49. Hans-Josef Klauck, *The Apocryphal Acts of the Apostles: An Introduction*, trans. Brian McNeil (Waco, TX: Baylor University Press, 2008), 32; cf. Eric Junod and Jean-Daniel Kaestli, eds., *Acta Iohannis*, CCSA 1 (Brepols: Turnhout, 1983), 2:493, where the Acts of John is not deemed docetic, since Christ maintains a physical body.

statement tries to maintain that "(Jesus) and the Father are one" (John 10:30) while denying that the Father could suffer.[50]

These are just a few examples of christological speculations that were in play by the end of the second century. Not everyone was reading all the same texts, and even the same texts lay open to multiple interpretations. Moreover, interpretations that were deemed heretical did not originate from people who self-identified as heretics; they likely just called themselves Christians. Nevertheless, "orthodox" means the straight or correct teaching, and proto-orthodoxy emerged by labeling certain texts and interpretations as heretical. "Heresy" (*hairesis*) literally means "choice," but the implication was that heretics had made the wrong interpretive choices—so much so that they dissociated from the orthodox/catholic church to form their own sects.

In the second half of the second century, Irenaeus of Lyons became the most prolific heresiologist up to that point. His five books *Against Heresies* laid out his strong opinions regarding the right interpretations of the right books. Irenaeus opposed more than a dozen arch-heretics, but for our purposes, he pointed out two heretical ditches that eventually became firmly entrenched.[51] One is the rejection of Adoptionism as too low a Christology. For example, the Ebionites erred by believing Jesus to be the biological son of Joseph and not the miraculous Son of God from his conception by Mary from the Holy Spirit (*Haer.* 3.21.1; 5.1.3). And while some assumed that Jesus did not become Christ until he was born, Irenaeus insisted that the preexistent Creator Logos had always been the Son of God who was truly born and suffered as a real human being (*Haer.* 3.18.1).

Irenaeus quotes John 1:3 to say that Jesus was the Logos who created all things (*Haer.* 5.21.10), and soon thereafter Irenaeus quotes Galatians 4:4 and Romans 1:3–4 to maintain that Jesus had to assume actual flesh from the Virgin Mary (*Haer.* 3.22.1). Jesus did not merely seem (*dokeō*) to be human: his coming in the flesh happened in truth (*alētheia*; *Haer.* 5.1.2). As too high a Christology, then, docetism lay on the other side of the christological highway.

I have switched metaphors from moving up and down a staircase to traveling a multilane road with ditches on either side. Adoptionism is the right-

---

50. The Acts of John asserted strong Monarchianism (the belief that the oneness of the Father and Son practically made them a single person) while rejecting Patripassianism (the belief that God the Father suffered on the cross).

51. Irenaeus was not without predecessors, of course. In the first half of the second century, Ignatius of Antioch defended Mary's virginity and her conception from the Holy Spirit (Ign. *Eph.* 18–19) as well as Jesus's actual—not seeming—human birth, life, death, and resurrection (Ign. *Trall.* 9). As in Thomas's confession in the Gospel of John (20:28), Ignatius also called Jesus God, not just Son of God (Ign. *Smyr.* 1.1; Ign. *Eph.* inscription).

hand ditch, since Jesus is not considered divine enough. The lowest acceptable Christology would be found in the nativity stories of Matthew and Luke, which occupies the slow, right-hand lane. Along with the nativity stories are the statements from Galatians and Romans that Jesus was born of the flesh but that he was also the Son of God who was sent into the world. Philippians travels the middle lane: its explicit declaration of Jesus's preexistence encompasses the texts in the slow lane to the right, and Philippians has steered well clear of the Adoptionist ditch. Driving in the fast lane to the left are Colossians, Hebrews, and the Gospel of John, all of which espouse Creator Christology. Creator Christology entails all the lower, acceptable christological statements. To the left of the fast lane, however, lies the ditch of docetism, since it appears to deny Jesus's humanity.

The takeaway is that Irenaeus stacked the canonical texts in precisely this way. For all practical purposes, the only begotten Logos–Creator theology from the Gospel of John became the lens through which all other statements about Jesus's humanity and divinity were interpreted. Moreover, any texts that seemed too high or too low were cast aside. To be sure, christological speculation did not end with Irenaeus. Centuries later, certain texts and Christologies that Irenaeus deemed heretical nonetheless continued to circulate.[52] Irenaeus's influence weighed heavily, however, particularly his efforts to solidify the fourfold gospel—that Matthew, Mark, Luke, and John were the only four gospels that should be read in the orthodox/catholic churches (*Haer.* 3.11.7–8).

JOHANNINE RECEPTION IN EARLY TRINITARIAN DOGMA

A funny thing happened on the way to Nicaea, the site of the first ecumenical council, which was convened by the emperor Constantine in 325 CE. The orthodox/catholic church had been following closely behind Irenaeus in the fast lane, but at high speeds the lines started to blur. To press the metaphor, there were vehicles running double-wide in the Creator Christology lane. These were the two positions: (a) to the right was the view the Father had begotten the Son as sort of a precreation event, and then the Son participated in creating the cosmos; (b) to the left was the belief that the Son had always existed with the Father.

---

52. For example, around the turn of the third century, Clement of Alexandria was likely reading the Acts of John; see Janet E. Spittler, "John, Acts of," in *Brill Encyclopedia of Early Christianity Online*, ed. David G. Hunter, Paul J. J. van Geest, and Bert Jan Lietaert Peerbolte, https://referenceworks.brillonline.com/browse/brill-encyclopedia-of-early-christianity-online. Also, the Nag Hammadi codices were produced in the fourth century.

Creator Christology, as found in the Gospel of John and disputed Pauline epistles, had successfully elevated Jesus's divine nature above other formulations found in some earlier texts. That was their purpose, but these Scriptures were not necessarily entertaining the question of the Son's origination or eternality. Nevertheless, later interpreters felt compelled to answer this question to establish a tradition to carry forward. The debate had begun long before the Council of Nicaea, and the controversy continued well after.

Around the year 200 in North Africa, Tertullian wrote in opposition to Praxeas, who allegedly claimed that in the beginning God created the Son. Tertullian argued that (a) since Jesus Christ the Son of God is equated with the Logos of John 1, (b) since Logos means "reason," and (c) since God must always have been reasonable, it follows that (d) God the Father was never apart from God the Son (*Prax.* 5). Tertullian's own reasoning relied upon the personification of Wisdom in Proverbs 8, but he subsumed the creation of Wisdom under the prior argument that God always possessed reason and wisdom (*Prax.* 6).

According to Tertullian, reason and wisdom are inseparable from God the Father, but the Son was presented distinctly at the beginning of creation. That is, light was day one of creation (Gen 1:3), and Jesus was the light that was coming into the world (John 1:9). From there, Tertullian clusters citations of Genesis 1:3, Proverbs 8:22, Colossians 1:15, and John 1:3 as harmonious attestations to the procession of the eternal, only begotten Son as the firstborn of creation (*Prax.* 7). Thus, there is a Father, a Son, and a Spirit who are distinguishable and yet inseparable from one another (*Prax.* 9). Tertullian's language of three persons united in substance (*Prax.* 2) would later become Nicene dogma.

In the early third century, Origen took up similar questions in Alexandrian Egypt. According to apostolic teaching, God the Father was the Creator of all things. Jesus Christ was the only begotten Son prior to creation, and all things were made by him too. Eventually the Son was conceived by the Virgin Mary from the Holy Spirt, and Jesus was truly born, lived, suffered, died, and resurrected. Regarding the Spirit, though, it was unclear whether the Holy Spirit was begotten as another kind of Son or whether the Spirit subsists innately. Origen summarizes these points in his preface (4) to *First Principles* (*De principiis*).

Origen associates Christ, the Son of God, with Wisdom, the first created thing according to Proverbs 8:22 (*Princ.* 1.2.1). Conversely, Origen deems it insensible to think that God the Father ever existed without Wisdom; in other words, there is simply no way for the human mind to comprehend the beginning of God's Wisdom (*Princ.* 1.2.2; 1.2.9). Origen quotes Colossians 1:15 regarding the firstborn of all creation, but he seizes on the preceding phrase regarding Christ being "an image of the invisible God" (*Princ.* 1.2.5). As a corollary, Origen quotes

John 1:9 regarding Jesus as the light coming into the world (*Princ.* 1.2.6). Moreover, according to 1 John 1:5, God is also light, and so the only begotten Son proceeds inseparably as light from light (*Princ.* 1.2.7)—another phrase that would become Nicene dogma. The only begotten Son is distinguished from all other divine beings, since incorporeal beings such as angels and demons were created by the Father through the Son (*Princ.* 1.7.1, citing John 1:1–3 and Col 1:16–18).

Even though they wrote independently of one another, Origen and Tertullian evince significant degrees of unanimity between Eastern and Western thought at the turn of the third century. But it would be mistaken to assume that everyone shared their views, for there were predecessors, contemporaries, and successors who developed strikingly different Trinitarian notions. For example, in the mid-second century, Justin Martyr not only subordinated the Son to the Father but also considered them too divisible to be acceptable in later centuries. Justin literally ranked the Trinity: Jesus Christ stood "in second position," and the prophetic Spirit was "in third rank" (*1 Apol.* 13.3);[53] the unity and equality of the three persons would become a sticking point in later centuries. Regarding divisibility, Justin described the Father's begetting the Son as one fire kindling another (*Dial.* 61.2). Granted, light and fire are closely related concepts, but a new fire is cut off from its source. By contrast, Tertullian and Origen envisioned the Son as a beam of light indivisible and yet distinguishable with regard to its source.

In fairness to Justin, he wrote approximately a century after the canonical gospels and Pauline epistles were composed. Those texts talk about a Father, Son, and Spirit, but there is relatively little specification about how the three are interrelated. For example, at the baptism, the Father calls Jesus the Son, and the Spirit descends (e.g., Matt 3:16–17), and the Gospel of Matthew concludes with the risen Jesus's commission to his remaining disciples that they make more disciples, who would be baptized "into the name of the Father and the Son and the Holy Spirit" (28:19). John's Gospel enclosed the most intricate model of the Trinity's inner workings, but those details took a long time to be disclosed. In the fourth century, Arius's Christology was much higher than Justin's earlier speculation, but Arius was the one declared a heretic.

The (First) Council of Nicaea in 325 CE

Debates concerning the Son of God's origination or eternality intensified over the centuries, and Constantine convened the (first) Council of Nicaea to settle

---

53. ἐν δευτέρᾳ χώρᾳ . . . ἐν τρίτῃ τάξει (*1 Apol.* 13.3).

the matter—regardless of which position prevailed.[54] In the end, key statements regarding the Son of God affirmed that he was "eternally begotten of the Father," "light from light," "begotten, not made," "consubstantial [i.e., of one being] with the Father," and that "through him all things were made." There were strong precedents for each of those statements. Arius was the one who allegedly interpreted Scriptures differently. His views were declared heretical at the council, though the debate continued long into the future.

Athanasius became bishop of Alexandria three years after he participated in the Council of Nicaea as a deacon. He wrote extensively against the priest Arius and his opinions, which Athanasius adjectivally called Arian. A succinct primary text is Athanasius's *Defense of the Nicene Definition (De decretis)*, which highlights rival interpretations. Regarding the Nicene catchword "consubstantial" (*homoousios*), Athanasius clarifies, "The Son of God is neither a creature nor something made nor something originated, but the Logos is begotten from the substance of the Father" (*Decr.* 3.3). The point of contention was the so-called Arian claim, "Not always Father, not always Son: for the Son was not prior to being begotten, but also he was begotten not from something; and not always has God the Father begotten the Son, but when the Son was begotten and created, then God was called his Father" (*Decr.* 6.1). Athanasius conceded that in ordinary human language and understanding, fathers precede sons, but he contended that God was always the Father of the Son in a way that transcends human comprehension (*Decr.* 12.2).

Athanasius preserves more of his opponents' argument: "In this way, we think the Son to have advantage over others, and on this account he is called 'only begotten' because he alone has been begotten only by God, but all the others have come to be via the Son, as by an assistant" (*Decr.* 7.1). Given the intensity of fourth-century Trinitarian controversies, it is easy to overlook just how high a Christology Arius was said to have promulgated. He took very seriously the literal Greek translation of Proverbs 8:22, whereby Wisdom was "created" at the beginning of the Lord's works (*Decr.* 13.1). As had long been established, Wisdom was identified with the Logos, and the Logos was identified with the Son of God. From Arius's perspective, it might have seemed like the Son of God was the beginning of God's creative activity, and that cornerstone idea could support the notion of Christ being "firstborn of all creation" according

---

54. See especially Lewis Ayres, *Nicaea and Its Legacy: An Approach to Fourth-Century Trinitarian Theology* (Oxford: Oxford University Press, 2004); see also Frances M. Young with Andrew Teal, *From Nicaea to Chalcedon: A Guide to the Literature and Its Background*, 2nd ed. (London: SCM, 2010).

to Colossians 1:15.[55] Thereafter, in accordance with John 1:3, everything else must have come into being through the Son.

In earlier centuries, Arius might have been lauded for his high Creator Christology, for he never veered toward the ditch of docetism and could hardly glimpse the ditch of Adoptionism. In the fourth century, though, the orthodox/catholic churches were all traveling in the same Creator Christology lane, and ultimately a so-called Arian Christology was deemed too low. Athanasius impugned a contradiction in his opponents' theology: "all things" could not have been made by the Son (John 1:3) if the Son himself was something made (*Decr.* 13.5). Similarly, Athanasius quotes Colossians 1 at length, including Christ being "firstborn of all creation" (v. 15). However, the ensuing phrase says that "in him was created the everything" (v. 16),[56] which Athanasius interpreted in light of John 1:3. To reiterate, the Son of God could not have been a created thing.

A non-Nicene interpreter might have insisted on the sequence of Colossians 1:15–16. That is, the Son of God is first said to be "firstborn of all creation" (v. 15), and then "everything was created by him" (v. 16), so "everything" might really mean "everything else"; if so, then "everything" in John 1:3 would likewise mean "everything else," and Colossians 1:15 would align neatly with Proverbs 8:22. Again, though, pro-Nicene interpretations disallowed any qualification to "everything," so the Son of God cannot have been made or created at any point—even at a point prior to the creation of angelic beings, who themselves existed before the cosmos. Regarding Proverbs 8:22, Athanasius offers a rather weak argument, differentiating that a person "creates a house but begets a son," thereby failing to address Proverbs' use of personification as a literary device (*Decr.* 13.4). Athanasius later presents a stronger argument by quoting Origen in saying that Wisdom, the only begotten Logos, was forever accompanying God (*Decr.* 27.3), for God always must have been rational.

The (First) Council of Constantinople in 381 CE

Origen believed Jesus to be the only begotten Son of God, but Origen was not sure how to describe the Spirit's relation to the Father and Son. Along similar lines, the Nicene Creed simply concluded with an expression of belief in the Holy Spirit. The decades between the councils at Nicaea and Constantinople

---

55. πρωτότοκος πάσης κτίσεως (Col 1:15).
56. ἐν αὐτῷ ἐκτίσθη τὰ πάντα (Col 1:16).

had been filled with treatises regarding the Trinity and the specific nature and role of the Holy Spirit.

Basil of Caesarea's *On the Holy Spirit* (*De Spiritu Sancto*) is a prime example. Basil quotes John 1:3 and Colossians 1:16 in support of Creator Christology (*Spir.* 8/19). He had also quoted John 5:19b, where Jesus says that "the Son cannot do nothing by himself" (*Spir.* 8/19). Basil quotes additional passages from the Fourth Gospel where the work of the Father and the Son is inextricable (*Spir.* 8/20).[57] Then comes the decisive move: the Lord considered the Spirit in conjunction (*synapheia*) with himself and with the Father in the baptismal commandment in the Great Commission (*Spir.* 10/24; cf. Matt 28:19). Consequently, the work of the three persons of the Trinity is coordinated, and each person is involved; this doctrine is sometimes called the economic Trinity.

In opposition to Marcion or the so-called gnostics, it had been necessary to identify God, the Father of Jesus Christ, with the Creator God of Judaism. In the development of Trinitarian dogma, however, it was necessary to explain that the Triune God harmoniously created the cosmos. According to Basil, the Father was the initial cause (*prokatarktikē aitia*); the Son was the craftsmanlike cause (*dēmiourgikē aitia*); and the Spirit was the finishing cause (*teleiōtikē aitia*; *Spir.* 16/38). There must be differentiation when it comes to specific roles (for example, the Son is the one who was crucified), but the Triune God must be united in every work.

In 381 CE, the Council of Constantinople elaborated the Nicene Creed, particularly by affirming that the Holy Spirit is "the Lord, the giver of life," that the Spirit "proceeds from the Father,"[58] that the Spirit is "worshiped and glorified with the Father and the Son," and that the Spirit "has spoken through the prophets." Basil had briefly mentioned that "one of the distinctions of the Spirit's gifts is prophecy" (*Spir.* 16/38). I would add that the model of prophecy set forth in the Gospel of John, coupled with accounts of prophecy in the Old Testament, provide precisely the kind of nuanced, economic Trinity that the Cappadocians were formulating.

Johannine Prophecy and the Economic Trinity

More than one hundred times in the Tanak, the word (Hebrew *devar*; Greek *rhēma* or *logos*) of Yahweh or the word of the Lord is something that "happens"

---

57. E.g., John 5:20; 12:49–50; 14:24, 31.

58. The much-debated Latin term *filioque*, the addition that the Spirit proceeds from the Father "and from the Son," lies beyond the scope of this discussion.

(Hebrew *hayah*; Greek *ginomai*) to prophets. So the "word" is the powerful force that comes upon the prophet, but the "word" can also be the message that the prophet receives from God and then conveys to God's people. Similarly, dozens of times the Spirit (Hebrew *ruakh*; Greek *pneuma*) of God or Yahweh empowers prophets and kings, as Samuel predicted would happen to Saul (1 Sam 10:6, 10).

Early Christians appropriated and recontextualized Jewish Scriptures in accordance with nascent Trinitarian theology. The term *sensus plenior* claims that there was a deeper of fuller meaning all along, although it's plain to see that the original meaning was often stretched considerably.[59] At least ten times in the Gospel of Matthew, the narrator quotes an Old Testament text and explains that something had happened so that Jesus could fulfill the Scriptures or what had been spoken through a prophet.[60] While Mark and Luke include no such fulfillment citations, John's narrator uses "it is written" and "fulfillment" language at least five times to make the same kind of points that Matthew's does.[61]

Zechariah's (9:9) prophecy about Israel's king coming on a colt is one prophecy that Matthew and John have in common.[62] When John refers to the prophecy, he explains, "These things his disciples did not understand at first, but when Jesus was glorified, then they remembered that these things had been written about him and they did these things to him" (12:16). That occurred at John's third Passover, but a similar statement occurs at the first Passover. When Jesus had talked about destroying the temple and raising it up again, John mentions that the disciples remembered it "when he was raised from the dead" (2:22).[63] Those who believe in Jesus would receive the Spirit, but not until he had been raised from the dead (John 7:39; 20:22). Only then could the prophetic significance of Jesus's actions be properly understood.

59. For example, Matt 2:18 quotes Jer 31:15 (ch. 38 LXX) regarding Rachel's weeping for her children "because they are no more"; in Matthew, the children are dead, but in Jeremiah, the children are alive and being taken into exile, yet Jeremiah's next sentence (v. 16) promises that they will someday return.

60. Matt 1:22–23; 2:15b, 17–18, 23; 4:14–16; 8:17; 12:17–21; 13:35; 21:4–5; 27:9–10.

61. John 2:17; 12:14–15, 38; 19:24, 36.

62. I have discussed this prophecy in great detail in *John's Use of Matthew*, Emerging Scholars (Minneapolis: Fortress, 2015; repr., Eugene, OR: Wipf & Stock, 2021), 63–92 (ch. 4).

63. I agree wholeheartedly with Jaime Clark-Soles (*Scripture Cannot Be Broken: The Social Function of the Use of Scripture in the Fourth Gospel* [Boston: Brill, 2003], 294–97), who says that the disciples' remembrance of Jesus's words as recorded by John and the disciples' remembrance of Israel's Scriptures are intended to place John's Gospel as Scripture equal to the Old Testament.

Centuries later, Basil of Caesarea would accentuate the Spirit's prophetic gift, and the Holy Spirit's having "spoken through the prophets" would be codified in the Niceno-Constantinopolitan Creed. While John could not have anticipated the extents of every christological controversy, the Fourth Gospel nonetheless provides a thoroughgoing economic Trinitarian model for God's prophetic activity. God speaks the prophetic Word, and the Word of God literally comes upon the prophet. The Spirit of God also comes upon the prophet, yet the Spirit's role is distinguishable from that of the Logos. The Logos is the revelation itself, but apart from the Spirit, the Word would remain incomprehensible.

To be sure, the Trinity is incompatible with Jewish theology and was not intended by the authors of Jewish Scriptures.[64] When it comes to Christian Scriptures, however, Paul Anderson has rightly observed that "Trinitarian theology did not originate out of a vacuum in the patristic era."[65] Harold Attridge similarly concluded, "The Gospel of John . . . has all the makings of a Trinitarian theology, even if it remains implicit."[66] And C. K. Barrett said that "more than any other New Testament writer, (John) lays the foundation for a doctrine of a co-equal Trinity."[67] I agree with those sentiments and would go so far as to say that the work of the Trinity was not something that patristic writers invented: significant aspects of fourth-century Trinitarian dogma were instead discovered in the emergent New Testament canon. Above all, the economic Trinity stood ready-made in the Gospel of John.

CONCLUSION

Christology is a wide-ranging topic, so this chapter has considerably expanded my usual scope of inquiry. I began with the Pauline epistles, since some of them are the oldest samples of Christian literature. Then in turn, I examined

64. For a nuanced qualification, though, see Daniel Boyarin, *Border Lines: The Partition of Judaeo-Christianity*, Divinations: Rereading Late Ancient Religion (Philadelphia: University of Pennsylvania Press, 2004), 112–27 (ch. 5): "The Jewish Life of the Logos: Logos Theology in Pre- and Pararabbinic Judaism"; the chapter elucidates early Jewish Binitarian speculation regarding the *Memra*/Logos and the angel Metatron.

65. Paul N. Anderson, "The Johannine Riddles and Their Place in the Development of Trinitarian Theology," in Beeley and Weedman, *Bible and Early Trinitarian Theology*, 108.

66. Harold W. Attridge, "Trinitarian Theology and the Fourth Gospel," in Beeley and Weedman, *Bible and Early Trinitarian Theology*, 83.

67. C. K. Barrett, *The Gospel according to St. John*, 2nd ed. (Philadelphia: Westminster, 1978), 92.

the Christology of the Synoptic Gospels, the Gospel of John, and several of the extracanonical gospels. I continued into the early church period, when Trinitarian dogma was established. The influence of John's Gospel cannot be overstated when it comes to orthodox/catholic determinations of the Father, Son, and Spirit's interrelated work.

Regarding New Testament texts, I began with the Pauline corpus; as was customary in previous centuries, I included Hebrews, even though Paul didn't write it.[68] Paul's letters (undisputed and disputed alike) repeatedly refer to Jesus as God's Son, but that title needs a definition. For example, angels are called sons of God in the Old Testament, so exactly what kind of divine being might Jesus be? At the lowest end of the christological scale, Jesus underwent a divine transformation via the resurrection (Rom 1:4). Elsewhere Paul described a more highly exalted Jesus: he was the Son of God before he was even born, but his human birth, life, and death involved an emptying of some divinity—otherwise he would have been incapable of dying; via the resurrection, Jesus reattained his divine, imperishable form (Phil 2:6–9). Rising even higher, Jesus's preexistence could reach before creation itself. According to this Creator Christology, everything came into being through the Son of God, and "everything" includes the angels, who were sons of God in a different sense (Col 1:16; Heb 1:3).

Romans 1:4 taken in isolation sounds like a type of Adoptionism, whereby Jesus was not really divine until the resurrection. A slightly higher form of Adoptionism could be derived from the Gospel of Mark, which begins with Jesus's baptism, when the Spirit descends upon Jesus and God calls him "my beloved Son" (1:10–11). By contrast, Matthew and Luke can hardly be labeled Adoptionist, since Jesus miraculously became the Son of God by the Virgin Mary and from the Holy Spirit. No angel became human in such a way, and demons themselves acknowledge Jesus's superiority and call him the Son of God. Then in the Gospel of John, we encounter Creator Christology once again. Here, the Son of God is not only the Logos through whom everything came to be but also the "only begotten" Son of God, lest he be confused with any angelic beings. The Gospel of John equates Jesus with God both in the prologue (1:1) and in Thomas's confession, "my Lord and my God" (20:28).

68. As I have pointed out elsewhere ("Historical-Critical Methods," in *The Cambridge Companion to the New Testament*, ed. Patrick Gray [Cambridge: Cambridge University Press, 2021], 363), Hebrews is now stuck in limbo between the Pauline and Catholic Epistles. As best I can tell, all of Douglas Campbell's (*Framing Paul: An Epistolary Biography* [Grand Rapids: Eerdmans, 2014]) arguments for the authenticity of Colossians (and Ephesians) could extend to Hebrews as well.

Some subsequent gospels attempted to reestablish an Adoptionist Christology by claiming that Jesus was adopted at the baptism, even though he was the biological son of Joseph and Mary. Other gospels aimed for such a high Christology that Jesus's could not really have been human at all; he only *seemed* human. I have described those respective positions of Adoptionism and docetism as two ditches that the proto-orthodox church avoided. By the early third century, there was strong momentum for Creator Christology to endure and to encompass any conceivably lower christological statements found in the emerging New Testament canon. But whenever two texts make slightly different statements on the same topic, the early church fathers wanted to harmonize those texts, so one text ended up subordinating the other. In other words, one text literally had to come out on top and become the lens through which the other was read.

A crucial example was whether—analogous to Wisdom's self-declaration in Proverbs 8:22—Colossians meant that the Son of God was literally the first-born of all creation (1:15), who then brought everything (else) into being (v. 16). The alternative was to give primacy to the Johannine prologue, which begins "in the beginning," an intentional echo of the creation story in Genesis 1. In that case, the Logos was always equal to God and was the one through whom everything came into being; John does not necessarily intimate a two-stage creation, first the Son and then the rest. This question would be debated long into the future, but there were two centuries of strong advocates for Johannine primacy. Such influential figures include Irenaeus, Tertullian, Origen, Athanasius, and Basil. The long story short is that Johannine Christology came out on top at the Council of Nicaea.

It would be anachronistic to call the Fourth Evangelist pro- or anti-Nicene. On the one hand, John's choice of the word "Logos" carries Stoic resonances, so John would likely agree God was entirely and eternally reasonable. On the other hand, the "only begotten" was literally "inside the Father's womb" (John 1:18b), which could still imply that the Son's begetting occurred at some mysterious, unmeasurable moment before creation. John's Gospel always lay open to different interpretations, and the author could not have foreseen every possible disputation. An overemphasis of "I and the Father, we are one" (John 10:30) leads to Monarchianism. But elsewhere Jesus says, "Father, glorify your name," to which the *bat qol* replies, "I glorified, and again I will glorify" (John 12:28). Similarly, the Father sends the Holy Spirit in the name of the Son (John 14:26). The Father, Son, and Spirit were thus distinguishable, even as their work was coordinated.

The precise role of the Holy Spirit remained an open question, so the subsequent Council of Constantinople offered clarification. I have argued that the Gospel of John inherently provides a nuanced model for the Spirit's role in prophecy. The Constantinopolitan summary statement that the Holy Spirit "has spoken through the prophets" can be elaborated in the following way when the Old Testament is read through a Johannine lens: God the Father speaks and sends the prophetic Word, but the Word can be comprehended only by God's Spirit. As I see it, the Gospel of John already contained an economic model of the Trinity that would ultimately become dogma. Granted, it would be naive to claim that John envisioned all the contours of christological controversies spanning centuries after his gospel was published. Nevertheless, it is no foreign imposition to see the economic Trinity at work in the Fourth Gospel. According to John, divine activity throughout the cosmos—whether it be creation itself, revelation through prophecy, or the incarnation—always involves the interrelated work of the Father, Son, and Spirit.

CONCLUSION

BY WAY OF CONCLUSION, I want to pull certain threads from earlier chapters and tie some ends together. I have scrutinized the interrelations of the Gospels simply by using ancient texts that are presently available to us. I have not appealed to hypothetical sources such as Q, a pre-Markan passion narrative, a pre-Johannine passion narrative, or a signs source. Another potential source underlying the Gospels would be oral tradition, but nowhere have I speculated about what might have been handed down before the Gospels were written down. I don't deny that sayings and stories of Jesus were transmitted. I just don't think we can know much, if anything, about what those traditions were.[1] Compared to most contemporary scholarship on the Gospels, I connect the dots much more simply, because I would rather oversimplify perennial questions than overcomplicate them.

I have not inquired about the historical Jesus. Anytime we compare the Gospels, it is a great temptation to ask, "What *really* happened?" But all we have are the texts, and they don't always agree. My go-to example is Jesus's disruption of commerce in the Jerusalem temple: according to John, it occurred two years before the crucifixion; in the Synoptics, the temple disruption was right before the crucifixion; but in the Diatessaron, the temple incident was just one year before the crucifixion. Sometimes we can discern why an evangelist relocated a story. But narrative and rhetorical rationales should not be confused with historical solutions. Compared with patristic thinkers, I am less like Augustine and more like Origen: I would rather avoid the dizziness that comes from trying to reconcile disparities across the Gospels. A later evangelist might "correct" an earlier one, but literary reinterpretations do not necessarily set the historical record straight.

---

1. Here I am in solidarity with Robyn Faith Walsh, *The Origins of Early Christian Literature: Contextualizing the New Testament within Greco-Roman Literary Culture* (Cambridge: Cambridge University Press, 2021), 156.

I have not speculated about church communities the gospel writers might have belonged to, spoken for, or written for. Generations of redaction-critical studies were replete with such reconstructions, but recent scholarship has forged a much more promising path. I join those who contextualize the evangelists as Greco-Roman writers trying to impress other writers.[2] To move farther along that path, I have emphasized the material production of ancient texts. Each gospel was most likely drafted on waxed tablets, the contents of which were then transferred to bookrolls. After however many rounds of revisions, the Gospels were most likely published as bookrolls, although codices emerged as a new medium around the time the Gospels were composed. My conclusions regarding the construction of the Gospels are based in part on several years of hands-on experience making and using waxed tablets, bookrolls, and single-quire codices.

Ancient writers were also readers who collected and studied highly similar literary works. Simultaneous comparison of two, three, or four source texts was nothing unusual, so any subsequent evangelist could handle all their predecessors' works. The Diatessaron harmonized all four canonical gospels line by line, so all of the canonical gospel writers had an easier job than Tatian had. Also, any gospel could have been written in a group setting or by an individual, although we can't know for certain who any of those individuals were. Nor can we know exactly when and where the Gospels were published, and there is no way to determine whether later gospels came along in rapid succession or after long intervals. Given what we know about book collection, though, we should not suppose that any subsequent evangelist reasonably expected to replace any—let alone all—of the preceding gospels.

JOHN AND THE SYNOPTICS

Several breakthroughs ushered in the modern era of gospel study. At least by the mid-eighteenth century, gospel writers were envisioned as transcribing their sources. Since the Gospels had been subjected to two centuries of textual criticism, source critics could clearly envision evangelists maintaining visual contact with source texts—whether writers copied verbatim or employed greater or lesser degrees of rewriting. Another breakthrough was the deduction of Mark as the first written gospel. That seems almost self-evident when teaching the Synoptic problem today, but Markan priority took centuries to discover,

2. Stanley Stowers, "The Concept of Community and the History of Early Christianity," *MTSR* 23 (2011): 238–56; Walsh, *Origins of Early Christian Literature*.

simply because Matthew had been placed first in the New Testament. Also, despite centuries of tradition claiming Mark as Peter's record keeper in Rome, the Gospel of Mark could finally be dissociated from the apostle Peter.

Markan priority was a quantum leap for solutions to the Synoptic problem, and I have defended the Farrer hypothesis: Mark wrote first; Matthew used Mark; and Luke used Matthew and Mark. On the macroscale, Mark began with Jesus being baptized by John the Baptist; Matthew began with Jesus's conception and birth; and prior to narrating Jesus's conception and birth, Luke told about the birth of John the Baptist. Matthew and Luke elaborated the middle of Mark's Gospel with many of the same teachings. And in the end, Mark left readers with an empty tomb, but Matthew added a resurrection appearance by Jesus, who promised to remain with the disciples forever; Luke clarified that Jesus ascended into heaven but would remain with the disciples in spirit.

The Farrer hypothesis also works on the microlevel, as when a slave owner departs and leaves his enslaved persons in charge.[3] Mark briefly uses that example in the apocalyptic discourse to prepare readers for imminent final judgment. In Matthew's apocalyptic discourse, the short saying about the slave owner is embellished into a full-blown parable, but the point is to delay final judgment, since the slave owner will be gone for a long time. Luke rewrote Matthew's parable and repositioned it long before the apocalyptic discourse to emphasize more strongly that the end was not nigh (19:11).

There is so much evidence for Markan priority that the Augustinian and Griesbach hypotheses should be ruled out. The two-source hypothesis gets Markan priority right, but Matthew's and Luke's departed slave owner parable is a quintessential example of the uncertainty about what Q might have said. For the sake of argument, either Matthew or Luke substantially rewrote Q's parable. In that case, some scholars find it easier to posit a direct relationship between Matthew and Luke. The Matthean posteriority hypothesis does well to dispense with Q and see Matthew and Luke as directly related. Yet the hypothesis falters in positing Matthew's use of Luke. I just see too many snowballs rolling from Mark to Matthew to Luke.[4] Today the Farrer hypothesis has rightfully gained a foothold as a viable alternative to the two-source

3. I have added a few insights of my own, but overall this example is indebted to Mark Goodacre, "Fatigue in the Synoptics," *NTS* 44 (1998): 45–58.

4. In the most extensive defense of Matthean posteriority thus far, Robert K. MacEwen (*Matthean Posteriority: An Exploration of Matthew's Use of Mark and Luke as a Solution to the Synoptic Problem*, LNTS 501 [London: Bloomsbury T&T Clark, 2015]) focuses on strings of verbatim agreement. I extol MacEwen's meticulous analysis, but strings of verbatim agreement necessarily exclude any example where a subsequent evangelist substantially

hypothesis, which held the consensus for a century, dating to the publication of B. H. Streeter's *The Four Gospels*.[5]

While I dissent from Streeter's solution to the Synoptic problem, his work commendably studied the relationship between John and the Synoptics as well. Along these lines, I have also found snowballing trajectories extend-

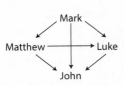

Figure 6.1. John and the Synoptics

ing to John. For example, Mark doesn't mention Samaritans; Matthew says that Jesus rejected the Samaritans; Luke says that some Samaritans rejected Jesus; but John says that Jesus himself evangelized a city of Samaritans who believed him to be the Messiah. The Samaritan question can best be answered if each subsequent evangelist added something to their predecessor(s). And if John becomes the lens through which the earlier gospels are interpreted, then their disparate accounts are reconcilable. As reiterated in figure 6.1, the sequence from Mark to Matthew to Luke to John best accounts for the data in many cases where John closely parallels synoptic material.

To be sure, there are many more cases where John doesn't closely parallel the Synoptics. Sometimes, though, John extensively rewrote the earlier accounts. The paralysis healing in John 5 is a clear example where nearly every detail of the synoptic version is changed. Counterintuitively, John is so different from the Synoptics that the differences must be intentional. I have borrowed the term *oppositio in imitando* from classical studies to describe John's tendency to turn synoptic stories inside out. I realize that this kind of rewriting is open to the critique of having it both ways: heads, I win; tails, you lose. Yet there are abundant examples of this literary technique in biblical and Greco-Roman literature. And if enough details are examined closely enough, then one can reasonably conclude, "Similarities as evidence of use; differences as evidence of writing."[6]

---

rewrote source material, and—as in the talents/minas parable—that's often where Luke's use of Matthew appears clearest.

5. B. H. Streeter, *The Four Gospels: A Study of Origins* (London: Macmillan, 1924).

6. Steven A. Hunt, "Jesus in Sharper Relief: Making Sense of the Fourth Gospel's Use of Mark 1.2–8 in John 1.19–34," in *John's Transformation of Mark*, ed. Eve-Marie Becker, Helen K. Bond, and Catrin H. Williams (London: T&T Clark, 2021), 134. Hunt was already using this terminology in *Rewriting the Feeding of Five Thousand: John 6.1–15 as a Test Case for Johannine Dependence on the Synoptic Gospels*, StBibLit 125 (New York: Lang, 2011) while

Some of John's most distinctive traits show up in the rewriting of episodes from the Synoptics. John likes to assign individual speaking parts where other gospels have "the disciples" seemingly speak in unison. In the feeding of the five thousand, Mark (6:37) has the disciples mention the sum of two hundred denarii, but John (6:8) gives that line to Philip; also, in all three Synoptics,[7] the disciples mention five loaves and two fish, whereas John (6:8) gives Andrew that line. Matthew had a group of disciples call Jesus the Son of God (14:33), and Simon Peter reiterated the point (16:16). Luke created a much larger crowd of disciples than just the Twelve. John's Gospel combined those ideas to multiply the characters who knew Jesus's true identity all along: John the Baptist (1:34), Nathanael (v. 49), and Martha (11:27) all call Jesus the Son of God. Those are not mere coincidences. John has read and intentionally rewritten the Synoptics.

BEYOND JOHN AND THE SYNOPTICS

As head of the Tübingen school in the nineteenth century, Ferdinand Christian Baur posited an early antithesis between Jewish and gentile Christians. The antagonism was most clearly represented by Peter and Paul's infamous food fight at Antioch (Gal 2:11–16).[8] Baur fit the Gospels into his schema, but he was working with the Griesbach hypothesis, so he paid virtually no attention to Mark. Baur was also incorrect to claim Matthew's strong opposition to Christian torah observance. Yet Baur rightly perceived a "Pauline tendency" in Luke; most perceptively, Baur read the book of Acts as reversing the roles of Peter and Paul to reconcile the differences between Jewish and gentile Christians.[9] According to Baur, the letters of Hebrews, Colossians, and Ephesians made the same attempt in different ways. Finally, Baur concluded that John's strong supersessionism transcended the Jewish-gentile rivalry altogether.[10]

By no means would I reinstate all of Baur's synthesis today, but I do think he was right to highlight early debates about torah observance and the rise

---

employing the painstaking methodology of isolating John's knowledge of the composition or redaction of each of the Synoptics. Similarly, I demonstrated John's knowledge of Matthean redaction in *John's Use of Matthew*, Emerging Scholars (Minneapolis: Fortress, 2015; repr., Eugene, OR: Wipf & Stock, 2021), but I was also invoking *oppositio in imitando*.

7. Matt 14:17 // Mark 6:38 // Luke 9:13b.

8. Ferdinand Christian Baur, *The Church History of the First Three Centuries*, 3rd ed., trans. Allan Menzies (Edinburgh: Williams & Norgate, 1878), 1:54–55.

9. Baur, *Church History*, 1:25–26, 30, 78, 132–36.

10. Baur, *Church History*, 1:114–15, 122, 155, 157, 159.

of supersessionism. In trying to explain the entirety of early church history, Baur instinctively analyzed the Pauline corpus together with the Gospels. New Testament scholarship has become too siloed with specializations in the Synoptics, John, or Paul. But it's increasingly clear to me that all four canonical gospels were already in dialogue with Paul. Besides studying John's relation to the Synoptics, then, we need to reexamine the Gospels' relation to the Pauline corpus.

I plot the Gospels along the following trajectory. It is crucial to begin with Mark and to see—as current scholarship may be trending—that Mark assumes a Pauline perspective.[11] For example, "making all the foods clean" in Mark 7:19 means that all of Jesus's disciples were not expected to follow "the tradition of the elders" (v. 5). Matthew used Mark's Gospel, but Matthew is the anti-Pauline gospel, which reinforced torah observance.[12] Jesus did not declare all foods clean, for Matthew's Jesus did not come to abolish torah (Matt 5:17), and no one should teach anyone to break a single commandment (v. 19)—a statement likely aimed straight at Paul.[13] In using Matthew and Mark, Luke attempted to split their differences: Luke's Sermon on the Plain omitted the strict torah observance of Matthew's Sermon on the Mount, but Luke followed Matthew by omitting Mark's line about all foods being made clean; conversely, in that instance, Jesus himself—rather than his disciples—transgressed the traditions of the elders.[14]

Matthew and Luke can still be read within Judaism,[15] but John distances Jesus from Judaism, and several times "the Jews" want to kill Jesus.[16] One can

---

11. Joel Marcus, "Mark—Interpreter of Paul," *NTS* 46 (2000): 473–87; Mar Pérez i Díaz, *Mark, a Pauline Theologian: A Re-reading of the Traditions of Jesus in the Light of Paul's Theology*, WUNT 2/521 (Tübingen: Mohr Siebeck, 2020); Cameron Evan Ferguson, *A New Perspective on the Use of Paul in the Gospel of Mark*, RSECW (New York: Routledge, 2021).

12. David C. Sim repeatedly emphasized Matthew's anti-Paulinism, beginning with *The Gospel of Matthew and Christian Judaism: The History and Social Setting of Matthew's Community*, SNTW (Edinburgh: T&T Clark, 1998).

13. David C. Sim, "Matthew 7.21–23: Further Evidence of Its Anti-Pauline Perspective," *NTS* 53 (2007): 325–43.

14. Luke 11:38; cf. Matt 15:2 // Mark 7:5. For Luke's literary dependence on Paul, see the careful analysis of Luke's harmonization of Mark 14:22–25 and 1 Cor 11:23–25 for the Last Supper by Cameron Evan Ferguson, "Paul's Possible Influence on the Synoptics," in *The Oxford Handbook of the Synoptic Gospels*, ed. Stephen P. Ahearne-Kroll (Oxford: Oxford University Press, 2023), 91–94.

15. E.g., Isaac W. Oliver, *Torah Praxis after 70 CE: Reading Matthew and Luke-Acts as Jewish Texts*, WUNT 2/355 (Tübingen: Mohr Siebeck, 2013); Joshua Paul Smith, *Luke Was Not a Christian: Reading the Third Gospel and Acts within Judaism*, BibInt 218 (Leiden: Brill, 2023).

16. John 5:18; 7:1; 10:31, 33; 11:8.

try to read the Fourth Gospel as though Jesus is a pious Jew making pilgrimage to Jerusalem for Passover, Sukkoth, Hanukkah, and another Passover. However, Jesus causes controversy at the temple every time he goes to Jerusalem, and he never explicitly participates in any Jewish rituals in John's Gospel. In the Synoptics, Jesus had commanded his disciples to prepare a Passover meal on the first day of the Feast of Unleavened Bread.[17] By contrast, John's Last Supper occurred "before the feast of the Passover" (13:1). While I am deeply remorseful about centuries of Christian anti-Judaism, in the end I think Baur accurately interpreted John's strong supersessionism.[18]

Torah observance has not been a theme throughout this book, but I have mentioned it here because supersessionism and Christology seem to go hand in hand: the higher the Christology, the stronger the supersessionism. That is another reason why I think the Pauline corpus should be compared with the Gospels. The authentic Pauline letters oppose compulsory torah observance (Gal 2:14). Instead, believers were encouraged to use their own conscience and accept others who held different convictions, which would include voluntary torah observance (Rom 14:5–6).[19] Those same letters establish a baseline Christology whereby Jesus is the Son of God who was also born from a woman (Gal 4:4; Rom 1:3–4). In the disputed Pauline letters, the original torah commandments become mere shadows (Col 2:17) and human commandments (v. 22). Torah has even been "abolished" (*katargeō*) so that Jews and gentiles can be one people (Eph 2:15).[20] That does not sound as though voluntary torah observance remains permissible,[21] and such strong supersessionism coincides with the claim that Christ created all things (Col 1:16).

17. Matt 26:17–20 // Mark 14:12–17 // Luke 22:7–14.
18. See especially Adele Reinhartz, *Cast Out of the Covenant: Jews and Anti-Judaism in the Gospel of John* (Lanham, MD: Lexington Books/Fortress Academic, 2018). For John's knowledge of some of Paul's letters, see Hunt, *Rewriting*, 235.
19. In the second century, Justin Martyr's *Dialogue with Trypho* (47) similarly permitted Christians to keep commandments such as Sabbath and circumcision as long as they were not compulsory for all Christians.
20. Rom 10:4 says that "Christ is the telos of torah." The Greek word τέλος is translated as the "end" of the law in the NRSV and ESV; cf. the "culmination" of the law in the NIV. Paul's point, though, is that Christ was always the telos in the sense of being the "purpose" or "goal" of torah—that the eternal mystery of God having a Son (Rom 16:25) would eventually be revealed. The point is that the telos of torah in Romans is not claiming the abolition of torah as in Ephesians.
21. In the second century, Ignatius of Antioch prohibited Christians from keeping distinctively Jewish commandments, especially Sabbath (Ign. *Magn.* 9.1), since he considered Judaism and Christianity to be opposites (10.1) and even contradictory (10.3).

Regarding Christology in the Gospels, the beginning of Mark allows room for an Adoptionist interpretation that the human Jesus became the Son of God at his baptism. On the contrary, Matthew and Luke emphasize Jesus's divinity from the moment of his conception. I have argued further that Matthew's and Luke's nativity stories are also compatible with Paul's claim of Jesus's preexistence (Phil 2:5–8). In particular, angels are literally called sons of God in the Old Testament, and demons are the ones who most frequently call Jesus "Son of God" in the Synoptics. Simply put, it takes one to know one: the demons have seen Jesus before, and they know that they will see him in the end when he condemns them at final judgment.

Despite Jesus's clear superiority over other divine beings in the Synoptics, John appears altogether uncomfortable with the notion of multiple sons of God. There are no exorcisms at all in the Fourth Gospel, so there is no room for demons to call Jesus "Son of God." John establishes from the beginning that everything came into being through Jesus (1:3), the only begotten Son of God (3:16, 18). The implication is that Jesus is substantially different from angelic beings, for he is in fact their Creator. The deutero-Pauline Letter to the Hebrews reveals the same set of concerns by endorsing Creator Christology and by calling Jesus the begotten Son who is superior to angels (1:2–6).

I've noted recent scholars who claim each evangelist's familiarity with at least some of Paul's letters, and I now see the Pauline corpus and the Gospels to be more intricately intertwined than I'd previously imagined. In terms of relative chronology, I've argued that John came after the Synoptics, and it is widely agreed that Paul's disputed letters came after the undisputed ones. I would summarize that Mark is Pauline; Matthew is anti-Pauline; Luke attempts a synthesis; and in a sense, John is deutero-Pauline. I have come far enough to cluster Colossians, Hebrews, and John based on their Creator Christology and strong supersessionism. I leave it to others to explore the possible directions of influence and literary dependence, particularly among the Gospel of John and the disputed Pauline letters. Honestly, I was surprised to find so many shadows of Pauline literature cast in so many corners of the Gospels.

When it comes to Christology, though, I have tried to clarify that I am not at all attempting to account for every swirling theological claim in early Christian literature. Not every text proceeded neatly in lockstep from lower to higher Christology. To press that point, I briefly addressed apocryphal gospels in chapter 5. A later text such as the so-called Ebionite harmony could excise the virginal conception and reassert a lower Christology. And the Gospel of Philip could reinterpret the Fourth Gospel such that Jesus was the son of Joseph and Mary, and then the Logos became flesh at Jesus's baptism. Although the canonical gospels have been my main focus throughout this book, the significance of extracanonical literature should not be discounted, and the interrelations of the gospels must be broadly construed to extend far beyond the fourfold gospel.[22]

My work has taken the paths of increasing skepticism toward Q and increasing acceptance of John's use of all three Synoptics. I have elucidated ancient reading and writing practices, particularly the material production of ancient books. I have also highlighted rewriting as an ancient literary technique. Those insights mark a significant advance not only for solving the Synoptic problem but also for understanding John's relation to the Synoptics. Not every alteration in a subsequent gospel reflects an author or community's theological convictions, but there are some christological claims that develop from one gospel to the next, and other aspects of the Gospels' Christologies connect with Paul's letters. Much has been written about the interrelations of the Gospels, and much work remains to be done. Just as no ancient gospel writer could reasonably expect to supplant any of the earlier gospels, I am deeply indebted to those who have come before me, and I hope to have made a positive contribution for those who follow.

22. For this line of inquiry, see especially Francis Watson and Sarah Parkhouse, eds., *Connecting Gospels: Beyond the Canonical/Non-canonical Divide* (Oxford: Oxford University Press, 2018).

Acknowledgments

The team at Eerdmans has been wonderful to work with, and my only regret is that I took so long to finish this book. The project was initiated by Allen Myers, who emailed in 2015 to ask whether a conference paper might turn into a book project. I'm very glad that I was able to thank Allen in person before he passed away in 2020. When the contract initially materialized, Michael Thomson was my editor, and I am grateful for his confidence in this project. And for the longest time now, Trevor Thompson has been my editor, whose abundance of patience and support has been much appreciated. In the final stages of production, I thank my project editor, Jenny Hoffman.

I owe an incalculable debt to my undergraduate mentor David Laird Dungan and to my graduate advisor Amy-Jill Levine. It was a privilege to study under them, and any success I achieve is a reflection of their devotion and guidance. Academia can be such an agonistic environment. However, in all the years I was considered a junior scholar, so many senior scholars were so gracious to me. A few people supported me in enormous ways, while many others happened to say or do the right thing at the right time—probably without ever realizing how much it meant. I hope that I have not left anyone out of the following list of those whose kindness should not go unacknowledged:

Paul Anderson, Harold Attridge, Jennifer Berenson, C. Clifton Black, Douglas Campbell, Mark Chancey, Jaime Clark-Soles, Neil Elliott, Simon Gathercole, Gregory Glazov, Patrick Gray, Leonard Greenspoon, Charles E. Hill, Teresa Hornsby, Larry Hurtado, Peter Judge, John Kaltner, Jennifer Knust, Eric F. Mason, Mark Matson, Steve McKenzie, Laura Nasrallah, Guy Nave, Wendy North, Elaine Pagels, Nicholas Perrin, Ray Person, Adele Reinhartz, Matt Rindge, D. Moody Smith, F. Scott Spencer, Jerry Sumney, Tommy Wasserman, Francis Watson, and Florian Wilk. Also, the unwavering friendship of Greg Carey, Mark Goodacre, Clare K. Rothschild, and Chris Skinner mean the world to me.

For several years, I attended the Midwest regional meeting of the Society of Biblical Literature. The Early Christian Gospels section, directed by Clare K.

Rothschild, was a delightful place to work through some of my earliest ideas for this project. For the entire time I've been writing this book, the Catholic Biblical Association's Continuing Seminar on the Gospel of John has been a stimulating and collegial venue to formulate and sharpen my arguments. I also gratefully acknowledge a 2022 research grant from the Catholic Biblical Association.

I am especially thankful for friends who read individual chapters and gave such thoughtful and helpful feedback. It sounds cliché to say, but it's true that any shortcomings remain entirely my fault. My sincerest thanks extend to Steve Hunt for reading chapter 1, Greg Carey for chapter 2, Hugo Méndez for chapter 3, Chris Skinner for chapter 4, Mark DelCogliano for chapter 5, and Robyn Walsh for chapter 6. I'm chuffed that Mark Goodacre read the entire book and wrote such a gracious foreword.

In the face of ongoing physical limitations, my doctor, Mike; chiropractor, Adam; physical therapist, Brad; and psychotherapist, Denise, help hold me together. Perhaps the least likely people ever to read this book are Jason Isbell, Julien Baker, Adam Granduciel (and the rest of the War on Drugs), and Michael Stipe (along with the rest of R.E.M.), yet their music and lyrics never cease to inspire me—particularly in dark times; to add one more artist from a different medium, I draw similar resoluteness from the work of Neal Brennan.

In the spring of 2023, I lost one of my closest friends, Shane. He was a constant source of empathy and encouragement to me (and many others), even as he experienced deep depression. I miss Shane dearly, and I know he would have been proud that I finally finished this project. In the fall of 2023, I lost my eight-year-old godson, Walter. He filled every space with joy and light. The world is darker without him, even as his memory is ever a blessing. Walter's mother, Maria, has been my dear friend for more than twenty years, and she is a brilliant scholar and editor. More than anyone else, Maria has boosted my confidence by encouraging me just to write what I know. In the final stages of writing, conversations with Robyn Walsh have emboldened my arguments and brightened my days.

I have been blessed immeasurably by a lifetime of love and support from my parents, James and Dianne, as well as my sister, Leanne. Finally, I dedicate this book to my wife, Katy; our children, Jacob and Hannah; and our cat, Pumpkin. You know that I love my research, but I hope you can somehow fathom how much more deeply I love you all.

Bibliography

Ancient Artifacts and Manuscripts

BL Royal MS 5 F XII. London.
Codex Augiensis: Trinity College (Cambridge) B.17.1.
Codex Bezae: Cambridge University Library, MS Nn.2. 41.
Codex Corbiensis secundus: Paris, Bibliothèque nationale de France,
    Latin MS 17225.
Codex Fuldensis: Fulda Bonifatianus I.
Codex Koridethi: Tbilisi, Inst. rukop., Gr. 28.
Codex Sinaiticus: British Library, Add. MS 43725.
Codex Vaticanus: Biblioteca Apostolica Vaticana, Vat.gr.1209.
Codex Washingtonianus: Washington DC, Smithsonian,
    Freer Gallery of Art 06.274.
Munich BSB Clm 14437.
P.Berol. 14004 = TM 69747. Berlin.
P.Mich. 3.166 = TM 78515. Ann Arbor, MI.
Papyrus 45: Chester Beatty Library BP I.
Papyrus 46: Chester Beatty Library BP II.
Papyrus 75: P.Bodmer XIV–XV.
Vatican MS Reg. lat. 1351.
Vienna hist. gr. 63.

Digital Resources

BibleWorks 10.
Google Maps. https://www.google.com/maps.
"Milman Parry Collection of Oral Literature." Harvard Library. https://curiosity
    .lib.harvard.edu/milman-parry-collection-of-oral-literature.
New Testament Virtual Manuscript Room. ntvmr.uni-muenster.de.

ORBIS: The Stanford Geospatial Network Model of the Roman World. https:// orbis.stanford.edu/.

Thesaurus Linguae Graecae. stephanus.tlg.uci.edu/.

EDITIONS

Aland, Kurt. *Synopsis Quattuor Evangeliorum*. 14th ed. Stuttgart: Deutsche Bibelgesellschaft, 1985.

Amgaglio, Delfino, ed. *Gli historikà hypomnemata di Strabone: Introduzione, traduzione italiana e commento dei frammenti*. Memorie 39, fasc. 5, pp. 377–425. Milan: Instituto Lombardo di scienze e lettere, 1990.

The Ante-Nicene Fathers. Edited by Alexander Roberts and James Donaldson. 1885–1887. 10 vols. Repr., Peabody, MA: Hendrickson, 1994.

Augustine. *De consensu evangelistarum*. PL 34:1041–1230.

Basil of Caesarea. *De Spiritu Sancto*. PG 32:67–218.

Begg, Christopher, ed. *Flavius Josephus: Translation and Commentary*. Vol. 4, *Judean Antiquities Books 5–7*. Leiden: Brill, 2005.

Biblia Hebraica Stuttgartensia. 5th edition. Stuttgart: Deutsche Bibelgesellschaft, 1997.

Biblia Sacra Vulgata. 5th ed. Edited by Robert Weber and Roger Gryson. Stuttgart: Deutsche Bibelgesellschaft, 1983.

Bonnet, Maximilien, ed. *Acta apostolorum apocrypha*. Vol. 2. Leipzig: Mendelssohn, 1903.

Butler, H. E., ed. *Quintilian: Institutio Oratoria*. 4 vols. LCL 124–127. London: Heinemann, 1920–1922.

Ceriani, Antonio Maria. *Codex Syro-Hexaplaris Ambrosianus*. London: Williams & Norgate, 1874.

Colson, F. H., G. W. Whitaker, Ralph Marcus, and J. W. Earp, eds. *Philo*. LCL. 12 vols. London: Heinemann, 1927–1962.

Cramer, J. A., ed. *Catenae in Evangelia*. Vol. 2. Oxford, 1841.

Dorandi, Tiziano, ed. *Diogenes Laertius: Lives of Eminent Philosophers*. CCTC 50. Cambridge: Cambridge University Press, 2013.

Elliott, J. K., ed. *The Apocryphal New Testament*. Oxford: Oxford University Press, 1993.

Evans, Ernest, ed. *Tertullian's Treatise against Praxeas*. London: SPCK, 1948.

Fairclough, H. Rushton, and G. P. Goold, eds. *Virgil: Eclogues; Georgics; Aeneid, Books 1–6*. LCL 63. Cambridge: Harvard University Press, 1916.

Goodspeed, Edgar J., ed. *Die ältesten Apologeten*. Göttingen: Vandenhoeck & Ruprecht, 1915.

Goulet, Richard, ed. *Macarios de Magnésie: Le Monogénès; Introduction générale, édition critique, traduction française et commentaire.* 2 vols. TT 7. Paris: Librairie Philosophique J. Vrin, 2003.

Gregory, Andrew, ed. *The Gospel according to the Hebrews and the Gospel of the Ebionites.* OECGT. Oxford: Oxford University Press, 2017.

Hicks, R. D., ed. *Diogenes Laertius: Lives of Eminent Philosophers.* Vol. 1. LCL 184. Cambridge: Harvard University Press; London: Heinemann, 1925.

Hock, Ronald F., ed. *The Infancy Gospels of James and Thomas.* The Scholars Bible 2. Santa Rosa, CA: Polebridge, 1995.

Hogg, Mr. and Mrs. Hope W., eds. "The Diatessaron of Tatian." Pages 42–130 in *Ante-Nicene Fathers.* Vol. 9. Edited by Allan Menzies. 5th ed. New York: Scribner's Sons, 1906.

Holl, Karl, ed. *Epiphanius: Ancoratus und Panarion.* 3 vols. GCS 25, 31, 37. Leipzig: Hinrichs, 1915–1933.

Holmes, Michael W., ed. *The Apostolic Fathers: Greek Texts and English Translations.* 3rd ed. Grand Rapids: Baker Academic, 2007.

Jerome. *De viris illustribus.* PL 23:601–720.

John Chrysostom. *Homiliae in Joannem 87.* PG 59:473–76.

Jones, Horace Leonard, ed. *The Geography of Strabo.* Vol. 5. LCL 211. Cambridge: Harvard University Press; London: Heinemann, 1928.

Junod, Eric, and Jean-Daniel Kaestli, eds. *Acta Iohannis.* 2 vols. CCSA 1. Brepols: Turnhout, 1983.

Keble, John, ed. *Five Books of S. Irenaeus, Bishop of Lyons: Against Heresies.* Oxford: Parker, 1872.

Kennedy, George A., ed. *Progymnasmata: Greek Textbooks of Prose Composition and Rhetoric.* WGRW 10. Atlanta: Society of Biblical Literature, 2003.

Kilburn, K., ed. *Lucian.* Vol. 6. LCL 430. Cambridge: Harvard University Press, 1959.

Koetschau, Paul, ed. *Origenes Werke.* Vol. 2, *Buch V–VIII gegen Celsus.* GCS 3. Leipzig: Hinrichs, 1899.

———. *Origenes Werke.* Vol. 5, *De principiis.* GCS 22. Leipzig: Hinrichs, 1913.

Lewis, Charlton T., and Charles Short. *A Latin Dictionary.* Oxford: Clarendon, 1879.

Lightfoot, J. B., ed. *The Apostolic Fathers.* 5 vols. London: Macmillan, 1889–1890. Repr., Peabody, MA: Hendrickson, 1989.

Marchant, E. C., and O. J. Todd, eds. *Xenophon.* Vol. 4. LCL 168. Cambridge: Harvard University Press; London: Heinemann, 1923.

Meyer, Marvin, ed. *The Nag Hammadi Scriptures.* International ed. New York: HarperCollins, 2007.

Munier, Charles, ed. *Justin: Apologie pour les chrétiens.* SC 507. Paris: Cerf, 2006.

Murray, A. T., and George E. Dimock, eds. *Homer: The Odyssey.* LCL 104–105. Cambridge: Harvard University Press, 1995.

Murray, A. T., and William F. Wyatt, eds. *Homer: The Iliad.* LCL 170–171. 2 vols. Cambridge: Harvard University Press, 1999.

The Nicene and Post-Nicene Fathers, Series 1. Edited by Philip Schaff. 1886–1889. 14 vols. Repr., Peabody, MA: Hendrickson, 1994.

Novum Testamentum Graece. 28th ed. Edited by the Institute for New Testament Research. Stuttgart: Deutsche Bibelgesellschaft, 2012.

Opitz, H. G., ed. *Athanasius Werke.* Vol. 2, part 1. Berlin: de Gruyter, 1940.

Perrin, Bernadotte, ed. *Plutarch.* Vol. 8. LCL 100. Cambridge: Harvard University Press; London: Heinemann, 1919.

Peter Comestor. *Historia evangelica.* PL 198:1537–1644.

Preuschen, Erwin, ed. *Origenes Werke.* Vol. 4, *Der Johanneskommentar.* GCS 10. Leipzig: Hinrichs, 1903.

Race, William H., ed. *Apollonius Rhodius: Argonautica.* LCL 1. Cambridge: Harvard University Press, 2008.

Rackham, H., ed. *Pliny: Natural History.* Vol. 4. LCL 370. Cambridge: Harvard University Press; London: Heinemann, 1945.

Radermacher, Ludwig, and Hermann Usener, eds. *Dionysii Halicarnasei quae extant.* Vol. 6. Leipzig: Teubner, 1929.

Rauer, Max, ed. *Origenes Werke.* Vol. 9, *Die Homilien zu Lukas.* GCS 49. Leipzig: Hinrichs, 1930.

Rehm, Bernhard, and Georg Strecker, eds. *Die Pseudoklementinen.* Vol. 1, *Homilien.* GCS 42. Berlin: Akademie, 1992.

Robinson, James M., Paul Hoffmann, and John S. Kloppenborg, eds. *The Critical Edition of Q.* Hermeneia. Minneapolis: Fortress, 2000.

Rousseau, Adelin, Louis Doutreleau, Bertrand Hemmerdinger, and Charles Mercier, eds. *Irénée de Lyon: Contre les hérésies.* 10 vols. SC. Paris: Cerf, 1969–1982.

Schwartz, Eduard, and Theodor Mommsen, eds. *Eusebius: Die Kirchengeschichte.* 3 vols. GCS NF 6. Berlin: Akademie Verlag, 1999.

Septuaginta. Edited by Alfred Rahlfs. Stuttgart: Deutsche Bibelgesellschaft, 1979.

Shackleton Bailey, D. R., ed. *Martial: Epigrams.* Vol. 3. LCL 480. Cambridge: Harvard University Press, 1993.

Singer, Peter, ed. *Galen: Selected Works.* The World's Classics. Oxford: Oxford University Press, 1997.

Thackeray, H. St. J., ed. *Josephus.* Vol. 1, *The Life and Against Apion.* LCL 186. Cambridge: Harvard University Press, 1926.

———. *Josephus: The Jewish War.* Vol. 3, *Books 5–7.* LCL 210. Cambridge: Harvard University Press, 1928.

Theophylactus of Ochrida. *Commentary on Matthew*. PG 123:143–488.

Tov, Emanuel, with the collaboration of R. A. Kraft and a contribution by P. J. Parsons. *The Greek Minor Prophets Scroll from Naḥal Ḥever (8ḤevXIIgr)*. DJD 8/The Seiyâl Collection 1. Oxford: Clarendon, 1990.

Urba, Karl, and Joseph Zycha, eds. *Augustine Opera*. Vol. 8, part 1. CSEL 60. Leipzig: Freytag, 1913.

Wartenberg, U., ed. "Apollonius Rhodius, *Argonautica* I (POxy 4413–4422)." Pages 79–101 in *The Oxyrhynchus Papyri*. Vol. 64. Edited by E. W. Handley, U. Wartenberg, R. A. Coles, N. Gonis, M. W. Haslam, and J. D. Thomas. GRM 84. London: Egypt Exploration Society, 1997.

Weihrich, Francisci, ed. *Augustine: De consensu evangelistarum*. CSEL 43. Leipzig: Freytag, 1904.

West, M. L., ed. *Greek Epic Fragments from the Seventh to the Fifth Centuries BC*. LCL 497. Cambridge: Harvard University Press, 2003.

Williams, Frank, ed. *The Panarion of Epiphanius of Salamis*. 2nd ed. 2 vols. NHMS 63, 79. Leiden: Brill, 2009–2013.

Secondary Sources

Allison, Dale C., Jr. *The New Moses: A Matthean Typology*. Minneapolis: Fortress, 1993.

Anderson, Paul N. *The Christology of the Fourth Gospel*. 2nd ed. Eugene, OR: Cascade, 2010.

———. *The Fourth Gospel and the Quest for Jesus: Modern Foundations Reconsidered*. LNTS 321. London: T&T Clark, 2006.

———. "The Johannine Riddles and Their Place in the Development of Trinitarian Theology." Pages 84–108 in *The Bible and Early Trinitarian Theology*. Edited by Christopher A. Beeley and Mark E. Weedman. CUASEC. Washington, DC: Catholic University of America Press, 2018.

Annet, Peter. *The Resurrection of Jesus Considered: In Answer to the Trial of the Witnesses*. London: Annet, 1743.

Attridge, Harold. "Intertextuality in the *Acts of Thomas*." *Semeia* 80 (1997): 87–124.

———. "John and Mark in the History of Research." Pages 9–22 in *John's Transformation of Mark*. Edited by Eve-Marie Becker, Helen K. Bond, and Catrin H. Williams. London: T&T Clark, 2021.

———. "John and Other Gospels." Pages 44–62 in *The Oxford Handbook of Johannine Studies*. Edited by Judith M. Lieu and Martinus C. de Boer. Oxford: Oxford University Press, 2018.

———. "Trinitarian Theology and the Fourth Gospel." Pages 71–83 in *The Bible and Early Trinitarian Theology*. Edited by Christopher A. Beeley and Mark E.

Weedman. CUASEC. Washington, DC: Catholic University of America Press, 2018.

Avioz, Michael. *Josephus' Interpretation of the Books of Samuel*. LSTS 86. London: Bloomsbury T&T Clark, 2015.

Ayres, Lewis. *Nicaea and Its Legacy: An Approach to Fourth-Century Trinitarian Theology*. Oxford: Oxford University Press, 2004.

Barker, James W. "The Acts of John within the Johannine Corpus." Pages 340–80 in *Studies on the Intersection of Text, Paratext, and Reception: A Festschrift in Honor of Charles E. Hill*. Edited by Gregory R. Lanier and J. Nicholas Reid. TENTS 15. Leiden: Brill, 2021.

———. "Ancient Compositional Practices and the Gospels: A Reassessment." *JBL* 135 (2016): 109–21.

———. "The Equivalence of *Kaige* and *Quinta* in the Dodekapropheton." Pages 127–52 in *Found in Translation: Essays on Jewish Biblical Translation in Honor of Leonard J. Greenspoon*. Edited by James W. Barker, Anthony Le Donne, and Joel N. Lohr. West Lafayette, IN: Purdue University Press, 2018.

———. "Historical-Critical Methods." Pages 348–68 in *The Cambridge Companion to the New Testament*. Edited by Patrick Gray. Cambridge: Cambridge University Press, 2021.

———. *John's Use of Matthew*. Emerging Scholars. Minneapolis: Fortress, 2015. Repr., Eugene, OR: Wipf & Stock, 2021.

———. "The Narrative Chronology of Tatian's Diatessaron." *NTS* 66 (2020): 288–98.

———. "The Reconstruction of *Kaige/Quinta* Zechariah 9,9." *ZAW* 126 (2014): 584–88.

———. Review of *Der vorjohanneische Passionsbericht: Eine historisch-kritische und theologische Untersuchung zu Joh 2,13–22; 11,47–14,31 und 18,1–20,29*, by Frank Schleritt. *CBQ* 74 (2012): 397–98.

———. Review of *Scribal Harmonization in the Synoptic Gospels*, by Cambry G. Pardee. *JTS* 72 (2021): 392–94.

———. *Tatian's Diatessaron: Composition, Redaction, Recension, and Reception*. OECS. Oxford: Oxford University Press, 2021.

———. "Tatian's Diatessaron and the Proliferation of Gospels." Pages 111–41 in *The Gospel of Tatian: Exploring the Nature and Text of the Diatessaron*. Edited by Matthew R. Crawford and Nicholas J. Zola. RJT 3. London: Bloomsbury T&T Clark, 2019.

———. "Teaching the Bible as a ~~Super~~Natural Book: Textual Criticism of Matthew's Parable of the Two Sons." *SMART* 25 (2018): 113–21.

———. "The Use of Sources in Ancient Compositions." Pages 44–62 in *The Oxford Handbook of the Synoptic Gospels*. Edited by Stephen P. Ahearne-Kroll. Oxford: Oxford University Press, 2023.

———. "Written Gospel or Oral Tradition? Patristic Parallels to John 3:3, 5." *EC* 6 (2015): 543–58.

Barker, James W., and Nicholas J. McGrory. "When Were the Gospels Written?" Paper presented at the Annual Meeting of the Midwest Region of the Society of Biblical Literature, Bourbonnais, IL, 7 February 2016.

Barr, James. "'Abbā Isn't 'Daddy.'" *JTS* 39 (1988): 28–47.

Barrett, C. K. *The Gospel according to St. John.* 2nd ed. Philadelphia: Westminster, 1978.

Barthélemy, Dominique. *Les Devanciers d'Aquila: Première publication intégrale du texte des fragments du Dodécaprophéton.* VTSup 10. Leiden: Brill, 1963.

———. "Redécouverte d'un chaînon manquant de l'histoire de la Septante." *RB* 60 (1953): 18–29.

Bauckham, Richard, ed. *The Gospels for All Christians: Rethinking the Gospel Audiences.* Grand Rapids: Eerdmans, 1998.

Baur, Ferdinand Christian. *The Church History of the First Three Centuries.* 3rd ed. Vol. 1. Translated by Allan Menzies. Edinburgh: Williams & Norgate, 1878.

———. *Kritische Untersuchungen über die kanonischen Evangelien: Ihr Verhältniß zu einander, ihren Charakter und Ursprung.* Tübingen, 1847.

Becker, Eve-Marie, Helen K. Bond, and Catrin H. Williams, eds. *John's Transformation of Mark.* London: T&T Clark, 2021.

Bellinzoni, Arthur J., Jr., ed. *The Two-Source Hypothesis: A Critical Appraisal.* Macon, GA: Mercer University Press, 1985.

Bing, Peter. *The Well-Read Muse: Present and Past in Callimachus and the Hellenistic Poets.* Hypomnemata 90. Göttingen: Vandenhoeck & Ruprecht, 1988. Repr., Ann Arbor: Michigan Classical, 2008.

Boismard, M.-É., Pierre Benoit, and A. Lamouille. *Synopse des quatre Évangiles en français.* 3 vols. Paris: Cerf, 1965–1977.

Bond, Helen K. *The First Biography of Jesus: Genre and Meaning in Mark's Gospel.* Grand Rapids: Eerdmans, 2020.

Botha, Pieter J. J. *Orality and Literacy in Early Christianity.* BPC 5. Eugene, OR: Cascade, 2012.

Bovon, François. *Luke.* Translated by Christine M. Thomas, Donald S. Deer, and James Crouch. 3 vols. Hermeneia. Minneapolis: Fortress, 2002–2013.

Boyarin, Daniel. *Border Lines: The Partition of Judaeo-Christianity.* Divinations: Rereading Late Ancient Religion. Philadelphia: University of Pennsylvania Press, 2004.

Bretschneider, Carolus Theoph. *Probabilia de evangelii et epistolarum Joannis, apostoli, indole et origine.* Leipzig: Barth, 1820.

Brodie, Thomas L. *The Birthing of the New Testament: The Intertextual Development of the New Testament Writings.* NTMon 1. Sheffield: Sheffield Phoenix, 2004.

Brown, Raymond E. *The Community of the Beloved Disciple: The Life, Loves, and Hates of an Individual Church in New Testament Times*. New York: Paulist, 1979.

———. *The Death of the Messiah: From Gethsemane to the Grave*. 2 vols. ABRL. New York: Doubleday, 1994.

———. *The Gospel according to John*. 2 vols. AB 29–29A. Garden City, NY: Doubleday, 1966–1970.

———. *An Introduction to the Gospel of John*. Edited by Francis J. Moloney. ABRL. New York: Doubleday, 2003.

———. Review of *L'Évangile de Jean* (*Synopse des quatre Évangiles en français*, vol. 3), by M.-É. Boismard and A. Lamouille. *CBQ* 40 (1978): 624–28.

Bülow-Jacobsen, Adam. "Writing Materials in the Ancient World." Pages 3–29 in *The Oxford Handbook of Papyrology*. Edited by Roger S. Bagnall. Oxford: Oxford University Press, 2009.

Bultmann, Rudolf. *The Gospel of John: A Commentary*. Translated by G. R. Beasley-Murray, R. W. N. Hoare, and J. K. Riches. Philadelphia: Westminster, 1971.

Burkitt, F. Crawford. *The Gospel History and Its Transmission*. Edinburgh: T&T Clark, 1906.

Busse, Ulrich. "Johannes und Lukas: Die Lazarusperikope, Frucht eines Kommunikationsprozesses." Pages 281–306 in *John and the Synoptics*. Edited by Adelbert Denaux. BETL 101. Leuven: Leuven University Press, 1992.

Calvin, John. *Commentary on a Harmony of the Evangelists, Matthew, Mark, and Luke*. 3 vols. Translated by William Pringle. Edinburgh: Calvin Translation Society, 1845–1846.

———. *Commentary on the Gospel according to St. John*. 2 vols. Translated by William Pringle. Edinburgh: Calvin Translation Society, 1847.

Campbell, Douglas. *Framing Paul: An Epistolary Biography*. Grand Rapids: Eerdmans, 2014.

Carey, Greg. "Moving Things Ahead: A Lukan Redactional Technique and Its Implications for Gospel Origins." *BibInt* 21 (2013): 302–19.

Carruthers, Mary. *The Book of Memory: A Study of Memory in Medieval Culture*. 2nd ed. CSML. Cambridge: Cambridge University Press, 2008.

Carson, D. A. *The Gospel according to John*. PNTC. Grand Rapids: Eerdmans, 1991.

Casey, Maurice. *Jesus: Evidence and Argument or Mythicist Myths?* London: Bloomsbury Academic, 2014.

Citroni, Mario. "Martial." *OCD* 904–6.

Clark-Soles, Jaime. *Scripture Cannot Be Broken: The Social Function of the Use of Scripture in the Fourth Gospel*. Boston: Brill, 2003.

Clinton, Bill. *My Life*. New York: Knopf, 2004.

Collodi, Carlo. *Le avventure di Pinocchio: Storia di un burattino.* Florence: Paggi, 1883.

———. *Pinocchio.* Translated by Mary Alice Murray. Wordsworth Children's Classics. Ware: Wordsworth, 1995.

Conzelmann, Hans. *The Theology of St. Luke.* Translated by Geoffrey Buswell. Philadelphia: Fortress, 1961.

Coogan, Jeremiah. "Rethinking Adoptionism: An Argument for Dismantling a Dubious Category." *SJT* 76 (2023): 31–43.

Crawford, Matthew R. "Diatessaron, a Misnomer? The Evidence from Ephrem's Commentary." *EC* 4 (2013): 362–85.

———. "Severus of Antioch on Gospel Reading with the Eusebian Canon Tables." Pages 215–33 in *Gospel Reading and Reception in Early Christianity.* Edited by Madison N. Pierce, Andrew J. Byers, and Simon Gathercole. Cambridge: Cambridge University Press, 2022.

Cribiore, Raffaella. *Gymnastics of the Mind: Greek Education in Hellenistic and Roman Egypt.* Princeton: Princeton University Press, 2001.

———. *Writing, Teachers, and Students in Graeco-Roman Egypt.* ASP 36. Atlanta: Scholars Press, 1996.

Cross, F. L., and E. A. Livingstone, eds. *The Oxford Dictionary of the Christian Church.* 4th ed. Oxford: Oxford University Press, 2005.

Curtis, Adrian. *Oxford Bible Atlas.* 4th ed. Oxford: Oxford University Press, 2007.

Damm, Alex. *Ancient Rhetoric and the Synoptic Problem: Clarifying Markan Priority.* BETL 252. Leuven: Peeters, 2013.

Davies, Malcolm. *The Greek Epic Cycle.* 2nd ed. London: Bristol Classical, 2001.

Davies, W. D., and Dale C. Allison Jr. *The Gospel according to Saint Matthew.* 3 vols. ICC. Edinburgh: T&T Clark, 1988–1997.

Derrenbacker, R. A., Jr. *Ancient Compositional Practices and the Synoptic Problem.* BETL 186. Leuven: Leuven University Press, 2005.

———. "The 'External and Psychological Conditions under Which the Synoptic Gospels Were Written': Ancient Compositional Practices and the Synoptic Problem." Pages 435–55 in *New Studies in the Synoptic Problem: Oxford Conference, April 2008; Essays in Honour of Christopher M. Tuckett.* Edited by Paul Foster, Andrew F. Gregory, John S. Kloppenborg, and Joseph Verheyden. BETL 239. Leuven: Peeters, 2011.

———. "Matthew as Scribal Tradent: An Assessment of Alan Kirk's *Q in Matthew.*" *JSHJ* 15 (2017): 213–23.

Dewey, Joanna. "The Survival of Mark's Gospel: A Good Story?" *JBL* 123 (2004): 495–507.

Díaz, Mar Pérez i. *Mark, a Pauline Theologian: A Re-reading of the Traditions of*

Jesus in the Light of Paul's Theology. WUNT 2/521. Tübingen: Mohr Siebeck, 2020.

Dinkler, Michal Beth. "Narrative Design in the Synoptics." Pages 136–51 in *The Oxford Handbook of the Synoptic Gospels.* Edited by Stephen P. Ahearne-Kroll. New York: Oxford University Press, 2023.

Dodd, C. H. *Historical Tradition in the Fourth Gospel.* Cambridge: Cambridge University Press, 1963.

Downing, F. Gerald. "Actuality versus Abstraction: The Synoptic Gospel Model." *Cont* 1 (1991): 104–20.

———. "Compositional Conventions and the Synoptic Problem." *JBL* 107 (1988): 69–85.

———. "A Paradigm Perplex: Luke, Matthew and Mark." *NTS* 38 (1992): 15–36.

———. "Redaction Criticism: Josephus' *Antiquities* and the Synoptic Gospels (I)." *JSNT* 8 (1980): 46–65.

———. "Waxing Careless: Poirier, Derrenbacker and Downing." *JSNT* 35 (2013): 388–93.

Dungan, David Laird. *A History of the Synoptic Problem: The Canon, the Text, the Composition, and the Interpretation of the Gospels.* ABRL. New York: Doubleday, 1999.

Eco, Umberto. *How to Write a Thesis.* Translated by Caterina Mongiat Farina and Geoff Farina. Foreword by Francesco Erspamer. Cambridge: MIT Press, 2015.

Ehrman, Bart D. *Did Jesus Exist? The Historical Argument for Jesus of Nazareth.* New York: HarperOne, 2013.

Ehrman, Bart D., Gordon D. Fee, and Michael W. Holmes. *The Text of the Fourth Gospel in the Writings of Origen.* Vol. 1. NTGF 3. Atlanta: Scholars Press, 1992.

Elder, Nicholas A. *The Media Matrix of Early Jewish and Christian Narrative.* LNTS 612. London: T&T Clark, 2019.

Elliott, J. K., ed. *The Collected Biblical Writings of T. C. Skeat.* NovTSup 113. Leiden: Brill, 2004.

Ennulat, Andreas. *Die "Minor Agreements" Untersuchungen zu einer offenen Frage des synoptischen Problems.* WUNT 2/62. Tübingen: Mohr Siebeck, 1994.

Esler, Philip Francis. *Community and Gospel in Luke-Acts: The Social and Political Motivations of Lucan Theology.* SNTSMS 57. Cambridge: Cambridge University Press, 1987.

Esler, Philip F., and Ronald A. Piper. *Lazarus, Mary and Martha: Social-Scientific Approaches to the Gospel of John.* Minneapolis: Fortress, 2006.

Eve, Eric. "The Devil in the Detail: Exorcising Q from the Beelzebul Controversy."

Pages 16–43 in *Marcan Priority without Q: Explorations in the Farrer Hypothesis.* Edited by John C. Poirier and Jeffrey Petersen. LNTS 455. London: Bloomsbury T&T Clark, 2015.

———. *Writing the Gospels: Composition and Memory.* London: SPCK, 2016.

Farmer, William R. *The Synoptic Problem: A Critical Analysis.* New York: Macmillan, 1964.

Farrer, A. M. "On Dispensing with Q." Pages 55–86 in *Studies in the Gospels: Essays in Memory of R. H. Lightfoot.* Edited by D. E. Nineham. Oxford: Basil Blackwell, 1955.

Fee, Gordon D. "Modern Text Criticism and the Synoptic Problem." Pages 154–69 in *J. J. Griesbach: Synoptic and Text-Critical Studies 1776–1976.* Edited by Bernard Orchard and Thomas R. W. Longstaff. SNTSMS 34. Cambridge: Cambridge University Press, 1978.

———. "Origen's Text of the New Testament and the Text of Egypt." *NTS* 28 (1982): 348–64.

Feldman, Louis H. *Studies in Josephus' Rewritten Bible.* JSJSup 58. Leiden: Brill, 1998.

Ferguson, Cameron Evan. *A New Perspective on the Use of Paul in the Gospel of Mark.* RSECW. New York: Routledge, 2021.

———. "Paul's Possible Influence on the Synoptics." Pages 81–99 in *The Oxford Handbook of the Synoptic Gospels.* Edited by Stephen P. Ahearne-Kroll. Oxford: Oxford University Press, 2023.

Fitzmyer, Joseph A. *The Gospel according to Luke.* 2 vols. AB 28–28A. New York: Doubleday, 1970–1985.

Fortna, Robert T. *The Gospel of Signs: A Reconstruction of the Narrative Source Underlying the Fourth Gospel.* SNTSMS 11. Cambridge: Cambridge University Press, 1970.

Fuller, Reginald H. *The New Testament in Current Study.* London: SCM, 1963.

Gamble, Harry Y. *Books and Readers in the Early Church: A History of Early Christian Texts.* New Haven: Yale University Press, 1995.

Gardner-Smith, Percival. *Saint John and the Synoptic Gospels.* Cambridge: Cambridge University Press, 1938.

Garrow, Alan. "Streeter's 'Other' Synoptic Solution: The Matthew Conflator Hypothesis." *NTS* 62 (2016): 398–417.

Gentry, Peter J. "Pre-hexaplaric Translations, Hexapla, Post-hexaplaric Translations." Pages 211–34 in *Textual History of the Bible.* Vol. 1A. Edited by Armin Lange. Leiden: Brill, 2016.

Giangrande, G. "'Arte Allusiva' and Alexandrian Epic Poetry." *ClQ* 17 (1967): 85–97.

Goodacre, Mark. *The Case against Q: Studies in Markan Priority and the Synoptic Problem.* Harrisburg, PA: Trinity International, 2002.

———. "Criticizing the Criterion of Multiple Attestation: The Historical Jesus and the Question of Sources." Pages 152–69 in *Jesus, Criteria, and the Demise of Authenticity.* Edited by Chris Keith and Anthony Le Donne. London: T&T Clark, 2012.

———. "Fatigue in the Synoptics." *NTS* 44 (1998): 45–58.

———. "The *Protevangelium* of James and the Creative Rewriting of *Matthew* and *Luke.*" Pages 57–76 in *Connecting Gospels: Beyond the Canonical/Noncanonical Divide.* Edited by Francis Watson and Sarah Parkhouse. Oxford: Oxford University Press, 2018.

———. "The Synoptic Jesus and the Celluloid Christ: Solving the Synoptic Problem through Film." *JSNT* 80 (2000): 31–43.

———. *The Synoptic Problem: A Way through the Maze.* London: T&T Clark, 2001.

———. "Taking Our Leave of Mark-Q Overlaps: Major Agreements and the Farrer Theory." Pages 201–22 in *Gospel Interpretation and the Q-Hypothesis.* Edited by Mogens Müller and Heike Omerzu. LNTS 573. London: T&T Clark, 2018.

———. Thomas *and the Gospels: The Case for* Thomas's *Familiarity with the Synoptics.* Grand Rapids: Eerdmans, 2012.

Goulder, Michael D. *Luke: A New Paradigm.* 2 vols. JSNTSup 20. Sheffield: JSOT Press, 1989.

Gregory, Andrew F., and Christopher M. Tuckett. "Reflections on Method: What Constitutes the Use of the Writings That Later Formed the New Testament in the Apostolic Fathers?" Pages 61–82 in *The Reception of the New Testament in the Apostolic Fathers.* Edited by Andrew F. Gregory and Christopher M. Tuckett. Oxford: Oxford University Press, 2005.

Griesbach, Johann Jakob. "A Demonstration That Mark Was Written after Matthew and Luke." Translated by Bernard Orchard. Pages 103–35 in *J. J. Griesbach: Synoptic and Text-Critical Studies 1776–1976.* Edited by Bernard Orchard and Thomas R. W. Longstaff. SNTSMS 34. Cambridge: Cambridge University Press, 1978.

———. *Synopsis evangeliorum Matthaei, Marci et Lucae una cum iis Joannis pericopis quae historiam passionis et resurrectionis Jesu Christi complectuntur.* 2nd ed. Halle, 1797.

Gullick, Michael. "How Fast Did Scribes Write? Evidence from Romanesque Manuscripts." Pages 39–58 in *Making the Medieval Book: Techniques of Production.* Edited by Linda L. Brownrigg. Los Altos Hills, CA: Anderson-Lovelace, 1995.

Haenchen, Ernst. *John.* Translated by Robert W. Funk. 2 vols. Hermeneia. Philadelphia: Fortress, 1984.

Hägerland, Tobias. "Editorial Fatigue and the Existence of Q." *NTS* 65 (2019): 190–206.

Haslam, Michael W. "Apollonius Rhodius and the Papyri." *ICS* 3 (1978): 47–73.

Hawkins, John C. *Horae Synopticae: Contributions to the Study of the Synoptic Problem*. 2nd ed. Oxford: Clarendon, 1909.

Head, Peter M. "Textual Criticism and the Synoptic Problem." Pages 115–56 in *New Studies in the Synoptic Problem: Oxford Conference, April 2008; Essays in Honour of Christopher M. Tuckett*. Edited by Paul Foster, Andrew F. Gregory, John S. Kloppenborg, and Joseph Verheyden. BETL 239. Leuven: Peeters, 2011.

Holmes, Michael W. "From 'Original Text' to 'Initial Text': The Traditional Goal of New Testament Textual Criticism in Contemporary Discussion." Pages 637–88 in *The Text of the New Testament in Contemporary Research: Essays on the Status Quaestionis*. Edited by Bart D. Ehrman and Michael W. Holmes. 2nd ed. NTTSD 42. Leiden: Brill, 2013.

Horst, Pieter W. van der. "Macarius Magnes and the Unnamed Anti-Christian Polemicist: A Review Article." Pages 181–89 in *Jews and Christians in Their Graeco-Roman Context: Selected Essays on Early Judaism, Samaritanism, Hellenism, and Christianity*. WUNT 196. Tübingen: Mohr Siebeck, 2006.

Houston, George W. *Inside Roman Libraries: Book Collections and Their Management in Antiquity*. SHGR. Chapel Hill: University of North Carolina Press, 2014.

Huggins, Ronald V. "Matthean Posteriority: A Preliminary Proposal." *NovT* 34 (1992): 1–22.

Hunter, Richard L. "Apollonius Rhodius." *OCD* 122.

Hunt, Steven A. "Jesus in Sharper Relief: Making Sense of the Fourth Gospel's Use of Mark 1.2–8 in John 1.19–34." Pages 121–34 in *John's Transformation of Mark*. Edited by Eve-Marie Becker, Helen K. Bond, and Catrin H. Williams. London: T&T Clark, 2021.

———. *Rewriting the Feeding of Five Thousand: John 6.1–15 as a Test Case for Johannine Dependence on the Synoptic Gospels*. StBibLit 125. New York: Lang, 2011.

Hurtado, Larry W. *Lord Jesus Christ: Devotion to Jesus in Earliest Christianity*. Grand Rapids: Eerdmans, 2003.

———. "Oral Fixation and New Testament Studies? 'Orality', 'Performance' and Reading Texts in Early Christianity." *NTS* 60 (2014): 321–40.

Jacobi, Christine. "Jesus' Body: Christology and Soteriology in the Body-Metaphors of the *Gospel of Philip*." Pages 77–94 in *Connecting Gospels: Beyond the Canonical/Non-canonical Divide*. Edited by Francis Watson and Sarah Parkhouse. Oxford: Oxford University Press, 2018.

Johnson, William A. *Bookrolls and Scribes in Oxyrhynchus*. Toronto: University of Toronto Press, 2004.

———. *Readers and Reading Culture in the High Roman Empire: A Study of Elite Communities*. CCS. Oxford: Oxford University Press, 2010.

Kazantzakis, Nikos. *The Last Temptation of Christ*. Translated by P. A. Bien. New York: Bantam Books, 1961.

Keener, Craig. *The Gospel of John: A Commentary*. 2 vols. Peabody, MA: Hendrickson, 2003.

Keith, Chris. *The Gospel as Manuscript: An Early History of the Jesus Tradition as Material Artifact*. Oxford: Oxford University Press, 2020.

Kelsey, Francis W. "A Waxed Tablet of the Year 128 A.D." *TAPA* 54 (1923): 187–95.

Kieffer, René. "Jean et Marc: Convergences dans la structure et dans les détails." Pages 109–25 in *John and the Synoptics*. Edited by Adelbert Denaux. BETL 101. Leuven: Leuven University Press, 1992.

King, Stephen. *On Writing: A Memoir of the Craft*. New York: Scribner, 2000.

Kirk, Alan. *Q in Matthew: Ancient Media, Memory, and Early Scribal Transmission of the Jesus Tradition*. LNTS 564. London: Bloomsbury T&T Clark, 2016.

———. "The Synoptic Problem, Ancient Media, and the Historical Jesus: A Response." *JSHJ* 15 (2017): 234–59.

Klauck, Hans-Josef. *The Apocryphal Acts of the Apostles: An Introduction*. Translated by Brian McNeil. Waco, TX: Baylor University Press, 2008.

Kloppenborg, John S. *The Formation of Q: Trajectories in Ancient Wisdom Collections*. Philadelphia: Fortress, 1987.

———. "The History and Prospects of the Synoptic Problem." Pages 3–26 in *The Oxford Handbook of the Synoptic Gospels*. Edited by Stephen P. Ahearne-Kroll. New York: Oxford University Press, 2023.

———. "Macro-conflation, Micro-conflation, Harmonization and the Compositional Practices of the Synoptic Writers." *ETL* 95 (2019): 629–43.

Kloppenborg, John S., and Joseph Verheyden, eds. *The Elijah-Elisha Narrative in the Composition of Luke*. LNTS 493. London: Bloomsbury, 2014.

Koester, Helmut. *Ancient Christian Gospels: Their History and Development*. Philadelphia: Trinity International, 1990.

———. "Written Gospels or Oral Tradition?" *JBL* 113 (1994): 293–97.

Konradt, Matthias. *Israel, Church, and the Gentiles in the Gospel of Matthew*. Translated by Kathleen Ess. BMSEC. Waco, TX: Baylor University Press, 2014.

Labahn, Michael. "Literary Sources of the Gospel and Letters of John." Pages 23–43 in *The Oxford Handbook of Johannine Studies*. Edited by Judith M. Lieu and Martinus C. de Boer. Oxford: Oxford University Press, 2018.

Larsen, Matthew D. C. *Gospels before the Book*. New York: Oxford University Press, 2018.

Lessing, Gotthold Ephraim. "Neue Hypothese über die Evangelisten als bloß menschliche Geschichtsschreiber betrachtet." Pages 45–72 in *Theologischer Nachlaß*. Berlin: Voß und Sohn, 1784.

Lieu, Judith M. *I, II, and III John: A Commentary*. NTL. Louisville: Westminster John Knox, 2008.

Lincoln, Andrew T. *The Gospel according to Saint John*. BNTC. London: Continuum, 2005.

Lord, Albert B. *The Singer of Tales*. Edited by Stephen Mitchell and Gregory Nagy. 2nd ed. Cambridge: Harvard University Press, 2000.

Lücke, Friedrich. *Commentar über die Schriften des Evangelisten Johannes*. Vol. 1. 3rd ed. Bonn: Weber, 1833.

Luz, Ulrich. *Matthew*. Translated by James E. Crouch. 3 vols. Hermeneia. Minneapolis: Fortress, 2001–2007.

MacDonald, Dennis R. *The Homeric Epics and the Gospel of Mark*. New Haven: Yale University Press, 2000.

———. *Two Shipwrecked Gospels: The Logoi of Jesus and Papias's Exposition of Logia about the Lord*. ECL 8. Atlanta: Society of Biblical Literature, 2012.

MacEwen, Robert K. *Matthean Posteriority: An Exploration of Matthew's Use of Mark and Luke as a Solution to the Synoptic Problem*. LNTS 501. London: Bloomsbury T&T Clark, 2015.

Mallon, Jean. "Quel est le plus ancien exemple connu d'un manuscrit latin en forme de codex?" *Emerita* 17 (1949): 1–8.

Marcus, Joel. *Mark*. 2 vols. A(Y)B 27–27A. New York: Doubleday, 2000–2009.

———. "Mark—Interpreter of Paul." *NTS* 46 (2000): 473–87.

Martindale, Charles, ed. *The Cambridge Companion to Virgil*. Cambridge: Cambridge University Press, 1997.

Matson, Mark. *In Dialogue with Another Gospel? The Influence of the Fourth Gospel on the Passion Narrative of the Gospel of Luke*. SBLDS 178. Atlanta: Society of Biblical Literature, 2001.

Mattila, Sharon Lea. "A Question Too Often Neglected." *NTS* 41 (1995): 199–217.

McNicol, Allan J., ed., with David L. Dungan and David B. Peabody. *Beyond the Q Impasse: Luke's Use of Matthew*. Valley Forge, PA: Trinity International, 1996.

Meer, Michaël N. van der. "Symmachus's Version of Joshua." Pages 53–93 in *Found in Translation: Essays on Jewish Biblical Translation in Honor of Leonard J. Greenspoon*. Edited by James W. Barker, Anthony Le Donne, and Joel N. Lohr. West Lafayette, IN: Purdue University Press, 2018.

Meier, John P. *A Marginal Jew*. Vol. 1, *The Roots of the Problem and the Person*. ABRL. New York: Doubleday, 1991.

———. *A Marginal Jew*. Vol. 2, *Mentor, Message, and Miracles*. ABRL. New York: Doubleday, 1994.

———. *A Marginal Jew*. Vol. 3, *Companions and Competitors*. ABRL. New York: Doubleday, 2001.

Melville, Herman. *Bartleby, the Scrivener: A Story of Wall Street*, in *The Texts of Melville's Short Novels*. Edited by Dan McCall. Norton Critical Editions. New York: Norton, 2002.

Méndez, Hugo. "Did the Johannine Community Exist?" *JSNT* 42 (2020): 350–74.

Metzger, Bruce M. *Historical and Literary Studies: Pagan, Jewish, and Christian*. NTTS 8. Grand Rapids: Eerdmans, 1968.

Metzger, Bruce M., and Bart D. Ehrman. *The Text of the New Testament: Its Transmission, Corruption, and Restoration*. 4th ed. New York: Oxford University Press, 2005.

Meyer, Elizabeth A. "Roman Tabulae, Egyptian Christians, and the Adoption of the Codex." *Chiron* 37 (2007): 295–347.

———. "Writing Paraphernalia, Tablets, and Muses in Campanian Wall Painting." *AJA* 113 (2009): 569–97.

Miert, Dirk van. *The Emancipation of Biblical Philology in the Dutch Republic, 1590–1670*. Oxford: Oxford University Press, 2018.

Mitchell, Margaret M. "Patristic Counter-evidence to the Claim That 'the Gospels Were Written for All Christians.'" *NTS* 51 (2005): 36–79.

Moloney, Francis J. *The Gospel of John*. SP 4. Collegeville, MN: Liturgical Press, 1998.

Mroczek, Eva. *The Literary Imagination in Jewish Antiquity*. Oxford: Oxford University Press, 2016.

Neirynck, Frans. *Evangelica: Gospel Studies*. Edited by Frans Van Segbroeck. BETL 60. Leuven: Leuven University Press, 1982.

———. "Les femmes au tombeau: Étude de la rédaction matthéenne." *NTS* 15 (1968–1969): 168–90.

———. *The Minor Agreements of Matthew and Luke against Mark with a Cumulative List*. BETL 37. Leuven: Leuven University Press, 1974.

———. "Note on Mt 28,9–10." *ETL* 71 (1995): 161–65.

Neirynck, Frans, with Joël Delobel, Thierry Snoy, Gilbert Van Belle, and Frans Van Segbroeck. *Jean et les synoptiques: Examen critique de l'exégèse de M.-É. Boismard*. BETL 49. Leuven: Leuven University Press, 1979.

Nelson, Scott Reynolds. *Steel Drivin' Man: John Henry, the Untold Story of an American Legend*. Oxford: Oxford University Press, 2006.

Nongbri, Brent. *God's Library: The Archaeology of the Earliest Christian Manuscripts*. New Haven: Yale University Press, 2018.

———. "Manuscripts: The Problem with the Synoptic Problem." Pages 152–74 in *The Oxford Handbook of the Synoptic Gospels*. Edited by Stephen P. Ahearne-Kroll. New York: Oxford University Press, 2023.

North, Wendy E. S. *What John Knew and What John Wrote: A Study in John and the Synoptics*. IJL. Lanham, MD: Lexington Books/Fortress Academic, 2020.

Oliver, Isaac W. *Torah Praxis after 70 CE: Reading Matthew and Luke-Acts as Jewish Texts*. WUNT 2/355. Tübingen: Mohr Siebeck, 2013.

Owen, Henry. *Observations on the Four Gospels: Tending Chiefly to Ascertain the Times of Their Publication and to Illustrate the Form and Manner of Their Composition*. London: Payne, 1764.

Pardee, Cambry G. *Scribal Harmonization in the Synoptic Gospels*. NTTSD 60. Boston: Brill, 2019.

Parsons, Mikeal C., and Michael Wade Martin. *Ancient Rhetoric and the New Testament: The Influence of Elementary Greek Composition*. Waco, TX: Baylor University Press, 2018.

Peabody, David B., ed., with Lamar Cope and Allan J. McNicol. *One Gospel from Two: Mark's Use of Matthew and Luke*. Harrisburg, PA: Trinity International, 2002.

Pelliccia, Hayden. "Two Points about Rhapsodes." Pages 97–116 in *Homer, the Bible, and Beyond: Literary and Religious Canons in the Ancient World*. Edited by Margalit Finkelberg and Guy G. Strousma. JSRC 2. Leiden: Brill, 2003.

Pelling, Christopher. *Plutarch and History: Eighteen Studies*. London: Duckworth, 2002.

Peterson, Jeffrey. "Matthew's Ending and the Genesis of Luke-Acts: The Farrer Hypothesis and the Birth of Christian History." Pages 140–59 in *Marcan Priority without Q: Explorations in the Farrer Hypothesis*. Edited by John C. Poirier and Jeffrey Peterson. LNTS 455. London: Bloomsbury T&T Clark, 2015.

Poirier, John C. "Luke and the Wax Tablet Revisited: An Assessment of Supposed Difficulties." Pages 335–55 in *The Synoptic Problem 2022: Proceedings of the Loyola University Conference*. Edited by Olegs Andrejevs, Simon J. Joseph, Edmondo Lupieri, and Joseph Verheyden. BTS 44. Leuven: Peeters, 2023.

———. "The Roll, the Codex, the Wax Tablet and the Synoptic Problem." *JSNT* 35 (2012): 3–30.

Poirier, John C., and Jeffrey Petersen, eds. *Marcan Priority without Q: Explorations in the Farrer Hypothesis*. LNTS 455. London: Bloomsbury T&T Clark, 2015.

Reinhartz, Adele. *Cast Out of the Covenant: Jews and Anti-Judaism in the Gospel of John*. Lanham, MD: Lexington Books/Fortress Academic, 2018.

Rhoads, David. "Performance Criticism: An Emerging Methodology in Second Testament Studies—Part I." *BTB* 36 (2006): 118–33.

Richardson, Alan. *The Gospel according to Saint John*. TBC. London: SCM, 1959.

Rothschild, Claire K. *Hebrews as Pseudepigraphon: The History and Significance of the Pauline Attribution of Hebrews*. WUNT 235. Tübingen: Mohr Siebeck, 2009.

————. Review of *Marcion and the Dating of the Synoptic Gospels*, by Markus Vinzent. *RBL*. 15 March 2016.

Rouse, Richard H., and Mary A. Rouse. "Wax Tablets." *LC* 9 (1989): 175–91.

Sammons, Benjamin. *Device and Composition in the Greek Epic Cycle*. Oxford: Oxford University Press, 2017.

Sanders, E. P. *Tendencies in the Synoptic Tradition*. SNTSMS 9. Cambridge: Cambridge University Press, 1969.

Sanders, E. P., and Margaret Davies. *Studying the Synoptic Gospels*. London: SCM, 1989.

Saulina, Chakrita M. "Competitive Traditions: Luke's and Matthew's (Con)Textualizations of the Beelzebul Controversy." Pages 233–75 in *The Synoptic Problem 2022: Proceedings of the Loyola University Conference*. Edited by Olegs Andrejevs, Simon J. Joseph, Edmondo Lupieri, and Joseph Verheyden. BTS 44. Leuven: Peeters, 2023.

Schleritt, Frank. *Der vorjohanneische Passionsbericht: Eine historisch-kritische und theologische Untersuchung zu Joh 2,13–22; 11,47–14,31 und 18,1–20,29*. BZNW 154. Berlin: de Gruyter, 2007.

Schnackenburg, Rudolf. *The Gospel according to St. John*. Translated by Kevin Smyth, Cecily Hastings, Francis McDonagh, David Smith, Richard Foley, and G. A. Kon. 3 vols. HThKNT 4. Repr., New York: Crossroad, 1990.

Shellard, Barbara. "The Relationship of Luke and John: A Fresh Look at an Old Problem." *JTS* 46 (1995): 71–98.

Shiner, Whitney. *Proclaiming the Gospel: First Century Performance of Mark*. Harrisburg, PA: Trinity International, 2003.

Sim, David C. *The Gospel of Matthew and Christian Judaism: The History and Social Setting of Matthew's Community*. SNTW. Edinburgh: T&T Clark, 1998.

————. "The Gospels for All Christians? A Response to Richard Bauckham." *JSNT* 84 (2001): 3–27.

————. "Matthew 7.21–23: Further Evidence of Its Anti-Pauline Perspective." *NTS* 53 (2007): 325–43.

Skinner, Christopher W. "ἐγώ εἰμι in Mark and John: Exploring the Johannine Trajectory of a Received Memory of Jesus." *BR* 69 (forthcoming 2024).

Smith, D. Moody. *John among the Gospels*. 2nd ed. Columbia: University of South Carolina Press, 2001.

————. *The Theology of the Gospel of John*. NTTh. Cambridge: Cambridge University Press, 1995.

Smith, Joshua Paul. *Luke Was Not a Christian: Reading the Third Gospel and Acts within Judaism*. BibInt 218. Leiden: Brill, 2023.

Speidel, Michael Alexander. *Die römischen Schreibtafeln von Vindonissa: Lateinische Texte des miltärischen Alltags und ihre geschichtliche Bedeutung.* VGPV 12. Brugg: Gesellschaft Pro Vindonissa, 1996.

Spittler, Janet E. "Is Vienna hist. gr. 63, fol. 51v–55v a 'Fragment'?" *Ancient Jew Review.* 6 May 2019. https://www.ancientjewreview.com/read/2019/4/30/is-vienna-hist-gr-63-fol-51v-55v-a-fragment?rq=spittler.

———. "John, Acts of." In *Brill Encyclopedia of Early Christianity Online.* Edited by David G. Hunter, Paul J. J. van Geest, and Bert Jan Lietaert Peerbolte. https://referenceworks.brillonline.com/browse/brill-encyclopedia-of-early-christianity-online.

Storr, Gottlob Christian. *Über den Zweck der evangelischen Geschichte und der Briefe Johannis.* Tübingen: Heerbrandt, 1786.

Stowers, Stanley. "The Concept of Community and the History of Early Christianity." *MTSR* 23 (2011): 238–56.

Strecker, Georg, ed. *Minor Agreements: Symposium Göttingen 1991.* GTA 50. Göttingen: Vandenhoeck & Ruprecht, 1993.

Streeter, B. H. *The Four Gospels: A Study of Origins.* London: Macmillan, 1924.

Thyen, Hartmut. "Die Erzählung von den bethanischen Geschwistern (Joh 11,1–12,19) als 'Palimpsest' über synoptischen Texten." Pages in 2021–50 in *The Four Gospels: Festschrift Frans Neirynck.* Vol. 3. Edited by Frans Van Segbroeck, Christopher M. Tuckett, Gilbert Van Belle, and Joseph Verheyden. BETL 100. Leuven: Leuven University Press, 1992.

Tomlin, R. S. O. "'The Girl in Question': A New Text from Roman London." *Brittania* 34 (2003): 41–51.

Tov, Emanuel. "Septuagint." Pages 191–210 in *Textual History of the Bible.* Vol. 1A. Edited by Armin Lange. Leiden: Brill, 2016.

Turner, E. G. *Greek Manuscripts of the Ancient World.* Princeton: Princeton University Press, 1971.

Verheyden, Joseph. "P. Gardner-Smith and 'the Turn of the Tide.'" Pages 423–52 in *John and the Synoptics.* Edited by Adelbert Denaux. BETL 101. Leuven: Leuven University Press, 1992.

Vinzent, Markus. *Marcion and the Dating of the Synoptic Gospels.* StPatrSup 2. Leuven: Peeters, 2014.

Wahlde, Urban C. von. *The Gospel and Letters of John.* 3 vols. ECC. Grand Rapids: Eerdmans, 2010.

Walsh, Robyn Faith. *The Origins of Early Christian Literature: Contextualizing the New Testament within Greco-Roman Literary Culture.* Cambridge: Cambridge University Press, 2021.

Warren, Meredith J. C. *My Flesh Is Meat Indeed: A Nonsacramental Reading of John 6:51–58*. Minneapolis: Fortress, 2015.

Watson, Francis. *Gospel Writing: A Canonical Perspective*. Grand Rapids: Eerdmans, 2013.

———. "Towards a Redaction-Critical Reading of the Diatessaron Gospel." *EC* 7 (2016): 95–112.

Watson, Francis, and Sarah Parkhouse, eds. *Connecting Gospels: Beyond the Canonical/Non-canonical Divide*. Oxford: Oxford University Press, 2018.

Weaks, Joseph. "Limited Efficacy in Reconstructing the Gospel Sources for Matthew and Luke." Pages 331–54 in *Empirical Models Challenging Biblical Criticism*. Edited by Raymond F. Person Jr. and Robert Rezetko. AIL 25. Atlanta: SBL Press, 2016.

West, M. L. *The Epic Cycle: A Commentary on the Lost Troy Epics*. Oxford: Oxford University Press, 2013.

———. "The Homeric Quest Today." *APSP* 155 (2011): 383–93.

Wheeler, Stephen M. "Ovid's Use of Lucretius in Metamorphoses 1.67–8." *ClQ* 45 (1995): 200–203.

Wilckens, Ulrich. *Das Evangelium nach Johannes*. NTD 4. Göttingen: Vandenhoeck & Ruprecht, 2000.

Windisch, Hans. *Johannes und die Synoptiker: Wollte der vierte Evangelist die älteren Evangelien ergänzen oder ersetzen?* UNT 12. Leipzig: Hinrichs, 1926.

Wire, Antoinette Clark. *The Case for Mark Composed in Performance*. BPC 3. Eugene, OR: Cascade, 2011.

Wright, Jacob L. *David, King of Israel, and Caleb in Biblical Memory*. New York: Cambridge University Press, 2014.

Yarbro Collins, Adela. "Paul and His Legacy to Trinitarian Theology." Pages 162–71 in *The Bible and Early Trinitarian Theology*. Edited by Christopher A. Beeley and Mark E. Weedman. CUASEC. Washington, DC: Catholic University of America Press, 2018.

Young, Frances M., with Andrew Teal. *From Nicaea to Chalcedon: A Guide to the Literature and Its Background*. 2nd ed. London: SCM, 2010.

Zahn, Molly M. *Genres of Rewriting in Second Temple Judaism: Scribal Composition and Transmission*. Cambridge: Cambridge University Press, 2020.

Zelyck, Lorne. "Irenaeus and the Authorship of the Fourth Gospel." Pages 239–58 in *The Origins of John's Gospel*. Edited by Stanley E. Porter and Hughson T. Ong. JS 2. Leiden: Brill, 2015.

Zumstein, Jean. *Kreative Erinnerung: Relecture und Auslegung im Johannesevangelium*. 2nd ed. ATANT 84. Zurich: Theologischer Verlag Zurich, 2004.

Music, Film, and Television

The Beatles. *Let It Be*. Apple Records, 1970.

———. *Let It Be: Special Edition (Super Deluxe)*. Apple Records, 2021.

Belafonte, Harry. "John Henry." *"Mark Twain" and Other Folk Favorites*. RCA Victor, 1954.

Callner, Marty, dir. *Jerry Seinfeld: "I'm Telling You for the Last Time."* Home Box Office (HBO), 1998.

Cash, Johnny. "The Legend of John Henry's Hammer." *Blood, Sweat and Tears*. Columbia Records, 1962.

Charles, Christian, dir. *Jerry Seinfeld: Comedian*. Miramax Films, 2002.

Clinton, Bill. Interview on *The Late Show with David Letterman*. Directed by Jerry Foley. CBS. 3 August 2004.

Drive-By Truckers. "The Day John Henry Died." *The Dirty South*. New West Records, 2004.

Fincher, David, dir. *Fight Club*. 20th Century Fox, 1999.

Ford, "Tennessee" Ernie. "John Henry." *This Lusty Land!* Capitol Records, 1957.

Garrone, Matteo, dir. *Pinocchio*. Archimede with Rai Cinema and Le Pacte, 2019.

Heyman, John, prod. *Jesus*. Warner Brothers, 1979.

Jackson, Peter, dir. *The Beatles: Get Back*. Disney+, 2021.

Jones, Terry, dir. *Monty Python's Life of Brian*. Orion Pictures, 1979.

Pasolini, Pier Paolo, dir. *The Gospel according to St. Matthew*. Arco Films, 1964.

Scorsese, Martin, dir. *The Last Temptation of Christ*. Universal Studios, 1970.

Sharpsteen, Ben, and Hamilton Luske, dirs. *Pinocchio*. Walt Disney, 1940.

Taylor, Alan, dir. *Mad Men*. Season 1, episode 1, "Smoke Gets in Your Eyes." Aired 19 July 2007 on AMC.

Toro, Guillermo del, dir. *Pinocchio*. Netflix, 2022.

Watson, Doc. "John Henry." *Doc Watson Sings Songs for Little Pickers*. Sugar Hill Records, 1990.

Zemeckis, Robert, dir. *Pinocchio*. Walt Disney, 2022.

Index of Authors

Index of Subjects

Index of Scripture and Other Ancient Texts